the GLOBAL ADVANTAGE

IMPROVING HUMAN PERFORMANCE SERIES

Series Editor: Jack Phillips, Ph.D.

Accountability in Human Resource Management
Jack Phillips

The Adult Learner, 5th Edition
Malcolm Knowles, Elwood Holton, and Richard A. Swanson

The Global Advantage
Michael J. Marquardt

Handbook of Training Evaluation and Measurement Methods, 3rd Edition
Jack Phillips

HR to the Rescue
Edward M. Mone and Manuel London

HRD Survival Skills
Jessica Levant

HRD Trends Worldwide
Jack Phillips

The Power of 360° Feedback
David A. Waldman and Leanne E. Atwater

Return on Investment in Training and Performance Improvement Programs
Jack Phillips

Technology-Based Training
Serge Ravet and Maureen Layte

the GLOBAL ADVANTAGE

How World-Class Organizations Improve Performance Through Globalization

Michael J. Marquardt, Ed.D.

Gulf Publishing Company
Houston, Texas

the GLOBAL ADVANTAGE

How World-Class Organizations Improve Performance Through Globalization

Gulf Publishing Company
Book Division
P.O. Box 2608 □ Houston, Texas 77252-2608

10 9 8 7 6 5 4 3 2 1

Library of Congress Cataloging-in-Publication Data

Marquardt, Michael J.
The global advantage: how world-class organizations improve performance through globalization / Michael J. Marquardt.
p. cm. — (Improving human performance)
Includes bibliographical references and index.
ISBN 0-88415-358-4 (alk. paper)
1. International business enterprises. 2. Organizational effectiveness. 3. Corporate culture. I. Title. II. Series: Improving human performance series.
HD2755.5.M364 1998
658′.049—dc21 98-29545
CIP

To my global family—

Eveline, my Swiss wife
Chris, my Peruvian son
Stephanie, my Salvadoran daughter
Catherine, my Russian scholar
Emily, my world traveler.

Thanks for making a wonderful world for me.

Contents

Acknowledgments

This book has been in my mind and heart for many years, and I owe a debt of gratitude to a large number of people for their help in getting it onto paper.

First, there are the many global practitioners who have offered help and ideas, as well as their practical experience—Bob Hoffman at Parke-Davis, Fred Ricci at Georgetown University, Jim O'Hern with Marriott, Paul Wright at JM Perry, Donna McNamara at Colgate-Palmolive, Nancy Snyder at Whirlpool, Peter Loan of U.S. Peace Corps, Phil Berg of Beloit Corporation, Angus Reynolds of Southern Illinois University, Arthur Byrnes of the U.S. Agency for International Development, Bren White of the World Group, Howard Schuman of East-West Capital Resources, Ray Rist at the World Bank, Barrie Oxtoby of Rover, Robert Kohls at San Francisco State University, Hans Geiser of the United Nations, Kevin Wheeler of National Semiconductor, Garth Andrus of Andersen Consulting, Tan Jing Hee at the Singapore Institute of Management, Les Pickett of the Australian Human Resources Institute, and Randy Maxwell at Nortel.

Next, I would like to acknowledge the wonderful students who have participated in my global human resource development course at George Washington University during the past twenty years. What I have learned from them about globalization would fill many books. The librarians at the university, especially Doug Carroll, were extraordinarily helpful and prompt in collecting resource materials for this book.

Special thanks go to my daughter Catherine, who assisted me in researching the numerous books and articles about globalization. And finally, I am very grateful to the talented and wonderful people at Gulf Publishing, especially Kelly Perkins, who has done a masterful job in editing the manuscript and guiding the publication.

Preface

We live in the global age. Technology, trade, travel, and television have created a global village. People around the world watch the same event on television or on the Internet at the same time. Many of us commute not just across city boundaries but across national boundaries. We communicate via e-mail instantaneously with colleagues around the world as if they were around the block.

Companies everywhere are rushing to globalize. Jack Welsh, CEO of General Electric, proclaims that "companies either globalize or they die." David Whitman, CEO of Whirlpool, says that "without global mind-sets we cannot globalize organizations." He goes on to state that the "key to globalizing an organization is to get everyone in the organization to think globally, not just a few."

Global organizations are places where people are adept at exchanging ideas, processes, and systems across national and functional borders. To do this, we need a new brand of global leadership that provides a unifying vision and philosophy to guide the organization's efforts. We need to globalize all operations, not just a few; we need to get everyone involved in globalization, not just the leaders. Kevin Barham and Marion Devine, noted global theorists, point out that the future is not only about global competition, but also about global learning.

The choice then is not whether to globalize, but how and how soon. Although we know we must do it, we still know so little about what needs to be globalized and how to do it. To date, few companies have successfully and totally achieved global status. The challenges are awesome, the difficulties immense, but the opportunities are endless and wonderful.

Two years ago, a large consulting firm that helps companies go global gave me a list of the ten most common questions its clients had about globalization:

1. How do you create a global culture?
2. What are the key components of globalization?
3. How do you create a global mind-set?
4. What kinds of skills should we look for in global managers?
5. Why do some people fail when going overseas?
6. How do we establish a global training program?
7. What experiences should we give our future leaders?
8. Should everyone in the organization become globalized?
9. Is there an order or process in which a company should go global?
10. Where can we go for help as we work toward globalization?

This list inspired me to write this book, for I realized that these questions had no easy answers and that only a handful of companies had resolved even a few of these issues. In addition, very little applied research and less analysis of successful global companies had been undertaken. In preparing the manuscript for this book, I was fortunate to work with a number of global executives and with global firms, both large ones and small ones, located in every part of the world. Some of these leaders considered themselves high on the globalization ladder, while others declined to accept the appellation, even though the press declared them to be such. Most, however, understood the true difficulties of globalization and recognized how far they had yet to go.

Overview of the Book

In Chapter 1, we examine **why** and **how** globalization emerged and the journey that organizations take to move from domestic to international, to multinational, and finally to global status. Climbing the globalization curve faster and better becomes the goal of any organization that wishes to succeed in the next millennium. Chapter 2 presents the fifteen powerful benefits and advantages available to global firms, as well as the challenges caused by culture, politics, and distance.

An overview of the six components of the *GlobalSuccess* Model is presented in Chapter 3. The focus is on the dimensions, the **what,** of a successful global enterprise. Chapters 4 through 9 then explore and illustrate these six components, namely corporate culture, human resources, strategies, operations, structure, and—perhaps most importantly—learning. Specific strategies and principles for globalizing the various dimensions of the organization are provided, as well as the best practices of more than forty successful global corporations.

Chapter 10 looks at the steps companies should take to move to global status. In the appendix is the *GlobalSuccess* Capability and Readiness Profile for measuring and guiding one toward globalization.

Enjoy the journey toward becoming a global organization!

I

A Global World

Signs of Globalization

More than two billion people watched the finals of the World Cup as they took place in France in the summer of 1998—understanding and cheering the same game. Products that are sold worldwide (such as, Coca-Cola, MasterCard, Nike, and Budweiser) were shown on televisions in homes and clubs throughout Europe, the Americas, Asia, Africa, and Australia. More than 180 countries had competed for the World Cup during the two years leading up to the final game. Now citizens from most of those countries filled the stadium.

We have entered the global age. We are a more global people; we share many global values and practices; we, more and more, work for global organizations. Globalization has caused a convergence of economic and social forces, of interests and commitments, of values and tastes, of challenges and opportunities. We can easily communicate with people 10,000 miles away because we share a global language (English) and a global medium for communication (computers and the Internet).

Four main forces have quickly brought us to this global age—technology, travel, trade, and television. These four T's have laid the groundwork for a more collective experience for people everywhere. More and more of us share common tastes in foods (hamburgers, pizza, tacos), fashion (denim jeans), and fun (Disney, rock music, television). Nearly two billion passengers fly the world's airways each year. People watch the same movies, read the same magazines, and dance the same dances from Boston to Bangkok to Buenos Aires.

Ever more of us speak English—a language now spoken by more than 1.5 billion people in more than 130 countries (often as a second, third, or fourth language). The English language, like all languages, carries with it implicit and explicit cultural and social values (such as, precision, individualism, active control, and clarity). English, despite the protests of the French, has become the global language of the airlines, the media, computers, business, and the global marketplace.

The Global Marketplace

The signs of the global marketplace are all around us.

- U.S. corporations have invested $1 trillion abroad and employ more than 100 million overseas workers; over 100,000 U.S. firms are engaged in global ventures valued at more than $2 trillion. Over one third of U.S. economic growth has been because of exports, providing jobs for more than 11 million Americans.
- 10 percent of U.S. manufacturing is foreign-owned and employs 4 million Americans; Mitsubishi USA is America's fourth largest exporter, and Toyota has displaced Chrysler as the third largest in U.S. auto sales. Foreign investment in the United States has now surpassed the $3 trillion mark.
- McDonald's operates more than 12,500 restaurants in 70 countries and is adding 600 new restaurants per year.
- Many of the oil-exporting countries on the Arabian Peninsula have more foreign-born workers than native population. More than 70 percent of the employees of Canon work outside Japan.
- Financial markets are open 24 hours a day around the world.
- Over half of the PhDs in engineering, mathematics, and economics awarded by American universities in 1997 went to non-U.S. citizens.
- Global standards and regulations for trade and commerce, finance, products, and services have emerged.
- More and more companies—InterContinental, Xerox, Motorola, Honda, Samsung, Pentax—are manufacturing and selling chiefly outside their countries of origin. We hardly know if a company is French, Japanese, Swedish, or American.
- Coca-Cola earns more money in Japan than in the United States.

- ❑ More than 70 percent of profits for the United States' $20-billion music industry comes from outside the country. Most big-bucks movies depend on global viewers for big profits.

Global Organizations

The global marketplace has created the need for global corporations. These organizations, in turn, have created an even more global marketplace. The growing similarity of what customers throughout the world wish to purchase, including the quality and price of those products and services, has spurred both tremendous opportunities and tremendous pressures for businesses to become global. More and more companies, whether small or large, young or old, recognize that their choice is between becoming global or becoming extinct [1].

Global organizations are companies that operate as if the entire world were a single entity. They are fully integrated so that all their activities link, leverage, and compete on a worldwide scale [2]. Global firms emphasize global operations over national or multinational operations. They use global sourcing of human resources, capital, technology, facilities, resources, and raw materials. They deem cultural sensitivity to employees, customers, and communications patterns as critical to the success of the organization [3]. Globalization of an organization has occurred when the organization has developed a global corporate culture, strategy, structure, and communication process [4].

According to Moran et al. [5, p. 296], globalization is "the art of positioning an organization beyond national boundaries, adapting to changing local environments wherever markets and resources may exist." It is "creating a world without walls, made possible by advances in communication and transportation technologies." Today's world involves "rapid technological advances, worldwide socio-economic and political changes, increasing environmental awareness, and other such forces impacting the global business environment."

Factors Creating the Global Marketplace and Global Organizations

A single global marketplace has been created by ten factors, or global drivers:

1. Global technology and telecommunication (enhanced by fiber optics, satellites, and computer technology)
2. Competitiveness of global corporations
3. Converging of global lifestyles and consumer values (accelerated by global language)
4. Emergence of global customers and global market drivers
5. Lowering costs of doing business globally
6. Globalization of financial markets, resources, and services
7. Emergence of the knowledge economy and era
8. Workforce diversity and mobility
9. Privatization and globalization of government services
10. Open and unrestricted free trade

Let's explore each of these globalization drivers and see how they have created a global marketplace, a global organization, and global customers.

Global Technology and Telecommunication

Alvin Toffler writes how the advanced global economy cannot run for thirty seconds without the information technology of computers and other new and rapidly improving complexities of production [6]. Yet, today's best computers and CAD/CAM systems will be Stone Age primitive within a few years. We are moving from information exchange to virtual organizations to Internet commerce, which can transform every process of global business, including buying, selling, and information flow.

The world has indeed entered an era of ever-increasing technological advancement—with new technologies such as optoelectronics, cyberspace, information highways, digital video discs (DVDs), informating, local area networks (LANs), wide area networks (WANs), groupware, virtual reality, and electronic classrooms. The power of computer technology has progressed from mainframe to desktop to briefcase-portable to user's hand. More and more of a company's operations are being totally automated and customized. The impact on organizational work and on learning has been overwhelming.

These new technologies have become necessary to manage the data deluge present in the fast-changing, turbocharged organizations of today. When working in a global economy in which being informed, being in touch, and being there first can make all the difference between success and second best, technology provides a big advantage indeed!

The impact of technology on globalization and in creating global organizations is still in its infancy stage. The emerging power and applicability of technology has turned the world of work on its head. Organizations will become more virtual rather than physical because of technology. People will be more linked to customers in Singapore or Moscow than to co-workers across the hall because of technology.

Already, we live in a world where virtual reality and interactive multimedia technologies are rapidly becoming commonplace. Personalized digitized assistants will soon be available as built-in, on-line experts to keep track of your appointments, priorities, and future. Artificial intelligence technologies (expert/knowledge-based systems, speech- and natural-language-understanding user interfaces, sensory perception, and knowledge-based simulation) will be commonly available. Intelligent tutoring systems will be used to allow learner-based, self-paced instruction. Desktop videoconferencing, collaborative software and group systems technology will be widely prevalent in the next five years [7].

And the speed and impact of technology on globalization continues to accelerate! Trying to figure out the capabilities and future directions of this rapidly changing technology is impossible. Let's look at just a few of the already existing powers of technology:

- ❑ New superconducting transmission lines can transmit data up to one hundred times faster than today's fiber optical networks. One line can carry one trillion bits of information a second, enough to send the complete contents of the Library of Congress in two minutes.
- ❑ Neural networks are advancing computer intelligence that has historically made process commands sequentially; a neural network

uses associative "reasoning" to store information in patterned connections, allowing the network to process complex questions through its own logic.

- ❑ Expert systems, a subset of artificial intelligence, are beginning to solve problems in much the same way as human experts.
- ❑ Telephones small enough to wear as earrings are being manufactured.
- ❑ New highly reliable connectivity has been developed that works regardless of time or place and is easy and affordable around the world.
- ❑ Cellular phones can now respond to e-mail.

One of the most amazing and transforming technological additions to our lives is the Internet. The use of the Internet is one of the fastest-growing phenomena the business world has ever seen—building from a base of fewer than one thousand connected computers in the early 1980s to more than ten million host computers today. Internet commerce is projected to grow from a mere $8 billion in 1997 to more than $327 billion in 2002.

Intranets (in-company internets) are rapidly catching up. The implementation of intranets is growing three times faster than that of electronic commercial applications, with more than 70 percent of major corporations currently having or planning intranet application. As the evolution of intranet sites continues, more and more features will emerge. For example, real-time training that combines a live mediator, on-line information, and several remote attendees is already possible. By the end of 1997, nearly 90 percent of all businesses had recognized the criticalness of developing comprehensive strategies for using both intranets and the Internet.

Some of the new high-tech learning machines, such as electronic performance support systems and virtual reality simulators, have been called "the most powerful learning tool(s) since the invention of the book" [8]. With virtual reality, the mind is cut off from outside distractions, and one's attention focuses on the powerful sensory stimulation (light-sound matrix) that bombards the imagination. It becomes possible for ideas and mental images to float in and out of a person's consciousness.

Technology, especially in such sectors as aerospace, advanced industrial systems, and automotive, is becoming more and more a part of all global products and the total gross national product (GNP). Already, nearly 20 percent of an automobile's value is the electronics within it. The computer service and computer software market has grown to be worth more than $420 billion, an increase of 50 percent in the last four years! Information technology is expected to form the basis of many of the most important products, services and processes of the future [7].

The continuous development of technology affects every process, procedure, and product in business, especially businesses that operate globally. Technology will serve as the principal tool for coordinating global production and distribution, exercising operational control, and driving policy formulation. Through the billion-byte global highway, cost performance is improved, and global billing is done via the Internet. Technology has become more and more valuable and less and less expensive for those who apply it well.

Technology also allows for the restructuring of industrial enterprises. The changing global labor market will force organizations to design better business processes and systems to make use of expert systems and data bases; the new informated organization will enable all levels of the hierarchy to have accessibility of information for control and decision making.

The increased power and capability of technology, illustrated in the following list, provides ever-expanding opportunities and advantages for global businesses:

- Reduced costs and more flexible use and application of telecommunication through developments such as Integrated Services Digital Network (ISDN), fiber optics, and cellular radio
- Miniaturization (tiny cameras, microphones, and small, high-resolution display screens)
- Increased portability through use of radio communication and miniaturization
- Expanded processing power through new microchip development and advanced software

- ❑ More powerful and user-friendly command and software tools, making it much easier for users to create and communicate their own materials [9]

The technology of the future will respond to our voices and extend our senses. It will simulate complex phenomena—weather patterns, stock market crashes, environmental hazards—solving problems and predicting outcomes at a price anyone can afford. Computers—or networks of them—will become ubiquitous as they are invisibly imbedded in other things. These machines will reconfigure themselves when new applications are required. A whole new metaphor for computing is taking shape, patterned on the natural resilience and elegance of biological organisms. Computers will learn to diagnose, repair, and even replicate themselves. Global companies will be affected by all these marvelous breakthroughs.

Competitiveness of Global Corporations

Global economic and marketing pressures are generating huge competitive pressures on all corporations. More than 25 percent of the *Fortune* 500 companies for a given year will not exist ten years later. Markets are rapidly changing and being competed for. Strong competitors from other countries have entered local markets. More and more of companies' sales will be to foreign markets. Domestic markets, with their ever-tighter niches, will no longer be sufficient.

Protected consumer markets dominated by national champions are disappearing. Nearly every industry is opening up to some form of competition from outside the traditional territory, even if it is only theoretical competition generated from the knowledge of the existence of better products in other markets. In any country of the world, there is a growing pool of more sophisticated customers with access to the best the world has to offer.

Global consumers will be pushing for new performance standards in quality, variety, customization, convenience, time, and innovation. They will increase the rapidity with which companies are compelled to move beyond domestic markets. Organizations will have no choice but to shop the world for customers, people, resources, technology, markets, and business partners. These new demands for quality, the constant change of consumer tastes, the existence of global fads, and short product-life cycles are forcing new global partnerships and alliances. Challenges raised by new niche markets, new and emerging industries, deregulation, fights over market share, and aggressive national competitors have created the need to merge global forces for survival.

Joining forces with other companies and in other countries has become a necessity for many companies because of:

- ❑ The rise of new competitors intent upon becoming global competitors (for example, in automotive and electronics industries).
- ❑ The growth of global networks, which makes countries and companies interdependent in particular industries (electronics).
- ❑ The increased need for strategic alliances (mergers/acquisitions) to share resources and gain access to other markets and technologies.

Converging of Global Lifestyles and Consumer Values

The influence of television, travel, and immigration has caused a growing similarity of global values and tastes, which then impact customer desires and expectations. The extent to which customers in different countries have the same or similar needs in a product or service category means that highly standardized global products are becoming more acceptable.

In the food and beverage areas where national taste seems dominant, the speed of change of eating habits has been dramatic. For example, the Japanese are now eating donuts, while the British are abandoning their warm "pint of bitter" beer for cold American and European-style lager. Heineken has successfully created a globally standardized beer that its adherents buy all over the world. Burger King and fast food have become popular in Paris, just as they are in Peoria; Coca-Cola and French mineral water can be found in Mongolia and in Mauritania as easily as in Miami and Melbourne. Yogurt is a health food in the nation of Georgia as well as the state of Georgia.

Global products are globalized, yet localized. McDonald's serves meatless hamburgers in India and guava juice in Malaysia. Both places, however, share the ambiance and the culture of Americanism—and the golden arches.

Global communication and marketing have increased consumers' awareness about possible products and services. Global competition has offered customers a larger variety and higher quality of choices. What has been created is a convergence of consumer needs and preferences. Consumers are now able to choose the products and services they want based on the best:

Cost. The product or service is the least expensive and/or most economical choice.

Quality. The product or service has no defects and meets and exceeds the customer's expectations.

Time. The product or service is available as quickly as possible.

Service. Service is pleasant, courteous, and available on products that are reparable or replaceable.

Innovation. The product or service is new, meaning that it's something not yet envisioned by the customer when produced (for example, Sony's Walkman).

Customization. The product or service is tailored to very specific needs.

Thus we now have global homogenous needs for better quality, price, and service regardless of the product's national origin.

Emergence of Global Customers and Global Market Drivers

Global travel has created global customers. Marriott, InterContinental, Holiday Inn, and ANA hotels are available worldwide, as are global restaurants such as Movenpick, Taco Bell, and Planet Hollywood. AT&T, Nokia, or MCI can service our telecommunication anywhere in the world, on the ground or in the air.

The per capita income has been converging among industrialized nations. Asian countries, led by Japan, Taiwan, Singapore, and Korea, have per capita incomes that are among the highest in the world. China's GNP is expected to be higher than that of the United States by the year 2025. Thus, there are vast new markets for the more pricey products of global countries. This is critical for companies that have saturated their home markets (such as Amway, Toys "R" Us, Honda, Canon, and Electrolux).

Companies are serving as global customers to each other. For example, AMP is a global supplier to many Japanese and American carmakers, while the World Health Organization represents billions of global customers in more than one hundred countries. There are now global telecommunication agreements, global brands (Levi's, Coca-Cola, Toyota), and global advertising (for example, Saatchi & Saatchi's commercials for British Airways).

Lowering Costs of Doing Business Globally

The cost of doing business abroad has dropped markedly during the past several years because of a variety of environmental factors and internal organizational efficiencies, including the following:

- Continuing corporate push for economies of scale and scope
- Leveraging of large capital and of development investments to reduce unit costs
- Acceleration of technological innovations
- Advances in transportation (such as the use of Federal Express to deliver urgent supplies from one continent to another)
- Emergence of newly industrial countries with productive capabilities and low labor costs (for example, Taiwan, Thailand, and China)
- Sourcing efficiencies
- Favorable logistics
- Products being exported are more knowledge driven (information and consultative services) and are lighter and less bulky because of technological advancements (such as computers)

Globalization of Financial Markets, Resources, and Services

The 1997-1998 downturn of Asia's markets in Hong Kong, Singapore, Tokyo, Jakarta, Manila, Seoul, Bangkok, and Kuala Lumpur demonstrates the globality of business and impact of one financial market on another. The Asian "flu" significantly affected the health of companies throughout the world. Financial markets are all globalized and significantly impact one another and, in turn, force companies to be involved in financial institutions on a worldwide basis in order to compete.

Companies, as a result, must be continuously involved in stock markets as the world turns since many of their competitors are making more money by managing money than by making it. They must seek global sources of capital as well as diversify their capital throughout the world.

Among the other drivers that have globalized finance and the workplace are:

- ❑ Globalization of stock markets (such as the listing of corporations on multiple exchanges)
- ❑ Global banks with branches throughout the world (Citibank, Hong Kong Shanghai, Irish Allied)
- ❑ CNN-FN, CNBC, AsiaWorld and other 24-hour financial news networks (essential information for all global companies)
- ❑ The connection of all currencies to the U.S. dollar
- ❑ Wireless, instantaneous transfer of financial resources

Emergence of the Knowledge Economy and Era

We now live in the **knowledge era;** the new economy is a **knowledge economy.** More and more, knowledge is providing the key raw material for wealth creation and is quickly becoming the fountain of organizational and personal power.

Knowledge is created continuously in every corner of the globe and doubles every three to four years simply because more people are creating more knowledge. It is becoming a company's most valuable asset and is absolutely critical for the survival of organizations competing with the world's brightest companies. Thomas Stewart, author of *Intellectual Capital,* asserts, "Every company depends increasingly on knowledge—patents, process, management skills, technologies, information about customers and suppliers, and old-fashioned experience. . . . This knowledge that exists in an organization can be used to create differential advantage. In other words, it's the sum of everything everybody in your company knows that gives you a competitive edge in the marketplace" [10, p. 44].

We are now employing more and more knowledge workers. Not only senior executives, but employees at all levels must be highly educated, highly skilled knowledge workers. In the new post-capitalist society, knowledge is not just another resource alongside the traditional factors of production, land, labor, and capital. It is the only meaningful resource in today's workforce. In an economy based on knowledge, the knowledge worker is the single greatest asset.

By the year 2000, three quarters of the jobs in the U.S. economy will involve creating and processing knowledge. Knowledge workers have already discovered that continual learning is not only a prerequisite of employment but is a major part of everyone's work.

Global companies can no longer focus only on products and services; their business increasingly depends on the specialized knowledge and the know-how of their employees. These knowledge employees are the critical core of the company, the essence of the business from which all revenues flow. And unlike other assets of the company, which lose value over time and use, the know-how of employees actually increases in value when used and practiced.

Workplace Diversity and Mobility

William Johnston, who recently completed an exhaustive study of global work patterns, identified four major implications of the mobile, culturally diverse workforce on global corporations:

Relocation. A massive relocation of people, especially young and better-educated, will flock to urban areas around the world.

Competition for labor. More industrialized nations will come to rely on, and even compete for, foreign-born workers.

Improved productivity. Labor-short, immigrant-poor countries, such as Japan and Sweden, will be compelled to improve labor productivity dramatically to avoid slow economic growth. The need for increased outsourcing of jobs to other countries is escalating.

Standardization. A gradual standardization of labor practices in the areas of vacation time, workplace safety, and employee rights is occurring around the world.

Johnston adds that nations that have slow-growing workforces but rapid growth in service-sector jobs (Japan, United States, Germany) will become magnets for immigrants. Nations whose educational systems produce prospective workers faster than their economies can absorb them (Argentina, Egypt, Philippines, Poland, Russia) will export people [11].

The combination of a globalized workforce with massive mobility compels organizations to be able to work with growing numbers of people with differing cultures, customs, values, beliefs, and practices.

Physicists at Bell Laboratories are as likely to come from universities in England or India as from Princeton or Massachusetts Institute of Technology (MIT). At research centers around the world, the native language of the biochemists is as likely to be Hindi, Japanese, or German as it is English or French. It is routine for U.S. hospitals to advertise in Dublin and Manila for nurses.

Global corporations will increasingly have to reach across borders to find people with the skills they need. These movements of workers to other countries are driven by the growing gap between the world's supplies and demands for those supplies. Much of the planet's skilled and unskilled human resources are being produced in the developing world. Yet, most of the well-paid, high-skilled jobs are being generated in the cities of the industrialized world.

Privatization and Globalization of Government Services

State-owned enterprises are being sold in every part of the world as the role of governments as producers and customers declines. The controlled economies of Eastern Europe, Asia, and Africa are being dismantled. Amid the failure of communism and other state-controlled models as well as because of the shortage of tax funds in free-market economics, governments around the world are seeking to unload public companies.

The Washington Post calls privatization the "biggest fire sale in history" [12]. From Australia to Argentina, Poland to Pakistan—all around the globe—countries are transferring their state-owned companies by selling them into private hands.

More than $100 billion worth of state-owned enterprises have been sold in the past three years. For sale are government-owned steel mills, once considered a badge of nationhood for less-developed countries; banks whose nationalization decades earlier was seen as a key to development; and government-owned newspapers that were used to maintain "government-think."

In a recent special report in *Business Week* titled "The Global Rush to Privatize" [13], the authors describe the following actions:

- ❑ *Privatizatziya* is the rage in republics of the former USSR. During the next three years, Russia wants to privatize 30 percent of its state-owned assets. Asea Brown Boveri (ABB) and Mitsui are planning investments in huge Siberian chemical plants; Coca-Cola is seeking a joint venture with a bottling plant in Kiev; new private companies plan to split up Aeroflot and create new airlines.
- ❑ State-owned companies in Indonesia, Hungary, Poland, France, and South Africa are up for sale.
- ❑ Proctor & Gamble purchased Czech detergent Rakona; Germany's Korf bought Hungary's OZD Steel.
- ❑ Mexico has sold its phone company, Banamex; Venezuela unloaded the state airline, VIASA; Brazil is preparing its steel company for privatization; Colombia is selling much of its coal business; Paraguay is auctioning off its cement plants and liquor distillery; Argentina sold its highways and even the Buenos Aires Zoo.

States and cities throughout the United States are privatizing services ranging from garbage collection to prisons to social services. Japan has sold its tobacco manufacturing and marketing company as well as its railroad and telecommunication systems. Great Britain long ago sold British Steel and British Airways. Sweden has reversed its long-standing collectivist model in favor of a deregulated free-market economy.

Roger Leeds, a former World Bank economist, calls privatization the "story of the 1990s." Joseph Linn, World Bank vice president, calls it a "worldwide trend . . . dominating what is going on economically in the 1990s and beyond" [13].

Global companies are buying up many of these former state enterprises. They will be challenged to transform the generally inefficient, wasteful, and bloated former state enterprises to make them more efficient and productive as well as to develop quality- , service- , and price-conscious corporate cultures.

Open and Unrestricted Free Trade

A final driver that has accelerated globalization is the actions of governments and international bodies to create greater free trade around the world and in different regions. Regional trade agreements are beginning to emerge. In 1992, with the creation of the European Common Market, Europe became the world's largest market with more than 350 million people and a GNP of more than $10 trillion, 43 percent of the world's total GNP. A single currency is scheduled to be introduced in Europe, and the free movement of labor, goods, services, and capital has begun. The North American Free Trade Agreement (NAFTA) brings together the economic might of the United States, Canada, and Mexico. Other regional trade agreements are being pursued or are already in place in Asia, Latin America, Africa, and the Middle East.

Other recent actions to remove trade barriers include:

- ❑ Reduction in tariff barriers (for example, NAFTA).
- ❑ Reduction in nontariff barriers (for example, Japan's gradual opening of its markets).
- ❑ Creation of trading blocks in Europe, the Americas, and Association of Southeast Asian Nations (ASEAN) countries.
- ❑ Harmonization of European Union regulations for banking and finance services, which permits the free flow of capital among member countries.

On the other hand, a number of restrictive trade elements, such as tariffs, indirect barriers, and retaliatory strategies, have also forced companies to globalize, namely:

- ❑ Demand for local content requirements by a growing number of countries (for example, by the United States and Europe for automobiles).
- ❑ Currency and capital flow restrictions.
- ❑ Requirements of technology transfer (for example, in China).
- ❑ Requirements for specific technical standards (for example, Motorola found electronics products excluded from the Japanese market because of different frequencies).

These ten drivers have thus created an environment that both enables and puts pressure on companies to globalize. They need to leave their existing domestic, international, or multinational status (distinctions between three terms will be presented in the next section of this chapter). However, the path to globalization is not easy, nor is the path always a direct route. In the next section, we will explore how some companies have historically made this journey from domestic to global.

Corporate Global Evolution—Moving from Domestic to Global Status

Adler [3], Eom [14] and Hordes et al. [15] have observed that companies typically go through four distinct, progressively more complex states or phases as they evolve toward global status, namely (1) domestic, (2) international, (3) multinational/multiregional, and (4) global. Each of these stages (and types of companies in these stages) has a particular philosophy and way of operating (see Figure 1-1).

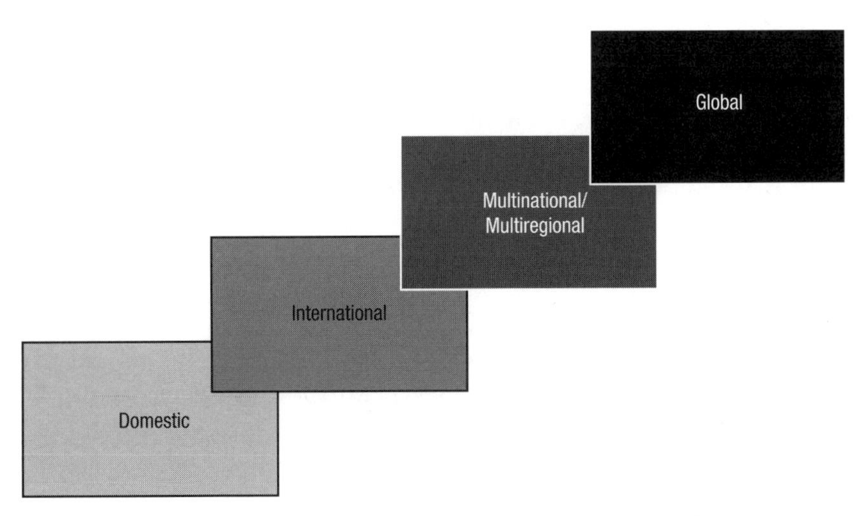

FIGURE 1-1. JOURNEY FROM DOMESTIC TO GLOBAL STATUS.

Domestic

Historically, all companies were domestic—each producing and selling its products or services within a single country. Going outside the domestic market was neither necessary nor, in most cases, even possible because of costs, the vastly different consumer values and needs in other countries, the availability of appropriate currency, and so forth.

Of course, many (too many) companies are still in this Phase I. These companies operate on domestic terms and focus solely on domestic markets. They emphasize either product or service, and technology is highly proprietary and protected. These companies perceive themselves as having relatively few competitors and are structurally centralized. The perspective is generally ethnocentric, and cultural sensitivity is relatively unimportant.

International

International, or Phase II, companies are those that begin to export their products or services abroad or begin importing raw materials needed for manufacturing. Usually, in such companies, only a small group of expatriate managers is involved directly in foreign operations. Structurally, the company is decentralized and often forms a single international division for its foreign operations. The corporate strategy is multidomestic. Cultural sensitivity begins to be important.

Moran et al. [5] describes the international organization as being typically ethnocentric, or home-country-oriented. Ethnocentric managers believe that home-country nationals are more intelligent, reliable, and trustworthy than foreign nationals. The operations of the company center on a domestic headquarters, and home-country nationals are recruited, trained, and transported for international positions. Foreign managers and employees are typically overlooked and underestimated. Ethnocentrism may occur because of biases of owners and stockholders, the influence of labor unions, or government emphasis on domestic markets. International companies have difficulty communicating in different languages and accepting cultural differences.

Multinational/Multiregional

Phase III is the multinational/multiregional phase. Companies focus on lowest-cost production with sourcing, manufacturing, and marketing worldwide. The parent company operates with a centralized view of strategy, technology, and resource allocation, but decision making and customer service shift to the national level for marketing, selling, manufacturing, and competitive tactics. There are many competitors, and profit margins are low. Products and services are standardized, and the primary orientation is price.

The headquarters is run by home-country nationals, while foreign nationals often run their respective local subsidiaries. The organization recognizes profit potential but does not understand how the foreign market functions, so they therefore leave foreign managers to run their local operations. These foreign nationals have little to no chance of receiving senior positions at headquarters.

The **multinational** enterprise shows more diversity in culture and organizational structure. In this type of organization, headquarters is less important, and each national/regional operation has more autonomy for operational decisions. Business process and technology are less of a one-size-fits-all and more based on local standards or optimization of local cost drivers. Headquarters provides guidance regarding policies, but there is great local discretion. At the multinational phase, the company usually functions on the idea that local people know what is best for them.

The **multiregional** organization is very similar to the multinational company but does begin to implement some of the linking and leverage characteristics of a global company. Multiregional companies capitalize on the synergistic benefits of sharing common functions across regions. Each region has a headquarters that organizes collaborative efforts among local subsidiaries and is responsible for implementing the plan provided by the world headquarters. Each region also has separate research and development (R&D), product innovation, executive selection and training, cash management, public relations, and so forth. The world headquarters is in charge of world strategy, country analysis, foreign exchange, selection of top management, technology transfer, and establishment of the corporate culture.

Global

In the global phase, the corporation operates without geographic boundaries. Global thinking and global competencies become critical for survival. The company is constantly scanning, organizing, and reorganizing its resources and capabilities such that national or regional boundaries are not barriers to potential products, business opportunities, and manufacturing locations.

Companies send their best, fast-tracked managers and senior executives for global assignments. Cultural sensitivity and language skills become critically important. Products are mass-customized. Imports as well as exports are part of the company's operations for manufacturing and sales. There are globally coordinated strategies, global structures, and a global corporate culture. Global learning becomes essential to remain competitive. Developing the thinking-global-and-acting-local mind-set is integral to operations and interactions [3, 16].

The truly global enterprise operates very differently from both the international and the multinational/multiregional enterprise. While the globalized company may have roots in one culture, it has created an organizational culture that values diversity. A few core values act as its major unifying force. Although it has a headquarters, the global enterprise is often managed by a team of managers from diverse locations. Its business process, policies, and technologies are often diverse with the exception of a few rigidly standardized policies, often centered on communication technologies and training of the workforce. Examples of global enterprises can be found in the pharmaceutical industry, management consulting industry, and consumer packaged goods industry.

Global organizations are geocentric, or world-oriented, and maintain a highly interdependent system. Their ultimate goal is creation of an integrated system with a worldwide approach. The organization simultaneously focuses on both worldwide and local objectives, with collaboration between headquarters and subsidiaries to achieve universal standards with local variations. The leaders are diverse, as the most competent people are sought to fill positions, regardless of nationality. Rewards are provided to encourage work toward worldwide objectives. There are no geographical borders; therefore resources and ideas flow through the organization freely. The global firm also overcomes political barriers by turning its subsidiaries into good citizens of the host nations. These companies also provide base countries with more hard currency, new skills, and the knowledge of advanced technology.

Global companies have globalized not only their operations and strategies but, equally important, also their corporate culture and structure. They have also globalized their people, as well as their learning. How companies globalize each of these areas will be explored in the remaining chapters of this book. Let us first look at how companies can determine their present status on the globalization curve.

The Globalization Curve

To assist organizations in identifying their location on the road to corporate globalization, the team of Bren White, Michael Marquardt, and Quentin Englerth has developed the Globalization Curve (Figure 1-2), which combines Adler's four phases with key corporate values, activities, and strategies [16]. As can be seen in the Globalization Curve, firms often begin their ascent toward global status by interna-

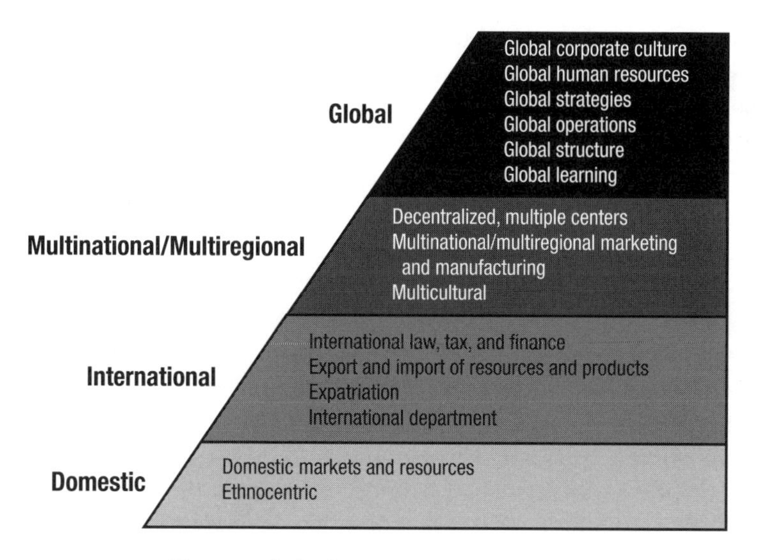

FIGURE 1-2. GLOBALIZATION CURVE.

tional travel before moving into exporting and importing, which requires knowledge of and involvement in international law, taxes, and finance issues. The multinational/multiregional phase includes a change in marketing, quality, service, and telecommunication systems. In the global stage, a corporation transforms its structure, policies, organizational dynamics, leadership, and corporate culture.

Of course, not all companies systematically and clearly traverse across each of the phases in a direct, clearly defined manner. For example, companies may be in Phase I (domestic) for some corporate activities, such as personnel, and in Phase IV (global) for other corporate activities, such as marketing or R&D. To the degree that this mixed-corporate evolution exists, so also exists ineffectiveness and probable dysfunctioning, and ultimately economic failure. Hence, a critical importance exists for global companies to have a clear understanding about the journey toward globalization and how to move upward on the Globalization Curve. That will be the focus of the remainder of this book.

Climbing the Globalization Curve—From Whirlpool to Worldpool

In 1989, Whirlpool, headquartered in Benton Harbor, Mich., acquired the $2 billion appliance division of N.V. Philips Gleoilampenfabriekin, headquartered in the Netherlands. In one fell swoop, Whirlpool had gone from an almost exclusively domestic company to a company with 40 percent of its operations overseas. With the Philips purchase, Whirlpool had suddenly become the largest home-appliance company in the world.

The significance of the challenge could be seen in the fact that many of the U.S. senior managers didn't even have passports! Yet Whirlpool leadership was acutely aware of the critical importance of the Dutch and American companies becoming an integrated global corporation. The people of Whirlpool would quickly need to integrate the forces of globalization, culture, language, communication, and workforce diversity. They wanted to leverage their new resources instead of having them merely be added deterrents.

Whirlpool, under the guidance of President and CEO Dave Whitwam and its human resources staff, developed several programs to globalize the company that now was called Whirlpool International B.V. These various strategies were so successful that Whirlpool was recognized by *Personnel Journal* as an Optimas Award winner in the global outlook category for the unique globalization efforts made to "succeed in the world marketplace" [17].

One of the key programs that enabled Whirlpool to learn as an organization to become global was its annual Global Conferences. The first Global Conference was held at Montreux, Switzerland, for one week in June 1990. Top executives from sixteen countries in Whirlpool's European and North American operations attended. The theme of the conference was "Winning Through Quality Leadership: One Global Vision."

Let's carefully examine the planning and learning strategies involved in the design of the first Global Conference. The first step was to determine the worldwide conference's goals. The conference designers identified four major goals:

- ❑ Advance a unified *vision* of the company's future
- ❑ Instill the idea of embracing the future as one global company
- ❑ Establish a keen sense of responsibility within the leadership group for creating the company's future
- ❑ Identify and initiate explicit steps toward integrating the various activities and ideas throughout Whirlpool's worldwide operations

Another important goal of the conference was to enable the participants to think first of each other as business partners—not as *foreigners*. The conference designers also wanted to be sure that the participants' own goals and interests for the conference would be met. So, beginning nine months before the conference, they surveyed the interests of all 140 managers.

The designers deemed encouraging cultural mix between the managers as crucial. The problem was that at typical international meetings managers gravitate toward their own "cultural cocoons." Planners tried to build in events to help managers get beyond their own national backgrounds and people of their own language.

The well-planned structure of the conferences freed the managers to involve themselves in the true, most critical part of a conference—the building of a global organization. Emphasis was on meeting, getting to know and trust, working with, and learning with their new global colleagues. Together, they could better focus on critical, challenging issues, such as the Whirlpool vision, strategic planning, and quality.

One element that built powerful learning among the global participants was the conference's ground rules, which encouraged attendees to take part, and to help others participate as well, in the meetings and informal activities. They were challenged to get beyond their comfort zones with these guidelines:

- ❑ Create situations in which you can meet everyone.
- ❑ Promote an atmosphere of worldwide learning.
- ❑ Remember that the only problems we cannot solve are the ones we don't identify.
- ❑ Remember we are all responsible for making the week productive.
- ❑ Be a good listener.

Whirlpool managers themselves prepared and conducted the various workshops. This tactic helped the leaders of the new Whirlpool become accustomed to acting as learning facilitators and teachers, as well as managers.

During the conference, managers were invited to identify which major areas of the company's operations could be improved. Small-group discussions identified 200 areas. These were then boiled down to fifteen topics, such as global management reporting systems, global quality initiatives, development of a global corporate talent pool, and concept to consumer-product delivery cycles. Fifteen cross-functional and multinational groups, called Whirlpool One-Company Challenge Teams, were then formed to examine these fifteen topics during the upcoming year and present their recommendations at the next Global Conference in Washington, D.C., one year later. Team members met regularly and reported their progress in *The Leading Edge,* the corporate newsletter for Whirlpool's worldwide leaders.

Whirlpool people felt that this first Global Conference was so successful that it "launched the company ahead in time by an estimated three to five years in the integration of its global management team, and saved the company millions of dollars in the process" [17, p. 39]. Whirlpool had quickly jumped up the Globalization Curve.

Launching Toward Global Status

Whirlpool, like a small but growing number of companies, has begun its journey toward becoming a global organization. It is not an easy or simple journey but one with tremendous benefits and payoffs for those who succeed. In the next chapter, we will examine those benefits that make global companies so much more powerful and successful than the domestic, international, and multinational companies they have left behind. We will also discuss the special challenges related to corporate culture, people, strategies, operations, structure, and learning that must be overcome to make it to the global stratosphere.

References

1. Dunning, J. H. *The Globalization of Business: The Challenge of the 1990s.* London: Routledge, 1993.
2. Marquardt, M. and Snyder, N. "How Companies Go Global—The Role of Global Integrators and the Global Mindset." *International Journal of Training & Development,* Vol. 1, No. 2, 1997, pp. 104–117.
3. Adler, N. *International Dimensions of Organizational Behavior,* 2nd ed. Boston: PWS-Kent, 1991.
4. Rhinesmith, S. *A Manager's Guide to Globalization.* Homewood, Ill.: Irwin Professional Publishing, 1993.
5. Moran, R., Harris, P., and Stripp, W. *Developing the Global Organization.* Houston, Tex.: Gulf Publishing, 1993.
6. Toffler, A. *Powershift.* New York: Bantam Books, 1990.
7. Tapscott, D. *Digital Economy.* New York: McGraw-Hill, 1995.
8. Gery, G. *Electronic Performance Support Systems.* Tolland, Mass.: Gery Performance Press, 1991.
9. Bates, A. W. *Technology, Open Learning and Distance Education.* London: Routledge, 1995.
10. Stewart, T. *Intellectual Capital: The New Wealth of Organizations.* New York: Doubleday, 1997.
11. Johnston, W. "Global Workforce 2000: The New World Labor Market." *Harvard Business Review,* Mar.-Apr. 1991, pp. 115–127.

12. Auerback, S. "Around the Globe, the Sale of a Century." *Washington Post,* Nov. 17, 1991, pp. H1 and H9.

13. Glosgall, W. et al. "The Global Rush to Privatize." *Business Week,* Oct. 21, 1991, pp. 49–54.

14. Eom, S. B. "Transnational Management Strategies: An Emerging Tool for Global Strategic Management." *SAM Advanced Management Journal,* Vol. 59, No. 2, Feb. 1994, pp. 22–27.

15. Hordes, M. J., Clancy, A., and Baddaley, J. "A Primer for Global Start-ups." *Academy of Management Executive,* Vol. 9, No. 2, 1995, pp. 7–11.

16. Marquardt, M. and Engel, D. *Global Human Resource Development.* Englewood Cliffs, N.J.: Prentice Hall, 1993.

17. Laabs, J. "Whirlpool Managers Become Global Architects." *Personnel Journal,* Dec. 1991, pp. 39–45.

2

Power and Challenges of the Global Company

> For all practical purposes, all business today is global. Those individual firms . . . that already understand the new rules of doing business in a world economy will prosper; those that do not will perish.
>
> **Ian Mitroff, professor**
> **University of Southern California**

Power of Global Companies

Companies that are able to globalize will blow the competition away. Their power to link and leverage, to move and manipulate resources, to provide superior services and products at low costs will overwhelm their non-global competitors. Global firms will exponentially increase their competitive edge as they acquire the best workers, produce the best products, and attract the best customers.

Why do global companies have such strength and power? What is the source of their robust capabilities? How do they link and leverage these overwhelming advantages? Many sources account for this power. In this chapter we will explore the fifteen sources identified most frequently by global executives and leading global theorists (see Figure 2-1).

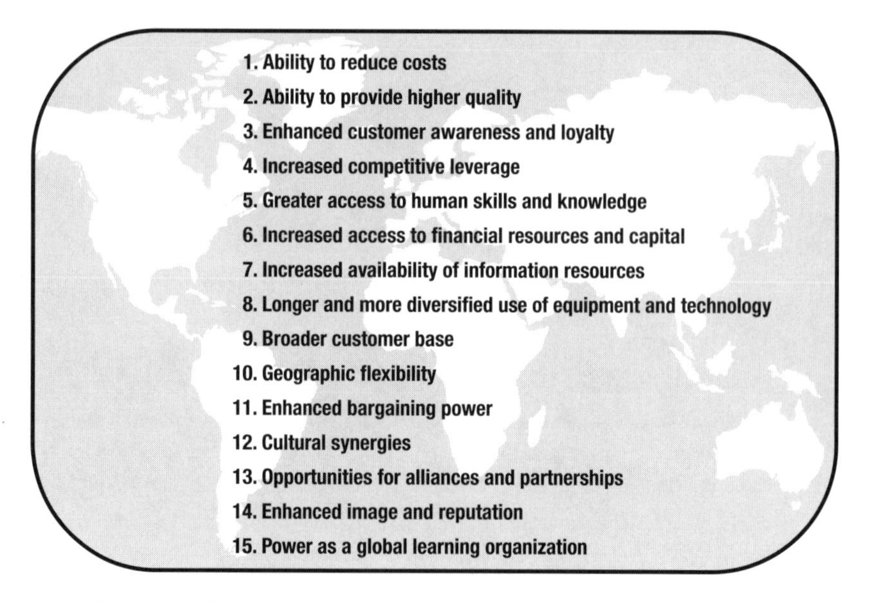

FIGURE 2-1. POWER SOURCES OF GLOBAL ORGANIZATIONS.

Ability to Reduce Costs

Global companies are able to reduce the cost of their products and services as a result of economies of scale, economies of scope, and focused production.

Economies of Scale

A global approach to activity location can help exploit economies of scale by pooling production or other value-adding activities. The production of large volumes of computers, cars, or fruits can result in economies of scale so that the cost per item is lowered. Global benefits of manufacturing, for example, are generally greater in the commercial aircraft business than in the apparel business. Why? Because achieving a minimumly efficient production scale requires a much higher share of the global market in aircraft than it does in apparel [1, p. 116]. Unlike multinational firms, global companies integrate production, marketing, and other activities from several countries or regions, thus permitting easier and quicker turnaround.

Economies of Scope

The global concentration of activities can exploit economies of scope by spreading activities across multiple product lines or businesses. It also reduces duplication of activities by eliminating and consolidating the identical activities occurring in many countries into one or two globally centralized locations.

For example, Unilever moved from thirteen factories for soap in Europe to three factories. Philips closed eighty factories to consolidate and reduce duplication. It is important to note that although a global approach to activity location means fewer locations than a multinational approach does, it may sometimes involve more locations and duplication than a pure export (international) approach.

A global organization can gain economies of scope over local competitors through lower costs, shorter delivery times, and/or broad assortments of standard products. Economies of scope are also obtained by:

- ❑ Gaining access to local, immobile factors of production and technological resources.
- ❑ Reducing transportation costs.
- ❑ Avoiding tariff and nontariff barriers.
- ❑ Satisfying some demands of and gaining benefits from local governments.
- ❑ Hedging against country-specific risks.
- ❑ Preempting competition.
- ❑ Not operating below full capacity in the various global locations.
- ❑ Gaining steep learning and experience benefits.

Focused Production

Reducing the number of manufactured products from many local models/brands to a few global ones is another way global companies can reduce costs. Typically, unit costs are lowered as the number of different products made in a factory declines. This reduces duplication of development efforts, as well as the costs of purchasing, production, and inventory. A global company can gain cost advantages by increasing volume of specific products—running fewer plants worldwide, buying inputs from fewer suppliers, and reducing duplication costs in research and development (R&D) and in engineering.

Global Cost Reductions at Becton Dickinson

Becton Dickinson's global strategy in the manufacturing of disposable syringes maximizes the global advantage of obtaining cost reductions. Becton built a global manufacturing network that concentrated production primarily in the United States, Ireland, Mexico, and Brazil, with each facility serving multiple markets. This concentration and coordination of production was made possible by the company's use of highly standardized global products and standardized production process. In addition to reducing duplication and increasing economies of scale, Becton Dickinson had the flexibility to take advantage of exchange rate fluctuations. For example, when the Mexican peso plummeted in value, Becton shifted much of the production in Mexico to serve the company's overseas markets. Sourcing out of Mexico gave the company a cost advantage vis-à-vis its competitors, who were locked into producing in higher-cost countries [1, pp. 117-118].

Ability to Provide Higher Quality

Because of economies of scale and scope, global companies gain significant advantages by focusing on a smaller number of products and programs than do the multinational companies, especially in the R&D and production activities.

The concentration in the R&D function, for example, allows a company to devote greater resources to the projects undertaken. At the same time, a concerted R&D function can also be the center of a global network that taps into the selected skills and knowledge available in any particular country.

A global concentration of production allows investment in better facilities and equipment than can be afforded under a multinational approach. These superior assets can then produce products of higher quality, as well as of lower cost. In highly globalized industries, combining high quality and low costs is particularly important because buyers have more choice of where they buy and have access to the best products or services offered in the world.

Another reason for superior quality in global companies is the fact that they are forced to improve quality via exposure to worldwide demanding customers and worldwide innovative competitors.

Global focus on quality is one of the reasons for the Japanese's success in automobiles. For example, Toyota markets a far smaller number of models around the world than does General Motors, even allowing for Toyota's unit sales being half that of General Motors. Toyota has concentrated on moving its few models, while General Motors has fragmented its development funds.

Enhanced Customer Awareness and Loyalty

Three complementary forces—global availability, global serviceability, and global recognition—can enhance customer preference through reinforcement of the image of the product. Yip refers to this global factor as "exposing customers to same mix in different countries." Coca-Cola, McDonald's, and Pizza Hut are leading examples of how to build worldwide customer loyalty.

Financial service companies (via credit cards and ATM machines), as well as hotels, also use this approach as they seek to reach the growing number of global travelers. Likewise, a manufacturer of industrial products can provide supplies to its global customer (for example, AMP for General Motors) with a standard product around the world.

Increased Competitive Leverage

Global companies achieve great competitive leverage over competitors by bringing the resources of the worldwide network to bear on the competitive situation in individual countries. Competitors that operate under an international or multinational approach are forced to deliver products and/or services provided by local facilities. Thus each subsidiary's competitive position depends on that subsidiary's own market share and revenues. So a subsidiary that loses market share under competitive attack also loses the operating scale needed to maintain the vast cost and quality advantages needed to defend its market position (as happened to Philips when its highly independent subsidiaries faced Japanese global strategies).

Greater Access to Human Skills and Knowledge

Global companies have access to the best people around the world, regardless of nationality. These people bring to the organization the experiences and learnings from their cultures, from their best universities, from their best organizations. Oftentimes this high quality of skill and knowledge is available at a much lower cost outside the United States and Western Europe. Russia, Eastern Europe, the Philippines, and India are sources of highly skilled, low-cost R&D workers for many global organizations. Local presence in countries such as these allows better opportunities to compete in their local job markets.

Local people also bring an understanding and sensitivity about workers and customers from their part of the world—for example, about buying habits, cultural consumer practices, motivational factors most likely to succeed, and management attributes that are effective in the local environment.

Global firms such as Arthur Andersen, Singapore Airlines, Microsoft, and General Electric pride themselves on obtaining the highest quality of people from and for each country in which they operate.

Increased Access to Financial Resources and Capital

Global companies have much greater access to capital and financial resources. They are able to be listed on multiple stock exchanges around the world—such as the stock markets of Hong Kong, Singapore, London, and Sao Paulo, to name a few. This provides the opportunity of selling stocks and raising capital from a greater array of sources.

Operating on a global scale allows companies to hold several currencies and to buy, sell, and leverage with financial institutions around the world. They are able to deal more forcefully with global, as well as local, banks.

When companies have a global presence, government restrictions that limit currency use and bank access to companies operating within its national borders do not apply to them. In addition, banks may be willing to provide more favorable loans to companies that they see and read about in the local newspapers and that have popular, local support.

Diversifying the company's assets and currencies allows for greater protections, as well as opportunities for moving in and out of currencies as an investment strategy. Currency exchange rates have a direct effect on relative country costs and therefore on the competitive positions of companies. The power of currency rates was dramatically shown several years ago when Caterpillar lost much of the Asian market to Komatsu, primarily because the U.S. dollar had increased by 50 percent over the yen.

Increased Availability of Information Resources

Information is often **the** competitive advantage of an organization. The organization with the most information (about new technologies, customers, sources of best employees, political happenings, and so forth) will generally be able to make better decisions and produce better products and/or services.

Global companies oftentimes deliberately establish a presence in countries that are a major source of industry innovation and have prestigious, high-quality universities. Global companies seek ways to be located near Cambridge or Silicon Valley or Singapore so they can gain more direct access to the many sources of innovation present in those locations. They will have more opportunities for face-to-face contacts with university researchers, to participate in technical and professional conferences, to acquire quicker access to publications (for example, many scientific journals are published only in Japanese and circulate little outside the country), and to hire the best local minds.

Longer and More Diversified Use of Equipment and Technology

Equipment and technology can be prohibitive in cost unless it can be amortized over longer periods of time and for a wider array of uses. Global companies have the ability to earn additional income on existing technology and equipment because of their wider and greater possibilities for application. Technology, equipment, and products can be reused as other new countries and/or companies seek to benefit from the product or service created by the technology (similar to the Format Painter on Microsoft Word that allows the user to apply what works well in one place to many other places).

Flexible manufacturing via computer-assisted design and manufacturing (CAD/CAM) also makes globalizing operations more feasible. Telecommunication technology, once the initial investments are made, oftentimes requires little or no additional costs, as it is utilized at sites worldwide.

Broader Customer Base

Global companies have a much greater consumer base. They see the entire world as their marketplace. With the opening up of the economies in China, India, and Russia, another 2.5 billion people are possible customers.

Global companies do not need to depend too heavily on one market. If the economy in one region falls or collapses (as occurred in several Asian countries in 1997–1998), the organization can divert marketing efforts, subsidize prices or losses, and ameliorate expenses.

The broader customer base serves another important purpose for global firms. Having a wider multitude of consumers generally expands the number of consumers demanding improved and customized products and services. These demands force the company (especially the R&D unit) to better understand present and future customer needs. For example, many firms have said that by attempting to meet the present demands of customers in California the firms acquire a predictive advantage, since Californians often are forerunners of what the rest of the American consumers will expect in the near future.

Geographic Flexibility

Global firms have much more geographic flexibility in determining where they will manufacture, carry out R&D, store supplies and products, and so forth. Choices are made based on a variety of factors, such as the level of political stability, government policies toward foreign investment, trade policies, tax policies, legal factors, the macroeconomic environment, and policies on international payments. The ideal location is one that is close to major global markets (lower costs for transshipment of raw materials, as well as intermediate and final products), yet where there is a low cost of raw materials, as well as a highly skilled labor force. A global manufacturing network also provides opportunities to set transfer prices and subsidiary remittances so as to minimize total tax liability.

Thus global companies have the option of moving manufacturing, production, or other activities to low-cost countries. Many European firms now manufacture cars in the United States because of lower production costs. American firms have done off-site manufacturing in Asia and on the Mexican side of the United States-Mexico border (at *maquiladoras,* which are factories at this border). Japan has plants in Malaysia and Thailand. Several U.S. credit-card companies and banks own data-processing facilities in Latin American and Asian countries to take advantage of low labor costs. Texas Instruments set up a software subsidiary in Bangalore, India, to access the low-cost, but highly skilled, technical workers available there. The subsidiary communicates with Texas Instruments' R&D center in the United States daily via satellite.

Global Locations of Banta Limited

Banta Limited, a small global firm headquartered in Canada, has established centers of excellence around the world to serve the needs of the rest of the organization. The Netherlands has become the R&D center; Indonesia provides the latest rubber footwear technology; Mexico is leading the plastic-injection molded footwear category; and Europe takes the lead in various retail marketing concepts [2].

Enhanced Bargaining Power

Global companies have the ability to switch production among multiple manufacturing sites and therefore possess bargaining power with suppliers, workers, and host governments. Global firms can also gain offensive and defensive advantages by having a presence in many markets, which enables a company to retaliate against attackers on its home ground. They also have more options to attack and counterattack against competitors. For example, Becton Dickinson, a major American medical products company, decided to enter three markets in its Japanese competitor's backyard.

Governments also seek to attract global firms. China, for example, has set up several economic development zones that provide tax breaks and other business incentives to attract global investment. The Chinese government also gives special tax treatment to joint ventures between domestic and foreign companies. Other countries, such as Ireland, Mexico, Thailand, and Malaysia, have provided similar economic incentives to attract foreign manufacturing to their countries.

Cultural Synergies

By being located in and by working with numerous cultures, global companies are able to "synergize" the strengths of differing cultures. This diversity should be seen as a primary source of new ideas when innovation is needed. Mobilizing the energy and the differences of various cultures can lead to multiple perspectives and the development of a wider range of options and approaches to problems and challenges. This increased creativity and flexibility proves invaluable in addressing culturally distinct clients and partners.

Opportunities for Alliances and Partnerships

Global companies not only have greater choices for alliances and partnerships but also are much more attractive to prospective suitors. As Rossbeth Kanter [3] eloquently states, "Globalization extends each partner's global reach while each contributes its local competence." Such global alliances and partnerships provide innumerable advantages for the global company, including:

- ❑ Combining of physical and human resources.
- ❑ Sharing of capital, equipment, and information.
- ❑ Easier and greater market access.

Enhanced Image and Reputation

Global companies are perceived, deservedly or not, by the public as having better products and services because of their globality. We believe that they must be superior or they would not be playing in the global arena. People who work for global enterprises are seen as the cream of the crop in terms of capability, compensation, opportunities, and fun (traveling to all those exciting places). A company's high reputation attracts a high quality of workers, who in turn create a high quality of products and services. In many countries, consumers buy products because of the global image; witness the success of McDonald's in Moscow or of Tommy Hilfiger in China or of Nike in the urban United States.

Power As a Global Learning Organization

Global companies have greater requirements, opportunities, and resources for acquiring, creating, storing, transferring, applying, and testing knowledge—the essence of a learning organization. The synergy of culture, the demand of global customers, and the challenges of global competition compels the organization to learn faster and continuously. Every employee needs to be a learner; every occasion needs to be a learning opportunity. Learning is necessary on an organizationwide basis and is tied closely with the business goals of the company. High-quality learners, customer demand for constant innovation, and cultural diversity all push global companies into becoming learning organizations [4].

Beloit Corporation—Going Global and Seeing the Benefits (by Pete Rosenberg, manager, corporate relations)

Beloit Corporation, one of the world's largest producers of paper products, has decided to go global. It began with the need to globalize the company's purchasing and materials management functions, which we expect will reap significant benefits in terms of both improving processes and reducing costs.

Jim Schneider is one of Beloit's biggest supporters of global product standardization, and for good reason. The vice president of sourcing and logistics says standardization/globalization is key to reducing the company's materials costs.

"Two things happen when you take advantage of standardization opportunities," says Schneider. "If a supplier makes the same part over and over, he becomes very proficient at doing it because he has a chance to optimize the process. And second, of course, you get the opportunity for volume discounts, which apply not only to products that go into Beloit equipment but also for production, maintenance, and repair materials.

"We spend millions of dollars every year on all kinds of general store items, such as cutting tools for example. If we can negotiate a contract for the same cutting tools to be used at all of our manufacturing facilities, each facility will pay the same lower price for those tools, whether they are a large or smaller user of the item."

This type of global purchasing is new to Beloit, which has purchased separately for most sites in the past. The new global plan will reduce the supplier base, as future suppliers must have the ability of servicing Beloit on a worldwide basis or, at a minimum, throughout the entire United States or all of Europe.

"We have put together a standard global contract for our stainless steel plate with Avesta, a Swedish company with plants all over the world," says Schneider. "Our past supplier was great but could only serve the U.S. With operations in other companies, we simply needed a global supplier. If a supplier cannot satisfy us on delivery, distribution, and quality and still be price competitive globally, he probably will not be a player in this business."

Beloit is actively developing partnerships with a number of global suppliers. For example, ABB provides complete electrical systems, headbox actuators, dryer hoods, and machine controls. And managing these complex interactions requires Beloit to have a much different relationship with these types of suppliers.

"In the past, these products would be brought by three or four different business units," Schneider says. "Typically no one would have any knowledge of the others' activities. Therefore we missed opportunities to leverage our buying power and also to understand the relationship of how these suppliers' products interact with one another."

This global partnership can also help Beloit improve processes, because long-term suppliers are more willing to transfer technologies and help Beloit use the suppliers' products in a more effective way. Schneider says, "If you sit down with a preferred supplier of welding equipment to discuss welding, for example, they may say, 'Here is a better way to do that.' Suddenly the global supplier is willing to spend time, money, and effort to help us improve our processes. It can get to the point where they almost become an extension of the company's own facilities. Their enormous technological capabilities can be transferred to Beloit."

One of the biggest challenges Beloit now faces involves using the current computer system for tracking materials and processes. With components being built at different Beloit locations around the world, it is critical to have a central global system for coordinating the supply of materials, potential order changes, and the transportation of finished product to the customers' mills.

Another area of focus involves getting people to work together to identify opportunities at the global level. The new Beloit Procurement Council plays an integral part by developing business units that use similar materials and leverage their buying power. Using global teams to improve processes and reduce cost is incredibly important to Beloit's future, and the payback is significant.

Schneider notes, "Right now, about sixty percent of the cost of manufacturing relates to the materials we buy. We know that we can save five to ten percent across the board by changing our scope from local and business group to global. By going global, we can save on some commodities by as much as thirty to forty percent!"

Corporate Challenges on the Path of Globalization

A global company operates without geographic boundaries, as if the entire world were a local marketplace. It is constantly scanning, organizing, and reorganizing its resources and capabilities in a way that national or regional boundaries are no longer barriers to potential products, business opportunities, and manufacturing locations. Global firms integrate activities so as to link and leverage every possible resource and opportunity. They use global sourcing to identify the best human resources, sources of capital, technology, facilities, and raw materials. Global companies have globalized not only their operations, structures, and strategies but, equally important, their corporate cultures, people, and learning.

However, three major tensions, or conflicting pressures, permeate every dimension of organizational life as companies seek to go global. These must be overcome to achieve global success.

1. **Culture**—Balance between a global corporate culture and local cultures around the world
2. **Politics**—Balance between global corporate politics and local political realities around the world
3. **Distance**—Balance between geographic distance and local proximity

Tensions of Culture

Simply defined, culture is a way of life shared by members of a group that older members pass on to new members. Culture consciously and subconsciously shapes the group's and each member's values, assumptions, perceptions, and behavior. It provides the group members with systematic guidelines for how they should conduct their thinking, their actions, their rituals, and their business. There are ethnic cultures, national cultures, corporate cultures, and, as already noted in this book, global cultures [5].

Culture provides a mighty challenge to global companies, because cultures create differences. Cultures cause employees to see reality very differently from each other and cause each individual to believe,

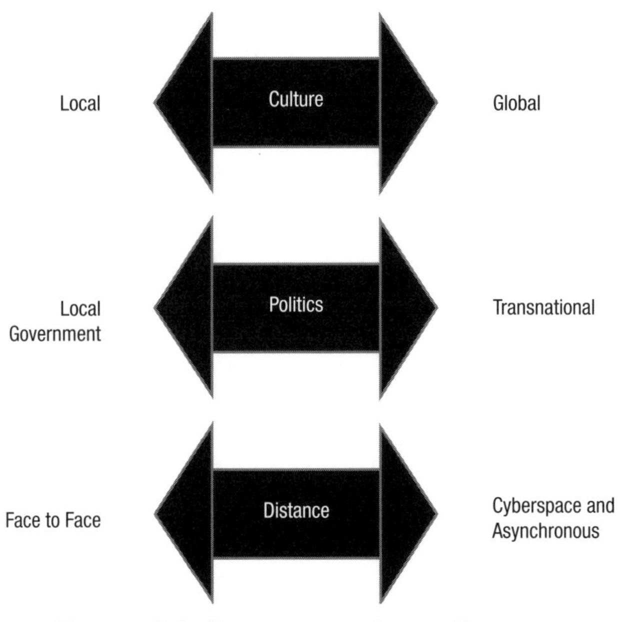

FIGURE 2-2. TENSIONS IN GOING GLOBAL.

of course, that his or her perception of reality is the correct one. Culture, which each of us learned at our mother's knee, leads us to believe that our way of thinking, acting, and doing things is the "only rational way of thinking, acting, and doing" [6]. To suggest or impose another way of seeing things and doing things seems strange, ridiculous, and/or unfair to someone of another culture.

Global companies need to recognize these differences, some of which may need to be changed and some of which need to be synergized (that is, building something better with the differences). The cultural tension revolves around how global companies seek to get their diverse populations, with local ways of thinking and acting, to share and agree on global ways of behaving and thereby to develop and achieve the global goals of the organization.

Tensions of Politics

Governments are dependent upon their local constituencies (if democratic) or themselves and the military (if totalitarian). Their allocation of power, as well as their regulation of access to resources and opportunities in their country, may be determined by what serves them best and not necessarily what serves the citizens or local or foreign corporations. Economic policies that might be best for the economy may not be best for the people who wield the power. Business opportunities may require ingratiating one's firm with the family in power (such as was true with the Suharto family in Indonesia) or abiding with strict religious customs (such as in Saudi Arabia).

Governments both shape and are shaped by culture. There are historical, religious, and cultural reasons citizens believe in or accept a certain form of political, governmental, or legal system. Governments may and do exclude or include specific groups on the basis of ethnicity, gender, age, or economic status; a government may even deem certain practices legal or illegal (for example, Islamic banks cannot charge interest). Who may be hired or fired, the status of unions, the role of government, and the possibility of rapid changes as in the case of coups—each of these factors can change a particular government's position for an industry or a corporation from support to opposition overnight.

Resolving the political tension revolves around having a global presence in all countries and yet determining which political risks and requirements are acceptable and/or likely in specific countries.

Tensions of Distance

The physical and psychological separation caused by geographic distance provides unique challenges for global companies. Although technology enables organizations to be both centralized and decentralized, numerous limitations still exist because of limited face-to-face contact. In many cultures, the personal contact is essential for the transaction of important business or for any progress in partnerships and promotions. Distance can cause people to feel cut off, be out of the loop, or have a sense of less importance. Headquarters' culture is often misunderstood or denigrated from afar.

Global business goes on 24 hours a day around the world. Important decisions may need to be made at 2 a.m., headquarters time. Workdays in some countries (for example, Saturdays and Sundays in the Gulf Region) are weekends in other countries.

The distance tensions revolve around the issues of integration and separation, collaboration and necessary independence, inclusion and exclusion, and being everywhere at the same time [7].

Each of these global tensions—culture, politics, and distance—significantly affects all dimensions of organizational life and activities, specifically the (a) corporate culture, (b) people, (c) strategies, (d) operations, (e) structure, and—most importantly for global companies in the knowledge era—(f) learning. We will examine these six global dimensions in Chapters 3 through 9. Here are a few of the challenges, conflicts, and/or tensions each organizational dimension encounters because of globality:

Corporate Culture

❑ Corporate headquarters' culture vs. local cultures
❑ Values of speed and efficiency vs. personal relationships and acceptance of fate
❑ Political expediency vs. truth and virtue
❑ Global mind-set vs. groupthink
❑ Technology vs. people

People

❑ Global competencies vs. local cultural skills
❑ Global vs. local recruitment
❑ Local vs. transnational vs. headquarters personnel
❑ Universal hiring/firing policies vs. local/government-mandated policies
❑ Management effectiveness across cultures
❑ Cultural and political reward systems and pay scales
❑ Staying close to distant staff

Strategies

❑ Costs of global vs. local coordination
❑ Global vs. local norms
❑ Alliances vs. franchising vs. doing it alone
❑ Political vs. economic access

- ❑ Inductive vs. deductive thinking
- ❑ Currency risks and incurring costs and revenues in different countries

Operations

- ❑ Location of R&D
- ❑ Metric vs. non-metric
- ❑ Financial borrowing—political vs. pragmatic
- ❑ Similarity vs. differentiation of products and services
- ❑ Distribution—political expediency vs. economic efficiency
- ❑ Global and local marketing and advertising
- ❑ Administrative bureaucracies and administrivia
- ❑ Flexible manufacturing vs. standardized products

Structure

- ❑ Non-hierarchical/seamless structure vs. steep hierarchical infrastructure required by cultural norms
- ❑ Projectized, multiple bosses vs. cultural aspects of loyalty
- ❑ Centralized vs. decentralized
- ❑ Need to accommodate local political and legal requirements
- ❑ Management of knowledge vs. restriction of knowledge
- ❑ Location and layout, including use of *feng shui* (Chinese belief in the importance of living in harmony with nature)

Learning

- ❑ Learning as an organization vs. learning as individuals
- ❑ Value and expectation of learning continuously
- ❑ Acculturizing learning materials and programs to local vs. headquarters' culture
- ❑ Providing worldwide learning via intranet and Internet yet maintaining need for instructor-learner familiarity
- ❑ Deductive vs. inductive; learner-centered vs. instructor-centered; lecture vs. experiential

These are just a few of the challenges that global companies must overcome on their journeys toward true and complete global status.

Global success depends on the company's systematic effort to globalize all six of the organizational dimensions described above. In Chapter 3, we will present an overview of the *GlobalSuccess* Model. Chapters 4 through 9 will provide specific strategies and steps for globalizing each of the six organizational components. Let's begin the global journey!

References

1. Yip, G. *Total Global Strategy.* Englewood Cliffs, N.J.: Prentice Hall, 1992.
2. Gorman, C. *Managing in a Global Organization.* Menlo Park, Calif.: Crisp Publications, 1994.
3. Kanter, R. *World Class: Thriving Locally in the Global Economy.* New York: Simon & Schuster, 1995.
4. Marquardt, M. and Reynolds, A. *The Global Learning Organization.* Burr Ridge, Ill.: Irwin Publishing, 1994.
5. Trompenaars, F. *Riding the Waves of Culture.* Chicago: Irwin Professional Publishing, 1994.
6. Storti, C. *The Art of Crossing Cultures.* Yarmouth, Me.: Intercultural Press, 1989.
7. Brake, T., Walker, D., and Walker, T. *Doing Business International.* Chicago: Irwin Professional Publishing, 1995.

3

The GlobalSuccess *Model*

The truly global company is a rare phenomenon and was only recently made possible by the four T's: technology, travel, trade, and television. Despite the urgency and absolute necessity of transforming themselves into organizations of global status, very few companies have thus far succeeded. Although some may have globalized their structures and corporate activities, most firms are still far from achieving the changes necessary to create a true global organization—one with a global corporate culture, global people, global strategies, global operations, global structure, and global learning.

Although many companies may believe they are global, in reality they are struggling along at the international or multinational stage. They have yet to comprehend and feel the power and speed of the global company.

During the past ten years, the author has researched and worked with hundreds of global executives around the world to discover the ways in which they are attempting to bring their corporations into the global stratosphere. The *GlobalSuccess* Model (see Figure 3-1) is built upon the experiences and ideas of these global leaders. It recognizes what successful global companies recognize—that to be a strong global player in the global marketplace, a company must develop globality in six organizational components: corporate culture, people, strategy, operations, structure, and learning.

Let's explore and define each of these six organizational components that form the *GlobalSuccess* Model.

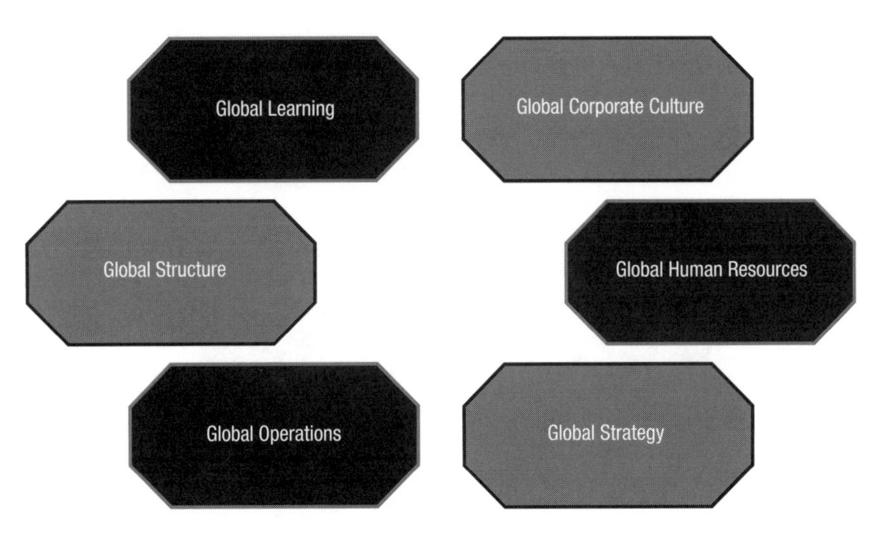

FIGURE 3-1. GLOBALSUCCESS MODEL.

Global Corporate Culture

Many global leaders, as well as leading global theorists (Rhinesmith, Adler, and Snyder among others), believe creating a global corporate culture is the most important, yet the most difficult, aspect of globalization. Changing structure and operations (external factors) is easier than changing internal factors, such as people's values and the way they think, act, and react. Transforming one's image of reality, attempting to be a world citizen in spite of having a national identity, and finding a new culture and ideology is immensely difficult.

And yet these cultural changes must be attained for a company to truly incorporate and implement the other five dimensions of globality. The new corporate culture—like any culture, be it national, ethnic, or corporate—involves a new mind-set, new values, new rituals and practices, new heroes and leaders. The *GlobalSuccess* Model's Corporate Culture component includes five dimensions: vision, mind-set, values, activities, and heroes (see Figure 3-2).

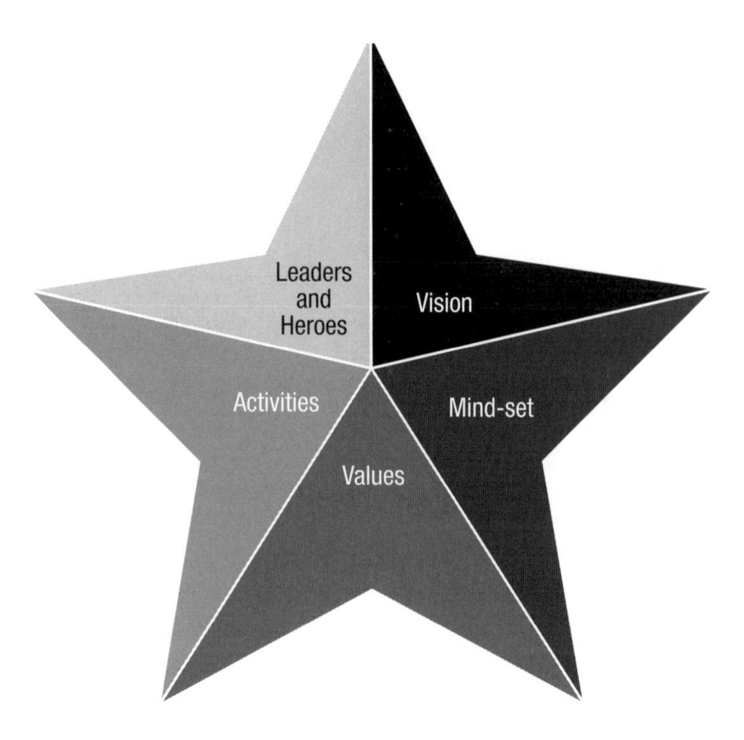

FIGURE 3-2. GLOBAL CORPORATE CULTURE.

Global Vision

A vision captures the organization's hopes, goals, and direction for the future. It is the image and dream that is transmitted inside and outside the organization. A global vision is borderless and multicultural with links and leverages worldwide.

Global Mind-set

Mind-set is a predisposition that directs people to see the world in a particular way. A mind-set sets boundaries and provides explanations for why things are the way they are while at the same time establishing guidance for ways in which one should behave; it is a filter through which we look at the world. A global mind-set thinks and see the world globally, is open to exchanging ideas and concepts across borders, and is able to break down one's own provincial ways of thinking. The emphasis is placed on balancing global and local needs and on being able to operate cross-functionally, cross-divisionally, and cross-culturally around the world.

Global Values

Values are the deep part of culture, oftentimes subconscious and passed from the present members to new members of a group. Values are what is meaningful and what provides purpose and reason for what one does. Global values include:

❑ Global thinking
❑ Cultural sensitivity
❑ Continuous learning
❑ Cultural customization of products and services
❑ Quality and continuous improvement
❑ Speed and timeliness
❑ Empowered global people
❑ Work life and humanization

Global Activities

All cultures have a variety of actions, rituals, events, activities, and norms that externalize and reinforce the desired internal values, mind-sets, and basic assumptions. Global companies undertake some of the following activities to build the desired corporate culture:

❑ Global seminars and conferences
❑ Global publications
❑ Global benchmarking
❑ Global language
❑ Global policies and procedures
❑ Global reward systems

Global Heroes and Leaders

Every culture has heroes whom group members are encouraged to emulate because of the qualities and successes of these heroes. Global companies seek to identify existing heroes (mentors) and to build future heroes via mentoring, training, development, and teams.

Global Human Resources

Global companies seek to identify, recruit, train, develop, provide global experiences for, recognize, and retain the best people from around the world, no matter their location or cultural background. Employing the top global people and benefiting from their capabilities and their learnings will result in better products, better services, and better success. The *GlobalSuccess* Model contains six dimensions under the category of Global Human Resources (see Figure 3-3).

FIGURE 3-3. GLOBAL HUMAN RESOURCES.

Global Competencies

Organizations need to identify the capabilities, attitudes, and skills necessary for implementing their missions and goals. The workers of global companies should have a number of special competencies, including cultural self-awareness, global perspectives, multilingual competence, tolerance for ambiguity and differences, cultural flexibility, and strong communication skills.

Global Recruitment

Global companies search worldwide for the best people using global and local recruiting firms. Recruitment and hiring policies reflect local customs and laws and are sensitive to appropriate and inappropriate questions. Local nationals and third-country nationals (expatriates from a country other than the one where a global company is headquartered), as well as expatriates, are considered for the applicant pool.

Global Training and Development

The ability of a company to compete globally depends heavily on the quality and level of global training in the organization. The training/career-development strategy includes the following steps:

- ❑ Connection of business goals to training
- ❑ Creation of a global training mission
- ❑ Examination of internal and external factors and resources related to global training
- ❑ Identification of training goals and objectives
- ❑ Identification of action steps to accomplish learning needs of organization
- ❑ Development of evaluation system to assess impact and needed changes of training and development strategies

Overseas Experience

In global companies, the overseas experience is a critical element in the development of global employees. Ideally, it should include the following elements:

- ❑ Be an integral part of career development and seen as a valued experience
- ❑ Be built upon solid selection criteria
- ❑ Include extensive predeparture, as well as ongoing, training
- ❑ Recognize the importance of the family
- ❑ Ensure ongoing communication and support
- ❑ Include plan for repatriation

Global Career Path

Retaining high-quality global workers and managers is much more difficult in the global arena. Identifying future leaders and providing them with the career opportunities and experiences needed for individual and corporate success is critical for institutionalizing globality. A career track that has a planned sequence of global career assignments, linked to the global business needs of the company, is essential.

Global Rewards and Recognition

Global companies need to expand the possibilities of how to recognize solid achievements and success on the part of workers. Performance appraisal systems and reward mechanisms need to be globalized, as well as localized, to accommodate corporate and cultural differences of employees.

Global Strategies

Global strategy is more than developing a core business strategy (which addresses products, customers, geographic markets served,

FIGURE 3-4. GLOBAL STRATEGIES.

major sources of sustainable competitive advantage, and so forth). It should be integrated and lead to worldwide business leverage and competitive advantage. Strategy considers the whole picture, determining when and where and how to act; it includes logistics, tactics, and policy. The Global Strategies category of the *GlobalSuccess* Model contains the following seven steps (see Figure 3-4):

Develop Global Mission and Philosophy

Among the most important tasks of global leaders are the duties of providing their workers with a sense of direction, defining the organization's global business, and developing a strategic mission. What type of organization do they wish to create? What markets do they seek to penetrate? What global attitude and philosophy do they wish to develop?

Undertake Analysis and Diagnosis of Global Opportunities and Threats

The second step in developing a global strategy is conducting a comprehensive analysis of opportunities and challenges that may be available on a worldwide basis. This environmental diagnosis includes both internal and external review of strengths and weaknesses, as well as opportunities and threats.

Establish Global Goals and Performance Targets

Step 3 involves the development of global goals in terms of the desired outcome to be achieved by the organization within a specified time period and with specific assignments of accountability.

Identify Strategic Alternatives and Choices

In this step, the organization seeks to examine its global-market positions, facilities, and investments so as to focus on leveraging and linking opportunities. Various competitive moves should be considered, as well as a number of strategic alternatives such as alliances, joint ventures, licensing, and franchising.

Form Strategic Contingencies and Plans

The next step in global strategizing explores the means to achieve the global ends or objectives. It examines the important entrepreneurial, competitive, and functional actions that are to be taken in pursuing organizational goals and that will thereby position the organization for sustained global success.

Implement Global Strategy Through Alignment and Integration of Resources and Organizational Units

This step involves executing a global plan alignment and integration of the following elements:

- ❑ Instilling a strong organizationwide commitment both to organizational objectives and to the chosen strategy
- ❑ Linking the motivation and reward structure directly to achieving the targeted results
- ❑ Creating an organization culture that is in tune with strategy in every success-creating aspect
- ❑ Installing policies and procedures that facilitate strategy implementation
- ❑ Developing an information and reporting system to track and control the progress of strategy implementation
- ❑ Exerting the internal leadership needed to drive implementation forward and to keep improving how the strategy is being executed

Evaluate, Modify, and Reapply Global Strategy

Based upon these analyses, as well as ongoing assessment of the success of the global strategy, the global strategic plan will probably require corrective adjustments and reformulations. Changing global conditions, the emergence of new opportunities or threats, a new corporate culture, and new learnings are all examples of what could necessitate reformulating the strategic plan and its implementation.

FIGURE 3-5. GLOBAL OPERATIONS.

Global Operations

All functions and operations of the global company should be globalized so that the linkages and leverages between them can be maximized and can complement one another. The *GlobalSuccess* Model includes twelve operations (Figure 3-5).

Global Research and Development (R&D)

R&D is a growing focus of companies in the highly competitive marketplace where innovative new products and services are critical for survival. Companies such as 3M and Rubbermaid recognize that 30 percent of their products will need to be invented and developed each year. Global R&D consumes big dollars, is centralized or regionalized to serve the entire global market, and is located where the world's top research is being conducted in that industry.

Global Manufacturing

Flexible manufacturing systems, self-directed work teams, and statistical engineering controls are part and parcel of global manufacturing. Global manufacturing allows greater access to local factors of production, reduces transportation costs, avoids tariff and nontariff barriers, creates efficiency of scale, and hedges against country-specific risks.

Global Product Development

To compete globally, product development needs to be strategized relative to diversity, innovation, scope, and design. Cultural awareness and customer values and buying habits are part of the product development mix.

Global Quality

Global quality must be able to compete with and be benchmarked against the world's best. Quality should be based on local and global aspects of conformance, aesthetics, perception, reliability, durability, performance, features, and serviceability.

Global Finance

Finance on a global level is more than just acquiring access to cash. Identifying financial resources with expertise and success on the local, as well as global, scale is equally important. Global companies need to know the currency conditions and regulations of countries and regions in which they operate. Global finance involves an understanding of tax policies and currency exposure issues worldwide, best locations for investment, and procedures for obtaining listing on multiple stock exchanges. Flexibility and speed, as well as rigid measurement and reporting systems, are a must in global finance.

Global Materials and Inventory Management

Global inventory management must answer several key questions:

- ❑ Do we have a consortium of suppliers that can deliver materials just in time?
- ❑ Do we have capital to invest in needed technology?

❑ Can inventory be shared across plants/regions/countries?
❑ Do we have software capabilities to access inventory data from centralized data bases?

Global sourcing considers price, quality, delivery, dependability, and service.

Global Marketing and Advertising

This operation carefully considers the cultural and global dimensions of the following:

❑ Appropriate customization and differentiation
❑ Global product strategies
❑ Global pricing
❑ Culture-based advertising
❑ World-class standards for quality and service
❑ Global sales and promotion strategies
❑ Global customer education

Global Distribution

A global distribution system examines the mix between global and indigenous distribution channels. The channels chosen are based upon what is appropriate between and within countries, recognizing cultural, political, economic, and distance factors.

Global Sales and Services

Promotion and sales strategies include worldwide, world-class standards that are tailored to provide local, decentralized customer service geared to meet the needs and expectations of the local culture.

Global Technology Systems

Technology includes both process technology and product technology. Technological systems should be integrated with all other eleven operations, along with value-added networks and global quality standards. Issues include cost, speed, quality, space, obsolescence, maintenance costs, customer service, dependability, and ease of use.

Global Telecommunication and Information Systems

Global telecommunication and information systems involve standardization necessary for gathering, processing, and distributing information through a variety of necessary, yet culturally appropriate, mechanisms. Connecting globally is enhanced by using identical desktop software and information systems in all parts of the world. E-mail that links its employees on a worldwide basis improves communication and productivity.

Global Administration

Administration for global companies includes coordination of a wide array of areas, such as immigration, transportation, work permits, pay differentials, family needs, schooling, safety and security, insurance, health care, and labor relations.

Global Structure

Globalization changes the spatial dimension of enterprises and creates the need for a more flexible organization. To more easily cross boundaries, whether across the hall or across the world, a new global structure is required. Since knowledge is rapidly becoming the most important advantage of global companies, this new global structure must be able to act more quickly and transparently to collect, store, analyze, distribute, apply, and test knowledge. Global structures, both organizationally and physically, are affected by the dimensions of culture and distance. Three elements are included in the Structures component of the *GlobalSuccess* Model (see Figure 3-6).

Global Integration of Functions, Operations, and Units

Global firms are matrixed and projectized, global yet local, seamless and streamlined, boundaryless and networked, flat and unbureaucratic.

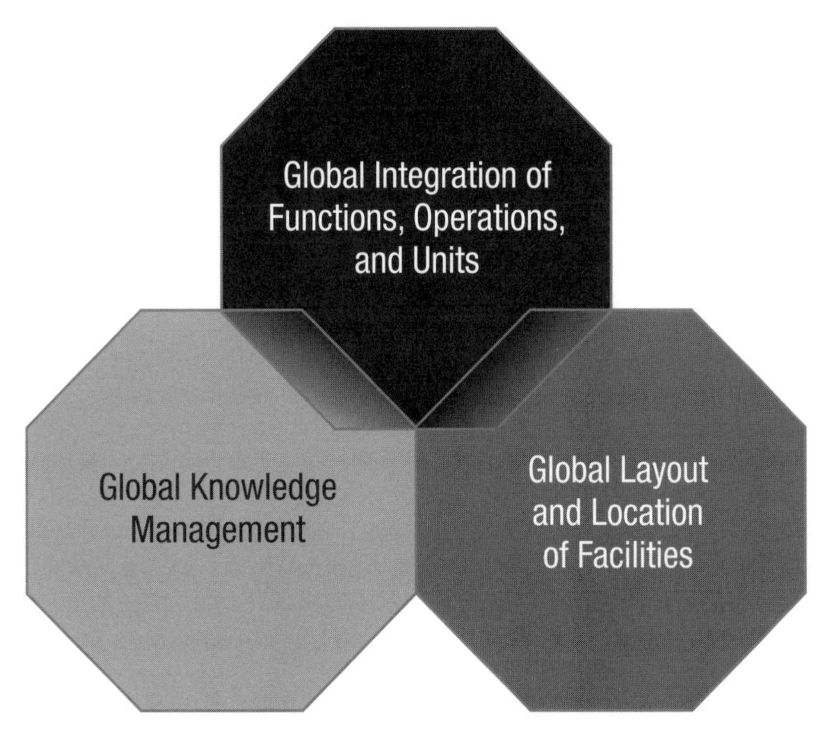

FIGURE 3-6. GLOBAL STRUCTURES.

Global Knowledge Management

Structures, together with technology and policies, are critical in facilitating and enhancing the flow of knowledge to, within, and out of global organizations. Knowledge should be acquired, stored, analyzed, transferred, and utilized on a worldwide basis.

Global Layout and Location of Facilities

Where to locate manufacturing and other facilities and how to arrange the layout are important management decisions that will relate directly and indirectly to corporate success, worker satisfaction, and customer belief in the organization. Cultural elements, such as *feng shui* (Chinese belief in the importance of living in harmony with nature), play significant roles in how local and global players participate in the company's day-to-day operations.

Global Learning

Increased speed and quality of learning have become absolutely critical components in global companies' ability to continuously improve the quality and speed of products and services demanded by the global customer. The Learning component of the *GlobalSuccess* Model examines the company's status as a learning organization, how all training programs are globalized and acculturated, and globalization of the learning curriculum (see Figure 3-7).

Global Learning Organization

The learning organization includes five subsystems:

- ❑ **Learning Dynamics:** Levels of learning (individual, group, and organizationwide), skills of learning, and types of learning
- ❑ **Organizational Transformation:** Vision, culture, strategy, and structures for learning
- ❑ **People Empowerment:** Leaders, employees, customers, partners, and community as learners
- ❑ **Knowledge Management:** Acquisition, creation, storage, and transferal of knowledge
- ❑ **Technology Application:** Information and learning technologies

Globalized Training Programs

Designing, delivering, and evaluating organizational learning programs requires an acculturation and globalization of each step and process to effectively reach the target learners.

Globalizing Curriculum

Learning materials—written materials, computer software, videotapes, and so forth—need to be adapted to fit the language and cultural needs of the users.

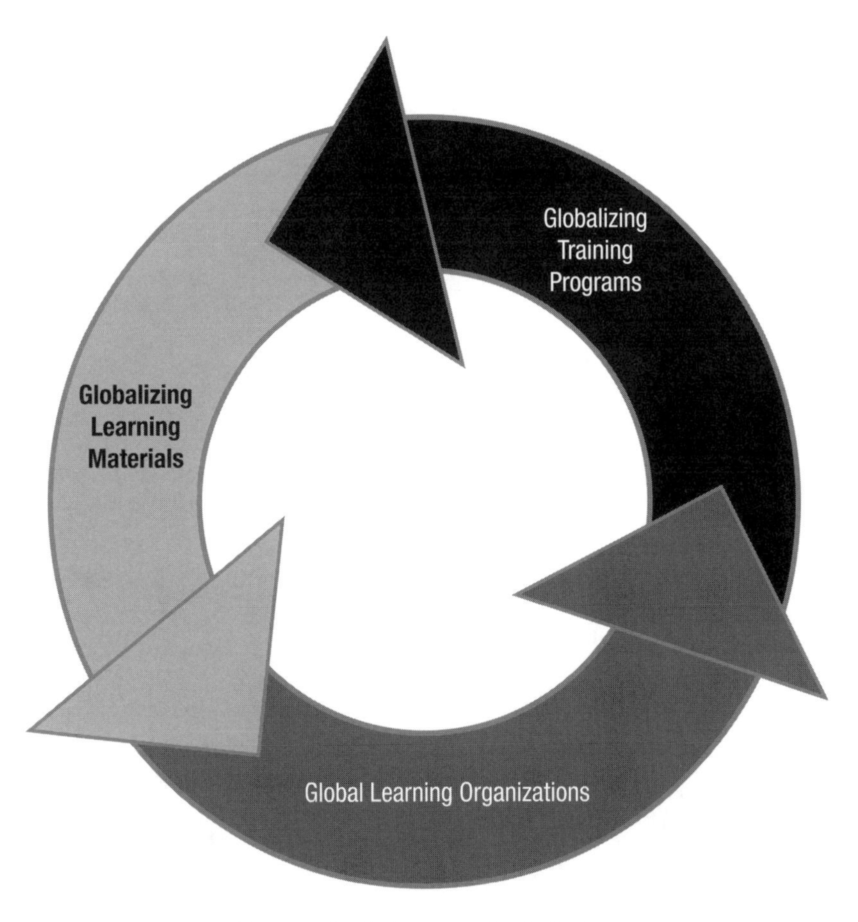

FIGURE 3-7. GLOBAL LEARNING.

Conclusion

In this chapter, we have identified the six organizational dimensions that must be globalized (the *whats*) for corporate success. In the next six chapters, we will examine *how* to globalize each of the components of the global organization. We will provide numerous examples and illustrations of the actions taken by top global companies to globalize each particular dimension of the *GlobalSuccess* Model.

4

Creating a Global Corporate Culture

Culture refers to the way a group of people thinks and does things. It represents the group's values, beliefs, practices, and customs. Culture guides and shapes perceptions and behavior, and thus has an overwhelming impact on how any group determines its way of surviving and succeeding in the world around it.

Just as nations and ethnic groups have distinct cultures, so do organizations. These corporate cultures, created intentionally and unintentionally, form unique ways of thinking and implementing action that are manifested by the vision, symbols, heroes, rituals, activities, and mind-sets of its members.

Corporate executives and organizational theorists recognize that the most important, most difficult, and yet most effective way of changing an organization is to change its corporate culture. Leaders who want to transform their companies into global companies begin by creating a global corporate culture—a culture with a global vision and with global values, mind-sets, and activities [1, 2]. By changing the corporate culture, these leaders know they will more easily and effectively change the other elements of the organization that need to be globalized. In this chapter we will explore the following components of corporate culture and identify ways in which they can be globalized:

1. Global Vision
2. Global Mind-set
3. Global Values

FIGURE 4-1. GLOBAL CORPORATE CULTURE.

4. Global Activities, Rituals, Practices, and Actions
5. Global Heroes and Leaders

Global Vision

Developing an organizational vision provides members of the organization with stars to steer by. A powerful vision guides and inspires, motivates and excites, and ultimately gives meaning and importance to the activities of people both inside and outside the organization.

It is hard to think of any organization that has achieved and sustained some measure of greatness without a vision. Taco Bell's vision is to "become No. 1 in the stomach," Federal Express delivers packages "absolutely, positively overnight," and Polaroid provides "instant photography." Each of these organizations was able to bind people together around a common identity and sense of destiny.

A vision captures a company's hopes, goals, and direction for the future. The vision is the image of the organization that is transmitted inside and outside the organization. As a company seeks to become a global organization, its global vision depicts and portrays the desired future picture of the company, in which:

- ❑ There are no geographic boundaries for opportunities.
- ❑ The entire world is the marketplace for customers, workers, and partners.
- ❑ Multiple cultures are present and synergized.
- ❑ Achieving the mission and goals of the organization requires global thinking and action.

Why is a global vision so important for becoming a global company?

1. A global vision provides the focus and energy for overcoming the existing corporate culture, where oftentimes a local-is-best mentality is present.
2. Without a pull toward some goal that people truly want to achieve, the forces of the status quo can be overwhelming. It is important to remember that people are not machines but individuals who live within various cultures. They need a collective sense of identity and fundamental purposes for living their lives. Visions should be exhilarating. They should create the spark and excitement to enable the organization to develop renowned, visionary products and services.
3. The loftiness of the target compels new ways of thinking and acting. It provides a rudder to keep the globalization process on course when stresses develop. Through a global vision, organizations can shape the direction—as well as create the structures, activities, and people—necessary to achieve global success.
4. Powerful, generative commitment toward globalization only occurs when people are truly committed to accomplishing things that matter deeply to them. The shared vision and values allow people to change, to accept new ways of thinking, and to be more able to give up deeply held views.

Jim Gannon, vice president of human resource planning and development for Royal Bank of Canada, underscores the decisive importance of a vision for globalization when he says, "Visions are what energize the organization. They represent the dreams that pull us forward [3]."

The global vision should be developed by as many stakeholders as possible—managers, employees at all levels, customers, partners, shareholders. The resulting shared global vision can and should guide strategic thinking and planning for the organization, as well as lead to multiple strategies and procedures for progressing on the path toward becoming a global organization.

Developing a shared global vision is only the starting point. Senior management must work hard to communicate the global vision, to publicly declare its commitment to global integration, and to demonstrate to employees, customers, and suppliers the critical importance that the vision holds for the company.

Colgate-Palmolive Vision and Values

VISION: TO BECOME THE BEST TRULY GLOBAL CONSUMER PRODUCTS COMPANY

VALUES:

- **Truly Global**—This means we bring together the world's best people, creative ideas, technology, and processes to meet the needs of our consumers wherever they live. We create and sustain superior business performance through global teamwork.
- **Continuous Improvement**—We are committed to getting better every day in all we do—as individuals and in our teams. By better understanding consumers' expectations and by always working to improve our products, services, and processes, we strive to become the best.
- **Caring**—We care about all Colgate people. This shared value means that each of us listens with respect, values differences, builds mutual trust, and supports our unity of purpose and action. We care also for the best interests of our consumers,

(Continued on next page)

our shareholders, our business partners, our many local communities, and the protection of the global environment.

- ❑ **Consumer focus**—We are committed to listening actively to consumers and responding to their needs and preferences. Through this unwavering consumer focus, we will achieve our end goal: To deliver quality products and services that exceed consumers' expectations.

Global Mind-set

Dave Whitwam, CEO of Whirlpool Corporation, emphasizes that the key to globalizing an organization is getting everyone in the organization to think globally, not just a few people. "You must create an organization where people are adept at exchanging ideas, processes, and systems across borders," he says [4, p. 137]. To do this, Whitwam believes that the leadership must build upon the unifying global vision and philosophy to help create a global mind-set.

A global mind-set is considered by global theorists as a critical part of the underlying subprocesses for building corporate globalization [5]. To have a global culture and become a global company, it is ultimately necessary to have a shared global mind-set throughout an organization [6]. Global mind-set is defined as "a predisposition to see the world in a particular way that sets boundaries and provides explanations for why things are the way they are, while at the same time establishing guidance for ways in which (members of the global company) should behave" [7, 8]. Mind-set is a filter through which we look at the world. The ideal global corporation has been described by Greenbaum [9] as one that possesses, among other business attributes, people who have the ability to manage change and think globally.

Rhinesmith [8] makes the following comparison between domestic and global mind-sets:

Domestic Mind-set	Global Mind-set
Functional expertise	Bigger, broader picture
Prioritization	Balance of contradictions
Structure	Process
Individual responsibility	Teamwork and diversity
No surprises	Change as an opportunity
Trained against surprises	Openness to surprises

Global mind-sets are not exclusive, but inclusive. People with global mind-sets, according to Rhinesmith, seek to continually expand their knowledge, have a highly developed conceptual capacity to deal with the complexity of global organizations, are extremely flexible, strive to be sensitive to cultural diversity, are able to intuit decisions with inadequate information, and have a strong capacity for reflection. A global mind-set thinks and sees the world globally, is open to exchanging ideas and concepts across borders, and is able to break down one's provincial ways of thinking. The emphasis is placed on balancing global and local needs, and being able to operate cross-functionally, cross-divisionally, and cross-culturally around the world.

Beyond having stamina, global workers must have exceptionally open minds. They must respect how people from different countries do things and have the imagination to appreciate why they do them that way. To build such a global culture of trust and technological exchange, Asea Brown Boveri (ABB), one of the world's leading global companies, created three forums:

1. A management board for each business area. These boards meet four to six times a year to shape global strategy, monitor performance, and solve big problems.
2. A rotating team of veteran managers, each of whom has worldwide responsibility for activities in a critical area, such as purchasing and R&D. They travel constantly, meet with the presidents and top managers of local companies, and drive the coordination agenda forward.
3. Functional coordination teams that meet once or twice a year to exchange information on details of implementation in production, quality, marketing, and other operations. The teams include managers with functional responsibilities in all the local companies, so they come from all over the world.

The building of global corporate culture involves the creation and sharing of a global mind-set among staff throughout the organization at both the individual and collective levels. Although many companies recognize the intrinsic, foundational value of the global mind-set as a global integrator, few have made much progress in breaking the provincial or nationalistic thinking of their employees.

Rhinesmith suggests some of the following programs for building global–mind-set thinking and skills in an organization:

1. Orientation programs for global cohorts across functions, regions, and product groups to instill common global visions and global corporate strategies and values
2. Global seminars on (a) how to scan social, economic, and political trends, (b) how to balance global integration needs for efficiency and global coordination for learning, and (c) how to accomplish effectiveness and local responsiveness by specific business, function, and task
3. Cross-cultural and multicultural skill training emphasizing problem solving, decision making, communicating, selling, negotiating, coaching, appraising, and leading in multicultural contexts
4. Right-brain/left-brain training for reframing and managing contradictions and complexities, ambiguity, and chaos and change, which all are part of the changing world of globalization

According to Moran et al. [10], a global mind-set can be promoted within the organization by encouraging employees:

1. To learn at least one additional language.
2. To utilize opportunities to work overseas. Short-term business exchange programs should be aimed at all employee levels, not just managerial levels.
3. To read books about other countries and cultures.
4. To vacation abroad and consider sending their children on summer exchange visits with children of the business counterparts.

Global Values

Values complement the pulling force of a company's vision by being the pushing drivers that enable a company to reach its vision. A number of globalization-oriented values characterize a corporate culture searching for and committed to global success. Abdullah [11] has identified several key global values: (a) global thinking, (b) appreciation of and sensitivity to various cultures, (c) continuous learning, (d) focus on quality and customer service, (e) speed and timeliness, (f) belief that people are important and should be empowered, (g) support for innovation, experimentation, and risk taking, (h) quality of work life, and (i) simplification of operations and processes.

Global Thinking

Global thinking, simply described, refers to the ability to search for global perspectives, to see global possibilities, and to look for the big picture, as well as the value placed on those things. Global thinkers are visionary, future-oriented possibility-finders. They look for ways to include other companies, other cultures, and other customers into the global mix.

To encourage and assist in global thinking, global human resource development (HRD) departments might offer training programs in areas such as cross-cultural communication, how to work in multicultural teams, global values and global thinking, and world-class customer service.

Many leading global enterprises regard ongoing briefings on various global business and cultural issues as critical for building global thinking and global skills. National Semiconductor, Royal Bank of Canada, and AMP all have periodic information exchanges about global trends, as well as political, social, and economic issues in different geographic regions. These briefings are supplemented by information provided in company newsletters and on bulletin boards. The ultimate goal of these efforts is to build the following organizational attitudes and competencies:

- ❑ Understanding and insight into global and regional geopolitical forces and changes, and their relationship to business
- ❑ Awareness of the existence of cultural differences and an understanding of the basis of these differences, especially as they occur between the native and foreign cultures
- ❑ Tools and techniques for developing and practicing effective business strategies within the foreign culture
- ❑ Global business strategies for establishing joint ventures and alliances
- ❑ Skill building in areas such as language, interpersonal communication, adjustment, and adaptation
- ❑ Leadership and management skills needed in global companies

Appreciation of and Sensitivity to Various Cultures

Global people must not only tolerate other cultures but possess a dedicated interest and enthusiasm in discovering more about these other cultures. To flourish in the global marketplace, they must appreciate and understand how people's different values influence productivity and performance, management orientations and values, and buying and selling [12].

As former U.S. Secretary of State Elliott Richardson once noted:

> The vastly expanded marketplace for innovative technologies and products will carry cultural identities across many borders. Cultural sensitivity, which is reflected in respect for national differences, may appear at first too intangible and unmeasurable to figure in the equation. But if one tries to identify all the various qualities distinguishing a corporation that has won respect and admiration in its quest for worldwide economic success, one finds that such sensitivity is invariably one of them.

Continuous Learning

The value of continuous learning is an absolutely critical value for global companies. With so much change occurring so rapidly across so many technical, cultural, and industrial borders, only by constant learning can an organization and its people have a chance of global success.

In global organizations, learning should become a habit and an integrated part of all organizational functions. Such a commitment to learning develops a rich adaptable culture, creates integrated relationships, and enhances learning by encouraging values such as teamwork, self-management, empowerment, and sharing. It is the opposite of a closed, rigid, bureaucratic architecture. Let's examine some of the specific learning values and actions global organizations should encourage:

A Corporate Climate in Which Learning Is Highly Valued and Rewarded

Global organizations should provide a facilitative climate where learning is highly encouraged and highly valued. Learners are the heroes. Learning gets recognized during performance appraisal time, at award ceremonies, and in the paycheck. Pay-for-knowledge incentive schemes are established to reward employees for their learning.

At 3M, learning is encouraged and rewarded. Workers are allowed up to 15 percent of their time to learn, to be creative, and to work on their own projects. 3M has also created the Pathfinder Award, which recognizes those who "develop new products or a new application of a product for a particular country or culture" [3]. In one year alone, sixty-seven different awards were conferred to different work teams; the value of those sixty-seven creative ideas in terms of sales and creativity was $522 million!

Responsibility for Learning Shared by All

Employees have responsibility for their own learning, as well as the learning of others. They must also understand how their responsibilities relate to the goals of the organization as a whole. Employees are expected to teach, as well as to learn from, their co-workers. The entire workplace culture is geared to organizationwide learning.

As a result of these paradigm shifts, members of the organization must gain a whole new mind-set and a whole new way of "seeing" organizations and the interplay between work and learning. Learning must take place as an ongoing by-product of people doing their work—in contrast to the traditional approach of acquiring knowledge before performing a particular task or job.

A New Form of Learning

Globalized companies emphasize a new form of learning in the following ways:

- ❑ It is performance-based (tied to business objectives).
- ❑ Importance is placed on learning processes (learning how to learn).
- ❑ The ability to define learning needs is as important as the answers.
- ❑ Organizationwide opportunities exist to develop knowledge, skills, and attitudes.
- ❑ Learning is part of work, a part of everybody's job description.
- ❑ What people and organizations **know** takes second place to what and how quickly they can **learn.**
- ❑ Learning skills are much more important than data.
- ❑ Penetrating questions are much more important than good answers.

Corporatewide, systemswide learning offers organizations the best opportunity to not only survive but to succeed. As foreseen by leaders of the Rover Automotive Group in England, "The prospect that organizational learning offers is one of managing change by allowing for quantum leaps. Continuous improvement means that every quantum leap becomes an opportunity to learn and therefore prepare for the next quantum leap. By learning faster than our competitors the time span between leaps reduces and progress accelerates" [13].

Focus on Quality and Customer Service

Customers throughout the world now have many more choices. They want high quality, low cost, continuous innovation, speed, customization, and total service. To succeed, global organizations must have employees committed to quality and must take continuous improvement seriously. Why? Because one question should never be far from everyone in the company: "How can this be done better?" Quality management requires that a comprehensive approach is present and that everyone is learning continually how to do everything better. A global culture seeks world-class standards in quality and service. There is pride and high self-esteem because of the high level of service, products, and operations.

Speed and Timeliness

Like quality, speed and timeliness has become crucial for satisfying customers. Global competition demands speed to the customer, or the customer will go elsewhere. The global corporation appreciates and values speed—speed of response to change, speed of response to customer demands, speed in organizational changes, speed of learning from successes and failures. The speed of change within the organization must be equal to or greater than change outside the organization, or the organization is in decline and may not survive.

Belief That People Are Important and Should Be Empowered

To respond to the challenges of the global marketplace, companies need to respect and empower their people. This reduces dependency and pushes responsibility as close as possible to the final action point. Group members should be treated as adults with adult capabilities, which include the ability to decide for themselves how to solve problems, to take actions, and to learn from these experiences. Of course, appropriate training and support are needed to enable this empowerment.

Honda is an exemplary company in empowering its people. Honda does not just talk empowerment; it permits people to set out and create the new cars. Robert Simcox, a plant manager, says Honda people are learning together because they have been "given the power to use their own creativity and imagination." On the shop floor, multifunctional teams take responsibility for the quality of Honda products. Problems encountered on the shop floor are solved by the workers. Frankness and creativity are necessary in Honda's factories [3].

Whirlpool has set a high standard of empowering its employees, customers, and partners. "People commitment" for Whirlpool means learning, listening to concerns and ideas, living the shared values in the workplace, and recognizing and rewarding performance. Workers are encouraged to feel like owners. Whirlpool's Excellence Systems (WES) give people the power to make decisions and thereby build their confidence and competence. Examples include a cross-functional team that developed Whirlpool's award-winning, super-efficient refrigerator; a learning group that devised a just-in-time system to supply product kits and components; and a project team that leveraged knowledge from North America into a new dryer designed for European customers.

Support for Innovation, Experimentation, and Risk Taking

Global organizations must be bold enough to encourage people to take risks, innovate, and get out of the habit of asking for permission and waiting for instructions. They realize that risks are necessary to achieve quantum leaps in product and service quality and to stay ahead of global competitors.

Responsible risk taking and an openness to new ways of doing things are promoted. In a global organization, there is no such thing as a complete failure—the company can always learn from them. Mistakes are not only allowed but valued, because they can be the source of new ideas and can help people discover new ways of doing things.

In companies like Ford and Harley-Davidson, the core values include intellectual curiosity, which means constantly challenging the status quo and looking for ways to improve learning and new ways to meet and exceed customer expectations.

Operational variety, which means hiring and bringing together people of diverse backgrounds to achieve, is also encouraged so as to generate more and more ways to accomplish organizational goals. An organization that supports variation in strategy, policy, process, structure, and personnel will be much more adaptable when unforeseen challenges arise. In global organizations, different management and working styles are recognized and appreciated. No single style is deemed as necessarily best, because an adaptive, innovative organization needs all styles, each of which can complement the deficiencies of the others.

Quality of Work Life

Global organizations are concerned not only with organizational productivity and profits but also with the quality of its members' working lives. They are committed to the development of the full range of human potential in an environment that invites participation and enjoyment. Work is exciting and challenging because one's mental, as well as physical, talents are being tapped. The social and physical surroundings encourage a respect for the total person. People care about each other.

Global companies are conscious of the growing pressures of workers to meet family and social obligations, and therefore they try to be family friendly by offering programs such as flexible work arrangement, dependent care services, and wellness programs. This concern for the whole person and his or her family is much more common in other cultures and countries of the world than it is in the United States.

Simplification of Operations and Processes

Global companies need to simplify operations and processes whenever and wherever possible by implementing the following:

- ❑ **Bureaucratic Elimination**—Removal of unnecessary administrative tasks, approvals, and paperwork
- ❑ **Duplication Elimination**—Removal of identical activities
- ❑ **Value-added Assessment**—Evaluation of every activity to determine its contribution to meeting customer requirements
- ❑ **Simplification**—Reduction of complexity
- ❑ **Cycle-Time Reduction**—Determination of ways to compress time while still meeting or exceeding customer requirements
- ❑ **Error Proofing**—Making the process difficult to do incorrectly
- ❑ **Simple Language**—Reduction of the complexity of the way the process or operation is described
- ❑ **Supplier Partnerships**—Improvement of supplier input
- ❑ **Standardization**—Commitment to doing it the best way all the time
- ❑ **Automation**—Automation of boring and routine activities

Too much complexity and too many delays result in too many costs and frustrations—spelling certain failure in the global marketplace.

Caterair International—A Company with Global Culture and Values

Caterair International serves more airlines worldwide than any other airline caterer, with more than 22,000 employees operating in twenty-three countries. Headquartered in Bethesda, Md., the company was formed in 1989 as a reincarnation of Marriott Corporation's airline catering division. Caterair controls about 40 percent of the domestic aviation catering market. It has a major global presence, with 44 percent of sales coming from international business. Caterair has kitchens in Australia, South Korea, Japan, and Taiwan. It also has joint ventures overseas—in Moscow with Aeroflot and in Sao Paulo with Varig. In 1997, Caterair catered approximately 200 million meals worldwide on approximately two million flights.

In its determination to become a global company, Caterair deliberately set about to create a global culture with a global vision, a global mind-set, and global values.

Caterair's Global Vision

Caterair decided that a clear corporate vision built on the cornerstone of globalness would provide the framework and direction for future expansion. This vision served as an integral part of the company's documents, discussions, and daily life (in other words, corporate rituals). Caterair's vision truly provided a clear picture of the stars to steer by for the company. The vision also furnished the framework that Caterair would employ to fulfill its goal of being the learning leader in the airline catering industry.

According to David Workman, former vice president of human resources, the company knew that the Caterair vision would be achieved only if there were agreement and strong support for the values underlying and supporting that vision. The values had to be developed organizationwide, and everyone in the organization would participate in Caterair's new "Mission, Vision, Values" training, discussions, and meetings. Top managers were trained to facilitate these efforts. Caterair decided that to be the global airline caterer of choice:

- ❑ Employees must experience a quality of life resulting from an environment of growth, fair treatment, and opportunity.
- ❑ Customers must receive value and consistent, superior service for the specified products.
- ❑ Airline passengers must perceive on-board food as a necessary and valuable feature.
- ❑ Shareholders must receive at least the required return on investment.
- ❑ The community must share in and benefit from Caterair's success and perceive it as a good corporate citizen.

CATERAIR'S GLOBAL VALUES

Caterair expressed its values under the categories of global mind-set, customer-driven, continuous improvement, teamwork, and empowerment.

Global Mind-set

- ❑ Communicate the fact that the airline business has become a world-as-a-single-market business.
- ❑ Every unit is a member of the Caterair global team.
- ❑ Remember that one unit's performance affects the success of all other units on the global team.
- ❑ Pursuing the world market offers the opportunity to grow and further secure our livelihoods.
- ❑ Maintain a Caterair world standard of quality.
- ❑ Pursue business opportunities with every airline.
- ❑ Look forward to and accept career opportunities throughout Caterair's world.

(Continued on next page)

Customer-driven

- ❑ Being the best in the eyes of customers is our No. 1 job.
- ❑ Treat each customer as if he or she were our only customer.
- ❑ There is no small customer or small customer base.
- ❑ All airline employees are our customers.
- ❑ Exceed customer expectations in all we do.
- ❑ Solve customer problems . . . fast!
- ❑ Prevent problems from recurring.
- ❑ Make and meet every customer commitment.
- ❑ Do the customer's work as if you were doing it for yourself.
- ❑ Recognize improvements that lead to customer satisfaction.

Continuous Improvement

- ❑ Communicate the need for continuous improvement—the intense competition in the airline business is making our customers demand more from us for the same money.
- ❑ Continually improve all that we do and how we do it—not only in big steps, but mostly in lots of little steps.
- ❑ Relentlessly pursue perfection—strive for zero defects.
- ❑ Don't think that you're the best, because it's the enemy of getting better.
- ❑ Find ways to prevent problems before they happen.
- ❑ Replace "We don't do it that way" with "Let's try."
- ❑ Continuous improvement requires **continuous learning.**

Teamwork

- ❑ Teamwork is an attitude, not a collection of players.
- ❑ Communicate team goals.
- ❑ There are no wins without the team winning.
- ❑ Solve problems as a team.
- ❑ Recognize team accomplishments, not just individual accomplishments.
- ❑ Argue among ourselves, but act with one voice.

- ❑ Think of the next person down the line as your customer.
- ❑ Think of yourself as the customer of the next person up the line.
- ❑ Pitch in and help others, even if it's outside your usual work.

Empowerment

The empowering motto of Caterair is "Caterair People Can." Caterair realizes that this can occur only if and because the organization will:

- ❑ Tolerate no blockage of essential information.
- ❑ Drive out fear and mistrust from every corner of the organization.
- ❑ Always strive for world-class standards in quality and service.
- ❑ Respect its people's knowledge.
- ❑ Solicit problem-solving ideas from its people.
- ❑ Encourage unsolicited problem-solving ideas.
- ❑ Encourage everyone within the company to listen to ideas different from their own.
- ❑ Respond in a timely way to 100 percent of people's suggestions.
- ❑ Put decision-making power in the hands of the person who knows the most about the task.
- ❑ Give people the authority to act when they must.
- ❑ Back up the person to whom Caterair gave the power.
- ❑ Find out why a mistake happens, learn from it, and prevent it from recurring.
- ❑ Forgive honest mistakes.

Role of Managers

Caterair managers see as their major responsibility the development of the people around them, which is accomplished by the following corporate cultural behaviors and norms:

(Continued on next page)

- ❑ Treat all people with respect, honor, dignity and fairness—take care of the people.
- ❑ Recognize a job well done.
- ❑ Help people feel free to ask questions.
- ❑ Supply people with the tools they need to do their work.
- ❑ Make and meet commitments to all our people.
- ❑ Increase our people's knowledge and skills.
- ❑ Encourage advancement and promotion.
- ❑ Increase confidence, self-esteem, pride, and professionalism.
- ❑ Seek out highly motivated people to join our team.

The Global Passport

Upon joining the Caterair corporate culture, employees are given a "global passport." Before an employee enters a new position he or she must have the relevant pages of this passport stamped (similar to having a visa stamped before entering a country) as a sign that the person has demonstrated competency and proficiency in the global work of Caterair. These skills are documented in the Caterair global data base, which allows the company to determine members' readiness for new global assignments and career progression.

Caterair believes in getting the word about being a global organization around. Its *Horizons* newsletter is published quarterly in six languages. In addition, there are also twelve regional newsletters. These provide a more localized focus on events and celebrations. Caterair also publishes a newsletter for its managers. Managers also benefit from a videotape series published for them in the second month of each quarter. The videos are distributed in French, German, Portuguese, Russian, and Spanish, as well as English, covering topics related to finance, marketing, and industry news.

A Global Environment

Looking ahead, it appears that the worldwide air travel market will continue to grow through the 1990s, nearly doubling in size by the year 2000. Caterair expects consolidation within the airline industry to continue for several more years. CEO Daniel J. Altobello says, "Far from being a disadvantage, we view the twin phenomena of growth and consolidation as strengthening the industry and providing additional business opportunities for Caterair. The traditional partnership between suppliers and customers will grow stronger with growth and consolidation."

Caterair's successful steps in building a global organization, as well as its reputation for quality and strong bonds with many of the world's airlines, will work to the company's advantage in the years ahead. Caterair International has quickly become a high-flying global organization [3].

Global Activities

The preceding three sections (vision, mind-set, and values) described the inner, deeper core of a culture—that which is such a part of an organization's thinking and acting that it becomes second-nature and subconscious. Most parts of a culture, however, are observed and demonstrated through their outer core—through their behaviors, their rituals, their language and communication, their activities, and very importantly, through their leaders and heroes. We will explore these elements of global corporate culture in the remaining part of this chapter, beginning with the activities of the global company—its global rituals, language, and programs.

Global companies utilize a number of activities to implement and demonstrate their globality: (a) communication, (b) their models for emulation (for example, those benchmarked), (c) global conferences, (d) global language, (e) global leadership and learning centers, (f) global policies and procedures that articulate hoped-for corporate behavior, and (g) sites for global learning.

Global Communication

To build the global culture, global companies talk about global events and happenings inside and outside their organizations. Internal newsletters and external press releases feature how the organization and its members have succeeded on the international scene. Rover's company newspaper constantly promotes global awareness and participation inside the organization. Honeywell's *The Global World* keeps people aware of the opportunities and resources available at its global resource center, which contains videos, brochures, cultural facts, and mobility assistance. British Telecom's management magazine, *Communique,* focuses on the numerous global successes of the company, while National Semiconductor's *International* prominently announces global goals and activities.

Acer has developed a wide variety of methods to keep employees aware of global programs. The company sends employees copies of *Acer News,* which is a biweekly on company products and strategy, and a cross-cultural monthly magazine, *Spectrum,* which focuses exclusively on cultural perceptions and practices in each country where Acer operates. The Beloit Corporation's weekly newsletter, *Dialogue,* is distributed via e-mail and bulletin boards in five languages for worldwide distribution. Beloit's bi-monthly, *Focus,* offers articles featuring global activities and the cultural aspects of working abroad.

Global Benchmarking and Best Practices—Identifying Both Internal Programs and Global Companies to Emulate

Another cultural global integrator used by many companies is their systematic process for acquiring and sharing best business practices information throughout the company. Whirlpool has its Quality Forum, an annual extravaganza of quality achievements around the world beamed to all employees via satellite. National Semiconductor has "sharing rallies," in which the best internal practices of each country and region are shared in festive, highly publicized events. Andersen Consulting has developed its own Globalization Assessment package for identifying internal and external best globalization practices. Kellogg recently conducted a comprehensive global assessment with its top seventy people. Johnson & Johnson and Whirlpool Corporation regularly conduct global culture audits.

Global Conferences

To demonstrate their desire to become and/or status as global companies, many organizations hold annual global conferences to bring together employees from various locations to share cultural perspectives and to develop global strategies, global projects, and global corporate culture (see Whirlpool example on pp. 22–24).

Beloit Corporation's First Global Conference

One message came through loud and clear during the company's first global Environmental, Health, and Safety Conference in Beloit recently: The health and safety of every Beloit corporation employee and the impact Beloit's manufacturing operations have on the environment are viewed by senior management as essential to Beloit becoming a world-class company. The conference focused on sharing knowledge and identifying common challenges faced globally. Groups discussed a wide variety of topics, including safety in the paper mill, cultural consideration in health and safety, global environmental perspectives, and specific plans to integrate environmental health and safety consistently into worldwide operations. Plans were developed to put the company's global environmental, health, and safety policies and procedures on the company intranet.

Global Language

Establishing a global language for the company, even if it is a different language than is spoken in the country where the headquarters is located, is important for globalizing the company. English has quickly become the global language of most Asian- and European-headquartered companies.

The common global language also includes unique corporate phrases, such as its advertising words, that capture the quality and power of the company, its products, and its values. Global companies, like any tightly united cultural group, need a common operating language to accelerate communication and to share values and perspectives. Global leaders recognize that language is both a creator and carrier of culture.

Global Leadership and Learning Centers

More and more organizations have established global leadership and learning centers. Honeywell's Global Center mission is "to spread awareness of globalization throughout the organization." It was created after an internal status and needs analysis showed that many people in the organization were unaware of globalization and were confused about the trade-off between global integration and local responsiveness. According to Honeywell literature, the Global Center plays a "lead role in fostering a culture and an environment within Honeywell that promotes a worldwide business perspective, cross-cultural sensitivity, multinational experience, and global management skills at all levels and in all operations."

British Telecom has an international leadership program for all its managers. Whirlpool's global education center at Brandywine Creek, Mich., has three primary goals: "To create a global mind-set, to develop skills necessary to win in the global marketplace, and to help each manager understand how his/her role fits into the strategic architecture."

Global Policies and Procedures

To guide activities, as well as to establish global norms and standards, companies set global policies and procedures, which in turn can be modified to address the needs and sensitivities of local cultures. Policies and procedures, of course, cover a wide array of expected corporate practices, including recruitment, performance appraisals, internal communication, and ethics. Royal Bank of Canada, for example, has created a number of such policies that optimize company resources and transcend borders, as well as capitalize on the strengths of the various cultures of the bank. Common core operating procedures worldwide can ensure quality and uniformity, as well as commitment.

Places for Global Learning with Other Global Learners

Learning along with other companies that are seeking to go global also helps build the global culture. Kellogg, for example, has discovered that its three-week global programs at Thunderbird International School have greatly increased globalized thinking and action at the company. British Telecom has also found staff attendance of global programs at business schools helped hasten globalization at BT.

Global Leaders and Heroes

The heroes in global organizations, according to Rhinesmith [2], are the past, present, and future leaders who are able to undertake the following six management actions for the company:

1. Manage competitiveness by allocating and aligning resources
2. Manage complexity by determining what must go according to plan
3. Manage adaptability by trusting process over structure
4. Manage teams by valuing diversity
5. Manage uncertainty by flowing with change
6. Manage learning by seeking to be open

Global companies identify and develop global heroes in a variety of ways:

Via Establishing "Glob-able" Competencies Among Their Leaders

Global competencies involve a mastery of identified global business skills, an ability to operationalize key globalization concepts, and a mastery of global competitive and organizational dynamics. AMP has identified what it calls the "glob-able" competencies needed by its leaders:

- ❑ Ability to describe clearly the forces behind the globalization of business
- ❑ Ability to recognize and connect global market trends, technological innovation, and business strategy

- ❑ Ability to outline issues essential to effective strategic alliances
- ❑ Ability to frame day-to-day management issues, problems, and goals in a global context
- ❑ Ability to think and plan beyond historical, cultural, and political boundaries, structures, systems, and processes
- ❑ Ability to create and effectively lead worldwide business teams
- ❑ Ability to help AMP adopt a functional global organization structure

Via Training

Developing global competencies for organizational leaders (that is, heroes) can be accomplished through a variety of training and development activities, such as:

- ❑ Individual profiling and consultations
- ❑ Global executive seminars
- ❑ Structured learning exchanges with other global executives
- ❑ Global briefings and conferences
- ❑ Executive retreats
- ❑ Leadership development programs

The American Society for Training and Development (ASTD) recently developed a skill model for the global executive, which included the following four skill areas:

1. Skills for *understanding* global business opportunities
2. Skills for *setting* an organization's direction—for creating vision, mission, and purpose
3. Skills for *implementing* the vision, mission, and purpose
4. Skills for *personal understanding and effectiveness* with multicultural teams and alliances in a global context

Training Management Corporation (TMC) has a two-day program titled "The Effective Global Manager," in which participants learn the skills and knowledge required to put top management's strategic plans into effect to penetrate and operate in global markets. Fostering global thought patterns and broadening cultural perspectives are primary objectives of the program. In the course, participants:

- ❑ Learn the distinctions between domestic, international, multinational, and global companies
- ❑ Develop corporate strategies and structures and learn how to manage the competitive process
- ❑ Examine the role of culture in business and the management implications of working with people who operate according to different cultural values and norms
- ❑ Identify U.S. cultural assumptions and values, examine how they are reflected in management practices, and contrast all of those with the values of key countries
- ❑ Apply cultural insights to management communication across national and organizational lines
- ❑ Explore the management competencies of a global leader
- ❑ Practice and apply techniques for multicultural team management
- ❑ Gain skills practice in analyzing and solving cross-cultural and organizational problems through case studies that simulate real-life situations

Via Mentoring

Companies such as Sime Darby, PPG, and Skandia see global mentoring as a key element in accelerating the globalization of their organizations. Respected and experienced global managers are chosen to guide and assist new managers into quickly becoming global managers.

Via Development

Other strategies used by global companies to develop global leadership qualities include:

- ❑ Rotating future leaders in and out of global assignments.
- ❑ Sending executives to visit key competitors in other countries.
- ❑ Teaching foreign languages on a just-in-time basis.

- ❑ Offering reentry programs for executives returning from foreign assignments.
- ❑ Establishing worldwide electronic study groups.

Global Brains at General Electric

Much of GE's success can be traced to corporate recognition of the need for global presence in its business units. GE's change of focus is really attributable to CEO Jack Welch, who decided that GE should be No. 1 or No. 2 globally in each of its businesses. GE's plastics business and jet engine business were already strong globally, and GE decided to learn from them.

Global Brains, a month-long executive program held at GE's training headquarters in Crotonville, N.Y., is recognized as one of the top corporate learning centers in the world. The curriculum has changed its focus from developing individual skills to seeking to bring about global organizational change.

GE believes that thinking globally requires more than just knowledge. People must actually learn how to manage in the complex, fast-moving global environment. As a result, GE decided to make its three key executive-development programs available overseas. Managers actually went on-site in various countries to work on real-world problems. And, at the same time that participants learn and solve problems, they build global networks together.

Global Culture As Key to Globalization

Creating a global corporate culture is perhaps the most difficult yet most important element necessary for an organization to achieve globality. In this chapter we examined how global corporate culture is built by developing global vision, mind-set, values, rituals (activities, practices, and actions), and heroes (that is, both past and present leaders). In Chapter 5 we will focus on how to best recruit, select, develop, retain, and reward the quality of global people needed to reinforce this global culture and work for the global company.

References

1. Marquardt, M. (Ed.) *Corporate Culture: International HRD Perspectives.* Alexandria, Va.: ASTD Press, 1987.
2. Rhinesmith, S. "An Agenda for Globalization." *Training & Development,* Vol. 45, No. 2, Feb. 1991, pp. 22–29.
3. Marquardt, M. and Reynolds, A. *The Global Learning Organization.* Burr Ridge, Ill.: Irwin Publishing, 1994.
4. Maruca, R. F. "The Right Way to Go Global: An Interview with Whirlpool CEO David Whitwam." *Harvard Business Review,* Vol. 72, No. 2, 1994, pp. 135–145.
5. Doz, Y. L. and Prahalad, C. K. "Managing MNCs: A Search for a New Paradigm." *Strategic Management Journal,* Dec. 1991, pp. 145–164.
6. Marquardt, M. and Snyder, N. "How Companies Go Global—The Role of Global Integrators and the Global Mindset." *International Journal of Training & Development,* Vol. 1, No. 2, 1997, pp. 104–117.
7. Rhinesmith, S. "Global Mindsets for Global Managers." *Training & Development,* Vol. 46, No. 10, Oct. 1992, pp. 63–68.
8. Rhinesmith, S. *A Manager's Guide to Globalization.* Homewood, Ill.: Irwin Professional Publishing, 1993.
9. Greenbaum, J. "View from the Top: Survival Tactics for the Global Business Arena." *Management Review,* Vol. 81, No. 10, Oct. 1992, pp. 49–53.
10. Moran, R., Harris, P., and Stripp, W. *Developing the Global Organization.* Houston, Tex.: Gulf Publishing, 1993.
11. Abdullah, A. *Going Global.* Kuala Lumpur, Malaysia: MIM Press, 1996.
12. Oviatt, B. and McDougall, P. "Global Strategies: Entrepreneurs on a Worldwide Stage." *The Academy of Management Executive,* Vol. 9, No. 2, 1995, pp. 30–43.
13. Marquardt, M. *Building the Learning Organization.* New York: McGraw-Hill, 1996.

5

Globalizing Human Resources

People are the most important resource for any company, global or otherwise. Global organizations need highly qualified people who are well-trained and well-supported in their global activities. According to most global executives, however, one of the most difficult tasks of the globalization process is the recruitment, selection, development, and retention of qualified global people. In this chapter we will explore six dimensions of the human resource process and how global companies can best perform these functions (see Figure 5-1).

Determining Competencies Desired for Global Staff

Based on numerous surveys of global and cross-cultural professionals, ten key competencies (see Figure 5-2) have proven to be essential for people who undertake global assignments [1, 2, 3, 4, 5]:

Knowledge of One's Own Culture (Cultural Self-awareness)

"Know thyself" is the most important intercultural competency of global professionals. Our behavior is influenced by our basic cultural values, beliefs, and assumptions. Unless we become conscious of these values and carefully examine them, we will not be able to understand why we act the way we do and react toward other cultures in the way that we do.

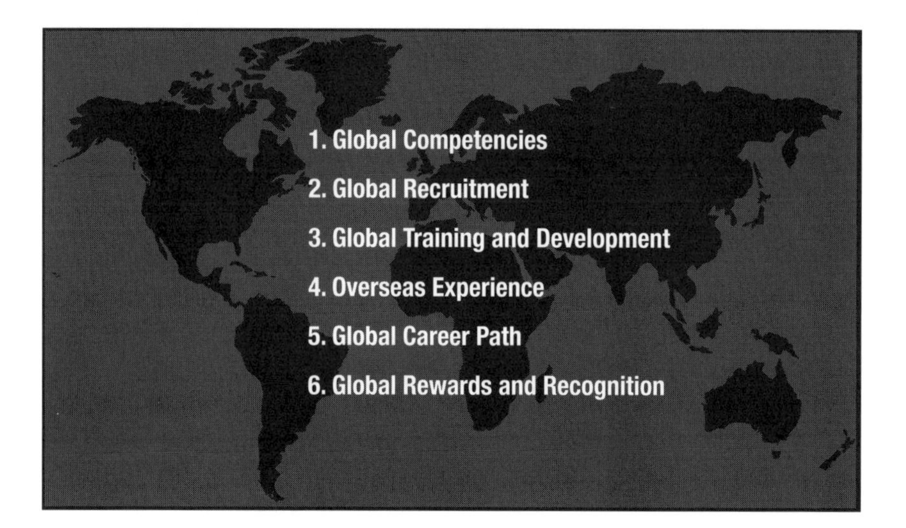

FIGURE 5-1. GLOBAL HUMAN RESOURCES.

FIGURE 5-2. TEN KEY GLOBAL COMPETENCIES.

Language Proficiency

More and more global specialists are stressing the importance of speaking or, as a minimum, understanding basic phrases, as well as the structural content, of the language. Language is important because it reflects cultural nuances and is a carrier of culture. As examples, Mandarin Chinese provides a sense of hierarchy, place, and order; the Thai language shows great respect for elders; the Spanish language reflects a passive locus of control.

In addition to the verbal, spoken language, nonverbal language is critical in understanding a culture. The body language, gestures, and environment of a high-context culture often speak more clearly and completely than the verbal language.

Almost everyone appreciates attempts by a non-native speaker to communicate in his or her native language. Often the show of goodwill is much more important than the degree of proficiency in the utterance.

Global Perspective and Mind-set

As we noted in Chapter 4, people with global mind-sets have the ability to continually expand their knowledge, have a highly developed conceptual capacity to deal with the complexity of global organizations, are extremely flexible, strive to be sensitive to cultural diversity, are able to intuit decisions with inadequate information, and have a strong capacity for reflection.

A global mind-set thinks and sees the world globally, is open to exchanging ideas and concepts across borders, and is able to break down one's provincial ways of thinking. The emphasis is placed on balancing global and local needs and on being able to operate cross-functionally, cross-divisionally, and cross-culturally around the world.

Respect for the Values and Practices of Other Cultures

Most Americans grow up learning that what they believe reflects the best ways of thinking and behaving; to think or act otherwise would be foolish and/or "uncultural." Our minds are "programmed" to think in a certain way [6]. Society through religion, schools, politics, and other cultural factors reinforces this ethnocentric way of acting. Americans, in particular, have been taught that their way is the best, that other ways are inferior and need to be changed.

It is difficult, therefore, to accept the fact that other ways of thinking and opposite values should be respected. Global employees should respect the other cultures. They should not view these other cultures as good or bad, but different. It is exactly this respectful, nonjudgmental attitude that is so critical for effective global activities or programs. Fellow workers and customers easily recognize if they and their ways of life are respected or rejected by the Americans.

Patience with and Tolerance of Ambiguity

Coping with the unavoidable stress of a cross-cultural setting is difficult. Yet patience with and tolerance of the ambiguities of new cultural situations are critical components for working and living abroad. The ability to react to new, different, and, at times, unpredictable situations with little visible discomfort or irritation is very important for anyone working overseas.

The *jiitsu* of adapting to an unclear and differently programmed environment requires a tremendous amount of patience. That we can control time and the future are fundamental American beliefs, but they may be totally opposite to the beliefs of other cultures. Waiting for consensus is extremely difficult for Americans, yet essential in working throughout the world.

Sense of Humor

Possessing a sense of humor, the humility and ability to laugh as one deals with the unexpected and the unknown, is surely needed to handle cross-cultural situations. This requires a healthy self-esteem and self-confidence but not arrogance or pride, which prevents a person from relaxing. Stress can be high in global situations where one is uncertain about what to expect and when one may be totally surprised by unexpected behaviors. A sense of humor is indispensable for dealing with the cultural mistakes and the faux pas every global worker will certainly commit.

Communication Skills

Listening and speaking is much more complex in cross-cultural settings, yet much more important. Understanding nonverbal as well as verbal messages requires a high level of communication skills, including the abilities to ask open-ended questions, to be silent, to paraphrase, and to reflect feelings. In some cultures, we may not even be able to ask questions to check out what we are experiencing because such inquisitiveness may be perceived as inappropriate or even rude.

Craig Storti, a noted cross-cultural specialist, identifies the following points as keys to communicating across cultures:

- ❑ Don't assume sameness.
- ❑ Monitor your instincts; what may seem natural to you may be, in fact, cultural.
- ❑ Familiar behaviors may have different meanings in different cultures.
- ❑ Don't assume that what you meant is what was understood.
- ❑ Don't assume that what you understood is what was meant.
- ❑ You don't have to like or accept "different" behaviors, but you should try to understand where they come from.
- ❑ Most people behave rationally; you just have to find the rationale [7].

Creativity

The global organizational environment—with its great need for adaptability, its high competition, and its often uncertain steps towards goals—requires a high degree of creativity on the part of the global professional. Solutions that may have worked in one's own culture may be unworkable or totally inappropriate in another culture. Problem solving with people of other cultures will require new approaches because techniques such as participative approaches and brainstorming may not be culturally accepted.

Emotional Resilience and Adjustment Skills

Typically, Americans begin a global assignment with euphoria and excitement. However, this is sooner or later followed by confusion, frustration, and psychological disorientation caused by the new culture. Emotional resilience enables a person to bounce back from frustrations and to be able to deal effectively with different situations. Unless the global employees are flexible and resilient, they are likely going to be unable to deal with this "cultural shock." To achieve a reasonable cultural adjustment level, the following strategies are recommended:

- ❑ Continue to learn more about the host country.
- ❑ Attempt to find the cultural reason behind everything in the new environment.
- ❑ Do not succumb to disparagement of the host culture.
- ❑ Identify sympathetic host-country people with whom to share confusion and frustration.
- ❑ Have faith in yourself and in the positive outcome of the experience.

Self-management of Learning

One should enter the global marketplace with a high degree of technical and psychological competence but recognize the need to continuously learn. Globalization has made change ever faster and convulsive. Technology and information pushes the need for continuous learning of new knowledge and skills. Global staff will need to learn even faster and better, quickly diagnose learning needs, and identify the sources necessary to provide such learning.

In addition to the ten competencies identified above, the three elements of (1) the organization, (2) motivation, and (3) family situation must also be considered in assessing the overall suitability of a person to work in a global organization [1].

Organizational Job Factors

- ❑ Technical skills
- ❑ Acquaintance with host-country operations and headquarters operations
- ❑ Administrative competence

Motivational State

- ❑ Belief in mission
- ❑ Congruence with career path
- ❑ Interest in overseas experience
- ❑ Interest in the specific host-country culture
- ❑ Willingness to acquire new patterns of behavior and attitudes

Family Situation

- ❑ Willingness of spouse to live abroad
- ❑ Adaptive and supportive spouse
- ❑ Stable marriage

Determining an Individual's Potential at Shell

Shell determines an individual's potential by assessing four qualities: (1) a sense of imagination; (2) a sense of reality; (3) the individual's power of analysis; and (4) the "helicopter quality," or capacity of the person to envision facts and problems in a wider context. "What appeared to distinguish the high-potential individuals at Shell was their capacity to see the big picture, to imagine the latent possibilities in a given situation, and yet at the same time to grasp detailed facts, realities, and constraints—linking the two through their analytic skill into constructive action" [8, pp. 132-133].

Criteria for Global Employees at Philips

Philips uses four criteria to guide (though not slavishly restrict) corporate judgments of potential global employees:

1. **Conceptual Effectiveness:** Vision, synthesis, professional knowledge, business directedness
2. **Operational Effectiveness:** Individual effectiveness, decisiveness, control
3. **Interpersonal Effectiveness:** Network directedness, negotiating power, personal influence, verbal behavior
4. **Achievement Motivation:** Ambition, professional interest, emotional control [9]

Global Recruitment

Once a global company has identified the "glob-able" attributes that will best assist the company toward global success, the next step is global recruitment. Global success begins with the recruitment and hiring of talented people who are predisposed and anxious to perform global work. Although training, enlightened career pathing, and other management-development techniques can help a company get the most from its people, these supports will work best on people who have an aptitude and capacity for global work.

Global recruiting includes not only selecting in-company and/or in-country employees with high-quality academic and professional experience but also searching worldwide for the best people, whatever their countries of origin. To facilitate recruiting and promoting from within, more and more corporations are moving toward global personnel systems, which permit them to tap their worldwide managerial talent pool.

Andersen Consulting suggests the following guidelines for global recruiting:

- ❑ Incorporate the global nature of the business in advertising designed to attract personnel.
- ❑ Use both global and local recruiting firms.
- ❑ Partner with MBA programs that have an international business focus.
- ❑ Recruit from foreign service or other fields with extensive international experience and exposure.
- ❑ Implement a system with automatic resume/applicant-skills tracking that can be used globally.
- ❑ Modify policies and procedures to reflect local customs and laws; be aware of culturally appropriate and inappropriate questions during the recruiting/selecting process; remember, that in some countries, once a worker is hired, it is almost impossible to terminate that worker without extensive, drawn-out procedures and costs.

- ❑ Use government reports from labor and state agencies to gain a realistic understanding of the skills available in the labor market where you are recruiting.
- ❑ Tailor the recruiting and selection process to fit local conditions.

Sources of Recruitment of Global Staff

Global organizations have essentially three options in recruiting for global positions: (1) expatriates, (2) local nationals, and (3) third-country nationals.

Expatriates

Expatriates are used (a) to provide the high level of technical or functional knowledge and experience that is required for a particular position; (b) to provide a promising executive with international experience; or (c) to transmit clearly the corporate image or a degree of home-office concern.

Although more and more global companies have begun elevating LNs to top-management positions, most senior positions are still occupied by expatriates. For example, at Fujitsu America, most expatriates are second- or third-level managers who have various U.S. citizens reporting to them. Besides occupying top-management slots, expatriates also staff many manufacturing and engineering positions. Expatriates are also key resources for companies with recent international acquisitions or for joint ventures.

Local Nationals (LNs)

Although many companies begin their global HR efforts by recruiting expatriates for global assignments, eventually they realize that LNs are generally much better acquainted with the local markets, government policies, and business scenes than are people from other countries. There are several reasons why the use of LNs is gaining popularity.

- ❑ **Reduced Cost.** Even in countries where qualified employees are in short supply, LNs typically enjoy a cost advantage resulting from savings in relocation costs, salary premiums, and housing, school, and other overseas allowances. In addition, LNs require no predeparture training. Bibiana Santiago, AT&T's human resource director for Europe, the Middle East, and Africa, estimates that the cost of maintaining an expatriate can be as much as three to four times the person's stay-at-home salary.

- **LNs Help Smooth Relations with Governments.** In most countries today, governments insist that LNs fill all jobs except when no qualified local national can be found. For example, the U.S. Immigration and Naturalization Service (INS) discourages the use of expatriates for technical, professional, and management positions at the U.S. subsidiaries of non-U.S. companies unless those companies can show that expatriates are essential to the operation of the business. Volvo AB contends that an INS application alone impedes the relocation of executives, because it requires the intervention of a U.S. immigration lawyer to expedite the processing of work permits and visa applications. It is widely acknowledged that Switzerland is especially restrictive vis-à-vis expatriates. Rank Xerox's experience there is fairly typical. "Switzerland," says Xerox's Debuisser, "has very tight rules regarding labor permits. You've literally got to prove that only this individual has the skills to prevent the company from going bankrupt."
- **Cultural Bonding.** LNs have a special advantage: They share a set of common cultural, linguistic, and religious antecedents with their fellow employees. This is particularly important in developing countries, where an expatriate is often seen as a tool of a former colonial power. Many companies therefore put LNs in the most visible positions, such as sales and marketing, because they speak the language and share a common background. IBM's director of executive resources and development, Don Laidlaw, says, "The people at IBM Japan in marketing are Japanese. Our marketeers in France are French." Philips' de Leeuw agrees: "A local national in a locally oriented job, like a sales job, knows the culture much better and is in a much better position to operate."

Third-Country Nationals (TCNs)

The third option for global companies is use of TCNs, known in some companies as "cross-poster" or international assignees. They are simply expatriates from a country other than the one where a global company is headquartered. Traditionally, TCNs have been the "hired guns" of international personnel. Often brought in to carry out layoffs, restructurings, or other difficult tasks, TCNs have acquired a reputation, particularly among LNs, of being a floating class of executives not linked to any one market and owing no particular allegiance to anyone in the company. It is precisely this freedom, however, that makes the TCN a great asset to headquarters. Having no identification with the home office or home country, a TCN is often ideally suited to supervise a restructuring and can help redirect what might otherwise be nationalistic sentiment against the parent company.

TCNs also serve as regional coordinators, most notably in Latin America and Asia. Not only do they speak the language and possess intimate knowledge of local conditions, they have already made the adjustment to the corporate culture and can pursue goals without bias. TCNs greatly expand the pool of candidates for significant positions in each country to include, theoretically, everyone with the proper background who speaks the language. This means that a country subsidiary's management can simply choose, to the extent permitted by the parent company's personnel system, the candidates with the best qualifications, no matter where they are located.

In the future, third-country nationals will become the norm for top leadership positions in the national and/or regional offices of global enterprises.

Global Training and Career Development

Companies now recognize that the ability to compete globally will be very dependent on the quality and level of global training in their organizations. For organizations seeking to compete in globalized markets, world-class global HRD can make the critical difference. Training is seen as the ultimate key to executing the bold vision and strategies needed for global success.

Although American companies spend more than $50 billion per year in workplace training, they spend little for global learning programs. In this respect, the United States is far behind Asia and Europe in preparing its employees for the global marketplace. Here are some facts:

- 70 percent of American businesspeople who are sent abroad are given no cultural training or preparation.
- 59 percent of the HRD executives surveyed by ASTD said their companies offered no international training for personnel taking assignments outside the United States, and another 5 percent didn't even know that such training existed!

The attitudes and actions of other countries are quite different from those of the United States. Japanese companies, for example, take up to three years to prepare managers for overseas assignments. Employers in France, Spain, the United Kingdom, Sweden and Germany, according to recent surveys, are much more likely to insist upon global training and experiences for senior and high-potential managers.

Why are Americans so far behind? Why is there such a large gap between recognized global business and the necessity of preparing staff for such assignments?

The fundamental reason is that American businesses simply do not believe global, cross-cultural training is necessary [10]. The assumption for many American executives is that American ways and business practices are the norm and that a manager or sales representative who is successful in Boston will be just as successful in Bangkok or in Buenos Aires. Furthermore, many American managers feel that foreign assignments are undesirable—a step off the career path.

By contrast, companies in Europe and Asia see global training and experience as an integral part of the employee's development and as mandatory for future senior executives. Therefore, these countries insist on more international experience and cross-cultural training.

The Importance of Global Training

More and more global corporations now recognize the critical need to train staff to work in an international environment. Global training and development, according to Sylvia Odenwald [11] have several benefits, including:

- Improved ability to identify viable business opportunities.
- Reduced waste of resources on ill-conceived ventures.
- Increased competitiveness around the world.

❑ Higher job satisfaction and retention of overseas staff.
❑ Less business lost because of insensitivity to cultural norms.
❑ Improved effectiveness in diverse business environments.

Developing a Global Training Strategy for the Company

A systematic training/development strategy to transform an organization into a global company requires the following six interrelated steps:

1. Connection of business goals to training
2. Creation of a global training mission
3. Examination of internal and external factors and resources related to global training
4. Identification of training goals and objectives
5. Identification of action steps to accomplish learning needs of organization
6. Development of evaluation system to assess impact and needed changes of training and development strategies

Bren White [12] recommends that headquarters staff members, from the CEO to the receptionist, become familiar with globalization and how it will affect every aspect of the company's operations. Many global companies now offer many of the following courses for their employees:

❑ Globalization 101: Concepts and Success Factors
❑ World-Class Customer Service
❑ The Global Learning Organization
❑ Working with Multicultural Teams
❑ Cross-cultural Communication Skills
❑ Global Marketing
❑ International Negotiating Skills
❑ The Global Business Team
❑ Global Leadership Perspectives
❑ Global Quality Management
❑ Effective Sales Presentations Across Cultures
❑ Global Account Management
❑ Project Management for the Global Corporation

- ❑ Global Trade and Finance
- ❑ Global Telecommunication and Information Management

Foreign Languages

In most European, Asian, and African countries, people speak three to four languages. Most Americans speak only one—their own. Although English is becoming a global language, only 5 percent of the world's population uses it as the mother tongue, or first language. Businesspeople from other language communities grow weary of the assumption that they are solely responsible for making the effort of speaking English to their English counterparts. The fact that the employees of firms do not know a foreign language has cost those firms millions of dollars, not to mention the damage done to their credibility and reputations.

Another reason for learning a language is that it enables one to get "inside" another culture [6]. Communicating effectively—essential for conducting business affairs—involves more than a proficiency in sending and receiving messages. Effective communication requires an understanding of how people think, feel, and behave. It involves knowing something about cultural values, attitudes, and patterns of behavior.

Speaking the local language provides considerable entrée into the world view of another culture. A language, through its structure and vocabulary, reveals the important values found in the culture; it gives insight into how directly or indirectly people in a particular community communicate with one another; and it reflects social realities, such as status differences. Language basically determines how you perceive the world; it determines your mind-set.

For example, the word *aunt* for Americans can refer to many different people (father's sister, mother's brother's wife, mother's sister, and father's brother's wife); in English, they are all linguistically equivalent and treated the same. Other linguistic communities, however, refer to and see these women-relatives as substantially different from each other, and they naturally behave toward them in different ways. English has one word that means "you," while Vietnamese has more than forty! Because of language and its use, different cultures value individual initiative and righteousness (United States), while others place much more value on group harmony (Japan).

Language is so powerful that if a language does not have a word for a particular idea, event, or phenomenon, people are unable to recognize its existence. For example, there is an aroma for roasted, ground sesame seeds for which no word exists in English. Therefore Americans do not perceive the aroma until the scent is painstakingly pointed out. Koreans, however, have a particular word for that scent and have no difficulty recognizing it when it fills the air.

For Americans, our language is explicit, direct, and unambiguous; we say what we mean as precisely and straightforwardly as possible; we "tell it like it is without beating around the bush." Likewise for Americans, we place great importance on words themselves and less on the context (we are therefore classified as a low-context culture). In many other cultures, the emphasis is on the nonverbal language, or the context (these are thus referred to as high-context cultures). High-context cultures tend to use fewer words and rely heavily on hidden, unspoken, implicit, contextual cues, such as nonverbal behavior, the social context, and the nature of interpersonal relationships. Words are only a part of the total communication system, and the words are inseparably interrelated to social relationships.

The purpose of language and communication in many eastern cultures is to promote harmony and social integration rather than to enhance the speaker's individuality through the articulation of words. People native to these cultures are suspicious of the limitations of words alone. They generally suppress negative verbal messages. Politeness and the desire to avoid embarrassment often take precedence over the truth. Therefore, in these cultures, there exists many ways to say, "Maybe."

Speaking our language is much more time consuming for us. Americans spend seven hours a day in conversations, twice as much as the Japanese. Language, both verbal and nonverbal, is very important in negotiations. For example, it is important to recognize the use of overstatement by Arab and Spanish speakers and the practice of understatement by many Asian cultures.

Staying Current on Global Issues

The acceleration of global change and global competition requires a regular, continual flow of relevant, strategic information entering the organization. Key professional journals and international newspapers should be made available, and appropriate global and technical computer networks should be identified. Workshops and roundtables on globally critical topics should be held. Educational seminars about topics such as global management issues in the 1990s, how to compete in the new Europe, the impact of a North American free trade zone, and global leadership in a high-tech world are needed in global organizations. Only then can the organization gain a strategic window on the world that is in tune with constantly changing global realities.

Managing the Overseas Experience

A high-quality global experience requires the six components shown in Figure 5-3.

Make Overseas Assignments Both an Integral Part of Managers' Career Development and a Valued Asset in Future Selection and Promotion Decisions

U.S. companies have historically undervalued the importance of overseas assignments. These assignments have been seen, at the very

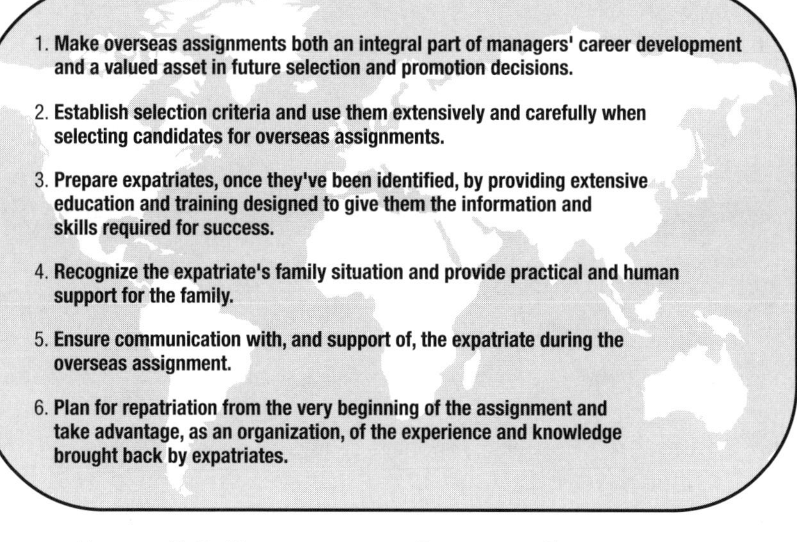

FIGURE 5-3. MANAGING THE OVERSEAS EXPERIENCE.

best, as a temporary switching of personnel to a side track while the express continued down the main line. At worst, the assignments were a signal that a career peak had been reached and was unlikely to be surpassed. These days, however, the continuing shock waves of global competition felt by American business have jarred this perception considerably. Increasingly, overseas assignments are seen as an integral concern in strategic planning. The survival of the company in the global marketplace is at stake. Assigning someone to an international project involves more than just getting the job done. It also involves selecting someone specifically for the benefit of the overall operation and for international career development—someone to get to know the worldwide networks and contacts for information and communication links and to help the firm itself integrate and develop into a global organization [13].

At Xerox, a heightened sense of global customer needs has resulted in an emphasis on overseas assignments. According to David Muxworthy, manager of senior management education, at least 80 percent of Xerox's top 300 managers has had international assignments:

> It's extremely important, not simply as an exercise. We think it's critical to really understanding the differences between business practices and markets in different countries. Most Americans, even if they've done a lot of reading about how the world has changed and what an international business really is, don't get a true feeling for that unless they've experienced it firsthand [14, p. 29].

In developing an overseas program, the following strategies should be implemented:

- ❑ Establish a career path that includes global assignments for managers.
- ❑ Develop a core group of managers who transfer every few years to new locations so as to broaden and share their knowledge of global business issues.
- ❑ Use global project teams as an introduction to working in foreign countries.
- ❑ Seek and build upon best practices from other industries.
- ❑ Set realistic development goals and recognize that the development of global expertise takes time.

- ❑ Establish a career management program that mandates global rotations so that global assignments are seen as a pathway to executive positions and not as out-of-the-loop assignments.
- ❑ Establish a leveling approach for compensation in foreign locations.

The overseas assignment should be seen as a first step in a process that, managed successfully, can lead one to senior positions in the global organization. One way to make this perception real is to dedicate significant upper management attention and company resources to the development of international career paths. Such commitment is seen in firms that participate in the University of Michigan's Global Leadership Program. The thirty-four corporate sponsors, including such global giants as NEC, Exxon, Philips, Sony, American Express, and Bull, not only send key executives to a five-week off-site program at the cost of $30,000 per participant but also commit to three years of action research on globalization within their own companies. Typical areas of research include assessing the company's progress in the globalization process, as well as the degree of internal operational management success. These companies are sending signals both internally and externally that global experience and career success within the organization go hand in hand [15].

Nakiye Boyacigiller, based on her study of major U.S. institutions, concludes that:

> International staffing decisions need to be tied to other strategic decisions. The emphasis during staffing should be on long-term organizational development and management development and, above all, on long-term commitment to learning about international markets. If high potential individuals are carefully selected and trained for overseas positions, they will not only facilitate the maintenance of an international network of operations in the short term but should be allowed to continue providing informational support upon their return to the U.S. The international education that future executives could acquire in these types of assignments cannot be replicated in any classroom [16, p. 154].

Establish Selection Criteria and Use Them Extensively and Carefully When Selecting Candidates for Overseas Assignments

A growing number of firms, led by global giants IBM and Philips, have developed systems that can identify talented executives throughout the world, ideally at early stages of their careers. Even if a company does not attempt to track "global" potential per se, it is well advised to develop a global system of personnel tracking to identify the best candidates for a job, wherever they may be.

Colgate-Palmolive taps into a worldwide pool of executive talent via a centralized committee that consists of the chief operating officer, the division presidents, the head of global business development, and a human resources representative. Using a corporate data bank, as well as firsthand knowledge, the committee prepares a list of potential candidates for each significant global assignment. This list encompasses employees at headquarters and all other locations.

NEC pinpoints talent in its system by performing a subjective evaluation of all executives every three years, specifically regarding their "ability to adapt to international environments," says Masaru Yamamoto, general manager of the international education division of the NEC Institute of Management.

Prepare Expatriates, Once They've Been Identified, by Providing Extensive Education and Training Designed to Give Them the Information and Skills Required for Success

To secure a successful adjustment to a new overseas assignment and to ease the pain of repatriation when an overseas assignment is completed, a comprehensive expatriate training program should typically encompass all or several of the following components:

Predeparture Orientation. Most companies find predeparture training a worthwhile investment. Significantly, the focus is squarely on the personal side because the majority of unsuccessful expatriate experiences are the result of the spouse's or family's inability to adjust. A comprehensive expatriate program should include assistance for the family, as well as the executive. Such programs should stress the firsthand experience of former expatriates and the realities of day-to-day life, both practical and emotional.

Moran, Stahl & Boyer, among the best-known American firms specializing in intercultural training, offers a multicultural communication program based on a four-phase training model. Contents and specifics vary depending on client needs and target cultures, but programs typically include these levels:

- Level 1 training raises participants' awareness of cultural differences and examines the effects these differences have on business situations.
- Level 2 focuses on cultural attitudes and how they are formed.
- Level 3 provides background knowledge and practical information about the target country.
- Level 4 concentrates on skill building in areas such as language, nonverbal communication, cultural stress management, and adjustment and adaptation.

Cultural Conditioning. In addition to predeparture counseling, many firms offer other types of cross-cultural training. These differ from conventional executive training because they stress cultural precepts that may run counter to traditional business behavior. Executives who work abroad may have to act in ways contrary to what they have learned from years of training and experience at home. For example, a Japanese manager who comes to the United States may have to act assertively in certain situations, whereas that kind of behavior at home would run contrary to custom. Similarly, U.S. executives who seek to do business in Japan must learn to be patient and deferential—two qualities that may actually hurt their careers back home.

Many corporations turn to consulting and training firms to provide specialized aspects of expatriate training and preparation. For example, the East West Group offers language and cross-cultural training that covers every region of the world. A typical cross-cultural program might last from two to five days and include video and other types of presentations, identification of the features and beliefs of the participants' own culture, cross-cultural simulations, and learning sessions with foreign informants from the target culture [15].

The goals of such a program are to enable participants to better:

1. Understand that their concepts of what's important in business (and in life) are culturally based and not universally shared.
2. Recognize the key areas in business where the target culture and the native culture differ in priorities and beliefs.
3. Apply verbal and nonverbal communication skills in job-related, cross-cultural communication.
4. Identify typical areas of cultural misunderstanding, such as directness, willingness to commit, trust, people orientation versus task orientation, authority and power structures, role of tradition and respect, time orientation, and profit and other motivations.
5. Understand and respond to target-culture business practices, protocol, and management styles.
6. Develop action plans designed to enhance cross-cultural communication and management skills.

Coaching in Local Business Practices. In addition to cross-cultural training, executives who work abroad may require additional instruction to put their functional and product expertise into a global, as well as cross-cultural, context. Often they need to acquire a knowledge of local marketing methods, financial practices, or technical standards [17].

Language Training. Although all companies offer intensive language training to employees prior to foreign posting, not all companies consider language proficiency crucial to success in a foreign position. Japanese firms are known to stress language ability—at least the ability to speak English. Typically, European firms prefer a degree of language proficiency. U.S. firms, on the whole, are less aggressive in stressing language training. However, the necessity to speak the local language will depend on the nature of the job.

In general, however, learning the host language has many important benefits:

- It helps to build rapport and sets the proper tone for doing business abroad.
- It builds trust; one is at a severe disadvantage in negotiations and marketing without language competence. Global business must be grounded in trust and mutual respect. What better way to gain that

trust and respect than by taking the time and energy to learn someone else's language?

- In certain cultures, particularly those in Latin America, business is conducted at a more leisurely pace. Time for speaking about social interests is very important in developing a personal relationship. Being fluent in Spanish allows one the opportunity to speak about the local culture and to gain both the respect and business of the foreign partner.
- Speaking the local language can also play a major role in adjusting to culture shock, because efficient communication can (a) minimize the frustrations, misunderstanding, and aggravations that face the linguistic outsider, and (b) provide a sense of safety, mastery, and self-assurance.

Management Training. Besides offering simple courses in business practices, companies have begun to provide more involved programs in global management. Once reserved for upper-level executives but now presented to lower-level managers, such programs typically serve as prestigious rewards for outstanding global managers and important tools to help expand their knowledge. Larger companies may create and offer such courses themselves, but many firms make use of advanced management-training courses offered by the top international business schools [18, pp. 10–12].

Recognize the Expatriate's Family Situation and Provide Practical and Human Support for the Family

In a survey about the issue of expatriate assignments within eighty U.S. companies [19], respondents were asked to indicate the most important reasons for expatriate failure in their companies. The No. 1 reason cited was "inability of the manager's spouse to adjust to a different physical or cultural environment." Also high on the list (No. 3) was "other family-related problems." These findings are consistent with other studies that show that poor family adjustment is a key factor in expatriate failure. Theoretically, one could respond to this problem by selecting candidates who are single, but it is well known that the loneliness built into an overseas assignment is even more overwhelming if the expatriate, in fact, goes alone.

Global companies are beginning to take steps to ensure, first of all, that family members and especially spouses are prepared, trained, and supported in much the same way the expatriate is. In the selection stage, interviewers should talk to the spouse, who often stays at home and is more likely than the employee to be able to predict the impact of the overseas assignment on the family and to identify any special situations that need to be addressed. His or her understanding of the challenge and willingness to meet it are also critical predictors of success. Preliminary trips to the host country for both the potential expatriate and the spouse are another good way to give both of them a chance to evaluate the life they might be choosing. Such a trip can also provide management with a realistic sense of their interest in, and suitability for, the assignment. It also allows for their introduction to other members of the expatriate community and local nationals who would become part of their everyday lives.

During the preparation stage, companies are increasingly providing training and orientation programs, not only for the prospective expatriate but also for the spouse and older children. Because the spouse is going to have to face the same cross-cultural adjustment challenges as the expatriate, there is equal reason to prepare and train both partners. These training programs are designed to make the employee, the spouse, and other family members more flexible and adaptive by providing them with information about, and insight into, the culture in which they're going to live.

Many European companies, for example, send their prospective expatriates and spouses to residential programs at the center for International Briefing at Farnham Castle in the United Kingdom. The center offers two types of residential programs: a four-day regional program and a week-long cultural awareness program. The former focuses on the historical, political, religious, and economic factors that shape the world view of the people of a particular region, and contrasts that world view with those of the participants. Through lectures, audiovisual presentations, and discussions with outside speakers, the center tries to help individuals adjust in a practical way to the work and community environments.

In contrast, the cultural awareness program does not focus on a specific region or country but seeks to broaden individual understanding of, and appreciation for, other countries through lectures and experiential exercises. Once the family arrives at the overseas location, company representatives or consultants should integrate them into the community as quickly as possible. Especially in those situations where there is no expatriate community, the company should contract with local firms to provide practical support during the initial stages of the relocation. These local sponsors should not only arrange social and professional introductions but also should provide practical assistance in finding housing and schools, connecting utilities, identifying shopping and recreational locations, and so on. Relatively simple procedures like getting the telephone hooked up can be endlessly complex and frustrating in a foreign country. The means of establishing relations with schools and local businesses are liable to be formidable, bewildering, and largely unknowable without local help. The sooner the family is able to get into new daily routines, the less likely the expatriate is to spend much of his or her time dealing with family crises.

Local orientation and language programs should also be made available soon after arrival. The degree to which the family members can function within the community in the native language will, in large measure, affect their abilities to adapt and adjust to their new surroundings. Their increased participation in the community will also provide the local people with an opportunity to observe and adapt to their visitors' appearance and behavior.

During the repatriation process, which is discussed at greater length later in this chapter, family concerns should be addressed systematically and practically. The spouse and children will likely be returning to a community and life that has changed in their absence, perhaps as much as they, themselves, have changed. While it might seem simpler in theory than the move overseas, in fact the transition back into the home community and culture can be just as complex and threatening. Particular attention should be paid to housing, groceries, changes in taxes, the cost of automobiles, technological developments, and the latest happenings in their communities; prior to repatriation, for example, the family should be encouraged to subscribe to a local newspaper and begin to reestablish links with old friends and neighbors.

From beginning to end, the expatriate process must recognize and provide for the family if it is likely to succeed. Failure to do so will often result in expatriates who are ineffective in their jobs, unhappy in their social lives and marriages, and subject to bouts of depression, substance abuse, feelings of alienation from others, lack of motivation, and inappropriate behavior both at work and home.

Ensure Communication with, and Support of, the Expatriate During the Overseas Assignment

Unless policies and practices are established to keep expatriates in the loop, once the expatriate and family are out of sight of headquarters it is likely they will also be out of mind. To avoid this unhappy and unprofitable situation, global companies are beginning to link overseas assignments with long-term strategies and are devising ways to ensure that such assignments are part of their day-to-day operating concerns. These firms support their expatriates in a number of formal and informal ways.

In selecting candidates for overseas assignments, the following guidelines have proved valuable for many global companies:

- ❑ Set realistic goals and be candid when discussing the local environment in which the expatriate will be working.
- ❑ Implement performance support tools for decision making and risk management.
- ❑ Establish policies and procedures that allow expatriates more freedom and autonomy in decision making while operating within risk management guidelines.
- ❑ Establish proficiency in a foreign language as a core competency (remember that language carries the culture and that one cannot fully understand a culture, much less communicate in it, if they do not speak the language).
- ❑ Visibly accept and support new methods (that is, more creative, less quantitative, and/or more qualitative ones) of analysis and decision making that may deviate from traditional methods [20].
- ❑ Create a referral program that refers expats to experienced expats who can guide employees and answer questions.
- ❑ Institute all available and appropriate communication channels (Internet, mailings, voice mail) to ensure that the expatriate is kept in the communication loop regarding the company's domestic activities, decisions, and news.

Some companies encourage their expatriates to call corporate or division headquarters as often as needed to ask questions, seek guidance, gain from the experience of returned expatriates, or just to talk with someone about concerns and problems. Others make an organized effort to inform the expatriate of any local support systems and to make introductions if desired. Local branches of clubs, such as Rotary or Lions, are identified. Religious congregations and alumni associations might also have local representation. Links can often be forged with expatriate communities of other home-based firms or subsidiaries.

To bridge the gap between headquarters and overseas and to help repatriated managers adjust, many companies have adopted mentor programs. Mentoring provides expatriates, on a one-to-one basis, with senior executives at the headquarters office who monitor their progress and watch out for their interests while they are abroad. Mentors—sometimes known as sponsors—follow expatriates' career development and accomplishments overseas, keep them posted on official and unofficial changes and goings-on at headquarters, and serve as troubleshooting liaisons between them and various headquarters departments. The mentor's responsibilities might include informal counseling, sponsorship of meetings to discuss problems and successes, communication of concerns back to the home office, and updating of local expatriates on new policies, strategies, and developments at corporate headquarters.

Rank Xerox sees the key role of sponsors as being a link between the assignee and the core unit, to keep him or her informed of what is going on at home and to take care of their reentry. AT&T has also implemented a mentor program. "Each person who goes overseas now has a sponsor back here in the U.S.," says Nancy Burgas, manager of global learning systems. "The sponsor is responsible for keeping that person informed of what's going on in the business." The company stipulates that mentors be at least two salary grades above the assignee. That way, says Burgas, "it's someone who's going to be a stable influence, so that even though you've left the organizational loop, you still have somebody to contact."

At least once a year, and more often as events dictate, expatriates should be brought back to headquarters for meetings and briefings that ensure communication in both directions. Truly global organizations should also rotate the location of major annual events so that expatriate locations can become better known and gain more credibility with home-based corporate management. Senior management visits and briefings held at regional locations throughout the company's sphere of influence also present opportunities for expatriates who are widely scattered within a region to meet, benefit from each other's experiences, and share resources.

Expatriates should also be included in ongoing training programs, both for their own personal growth and to enhance their effectiveness on behalf of the company. Gerald Jones, vice president in charge of international operations at the Forum Corporation, points out, for example, that managers who are closest to a country's customers are those who can most benefit from training in flexibility. "People in direct contact with the customer must be able to change quickly. They need training not in traditional topics, but in innovation, agility, and adaptability," he says. Jones sees the link between global strategy and expatriate training as essential. He suggests that companies must "create the strategy and, through training, communicate it. What's happening now is that the linkage is taking place much closer to the marketplace, and both training and strategy are being developed closer to the customer" [14, p. 32].

Plan for Repatriation from the Very Beginning of the Assignment and Take Advantage As an Organization of the Experience and Knowledge Brought Back by Expatriates

The repatriation process can be seen from two perspectives: that of the expatriate and that of the organization. From the expatriate's point of view, the transition back home should be orderly and should support personal and career needs. The organization should see it as an opportunity to gain additional benefit from the now-completed overseas assignment.

Ideally, the repatriation process should begin at the initial stage, when expatriate candidates are recruited. This helps avoid the problem of the expatriate being forgotten, ignored, and in fact being invisible until he or she suddenly reappears back at headquarters. If the repatriation plan is not considered from the beginning, career opportunities are lost, his or her track record and capabilities are forgotten, and doors are closed by events and changes of personnel [21].

Andersen Consulting recommends the following action for repatriation programs:

- ❑ Set up a repatriation team to support the expatriate's return to the home office. The team should consist of the expatriate's manager, an expatriate who has previously returned from the location, and a corporate human resource professional.
- ❑ Map out the career path for returning expatriates, and highlight the role a foreign assignment plays in meeting the expatriate's career goals.
- ❑ Plan the specific return position to be consistent with the original strategic purpose of the global assignment.
- ❑ Ensure that the challenges and responsibilities of the return position match or exceed the expatriate's prior responsibilities.
- ❑ Create opportunities for the expatriate to share his or her global experiences with other returned expatriates.
- ❑ Allow time for transition concerns (settling into accommodations, arranging for schooling, administrative tasks).
- ❑ Acknowledge that the adjustment can be difficult after one has acclimated oneself to another culture [20].

Many aspects of the reintegration process are similar to those seen in preparing the expatriate and family for the overseas assignment. Returnees may feel alienated in their own country. Their international experience may have put a social and psychological distance between them and their home environment. They may have developed broader perspectives that are difficult to explain to family and friends. They may experience a culture shock when confronted with the changes that have taken place in their absence. Finally, they may be returning to a lifestyle that is considerably less grand than the one they enjoyed overseas.

Information and training should be provided to address these and other issues. Support should be given in practical matters such as housing, taxes, and schools. Repatriates should be encouraged and helped to reintegrate into their families, communities, and social organizations.

Repatriation is an important part of global strategy and needs to be carefully considered as such. From the company's point of view, returning expatriates offer a resource that should not be overlooked. They bring back considerable experience, information, and expertise that can be applied immediately and in the future. These returning expatriates can help in the expatriate selection and training process by providing insights into the realities that have to be faced by those on overseas assignments. They are likely to be in-house experts in the culture of the country and region of their own assignment and probably have invaluable contacts and tips that can be passed along. They can provide reality testing for candidates preparing to go overseas and can give real-world credibility to the preparation and training process. They can be used to support the return of other repatriates and to act as sponsors for expatriates still overseas. Finally, they can be a source of valuable input in both global and regional strategic planning.

Global Career Path

Identifying and planning for global-minded employees to be the future leaders in the company is critical in institutionalizing globality. Developing the high-potentials as future global leaders is essential. Work experience is the best training and preparation for developing a succession plan for future global leaders of the company. To develop global executives of the future, many companies are sending high-potential junior executives abroad at an early age.

Colgate-Palmolive's Human Resource Strategy

Building its global human resources is at the heart of Colgate-Palmolive's global strategy for success. Unleashing the power of Colgate people represents the best source of sustainable competitive advantage. Strategic advantage is gained through:

- **Colgate Competencies**—The knowledge, skills, and abilities defined as critical to continued business success, and the values and behaviors that ensure unity of vision and performance excellence. People are selected and developed with current and future organizational needs and performance goals in mind.

- **Best Talent**—The process that provides organizational access to the global diversity of talent for existing and future business needs, through internal and external sourcing of the world's best people and effectively deploying them. This includes the processes of attracting, assessing, selecting, orienting, mentoring, and retaining people to meet business challenges.
- **Career Tracks**—The planned sequence of career assignments that develop leadership, management, category, and functional competence. This is necessary to meet future business opportunities and involves (1) understanding of career options, (2) timing, and (3) competency requirements of Colgate people.

Recognizing, Rewarding, and Retaining Global Employees

Among the critical issues facing global human resource officers is how to compensate and reward overseas employees. Challenges include:

- Overcompensation of senior execs and expats relative to other employees, which can demotivate the rest of the workforce.
- Long-term impact of rewarding according to financial performance.
- Cultural aspects of how to reward—according to what is legal, adequate, motivating, and equitable, according to income security, and according to cost-benefit effectiveness.

Mendenhall and Oddou [4] offer the following steps on how to appraise and reward an employee's global performance:

1. Determine the difficulty of the assignment. For example, it is generally much more difficult for an American to work in China than in Canada. The degree of difficulty depends on variables such as language, cultural differences, economic and political stability, and so on. Remember, local situations, events, and differences may make success much more difficult to achieve and require greater efforts with fewer results.
2. Objectify the performance assessment by means such as utilizing former expats from the same location in the appraisal process and involving on-site and home-site managers. Recognize that appraisal by a supervisor of another culture will involve that culture's values, ways of acting, and judgments. Take into account input from co-workers within the culture in which the expat is working (these evaluations, however, can be problematic, because they will be evaluating the expat's performance from their own cultural frame of reference and set of expectations; for example, the co-workers might see a participative manager as incompetent because the expat is not enough in control and does not have enough expertise).
3. Consider all the aspects of the expat's experiences and realize that he or she is not only performing a specific function but also broadening his or her understanding of the firm's total operations.
4. In determining pay, local markets generally are the biggest determinant of equity. An employee in Pekanbaru, Indonesia, doing the same job as an employee in Houston may be paid one tenth the Houstonian's salary. Consider the cost of living, the replacement cost of hiring and firing, and the availability of qualified labor factors into fair compensation. Within local markets, companies should maintain equitable pay according to job class and tenure with the company.

Andersen Consulting offers the following guidelines in assessing and rewarding global assignments:

- ❑ Standardize performance measurement systems across all locations, make adjustments with guidelines to account for local nuances, and compensate based on performance and achievement of goals.
- ❑ Consider non-monetary forms of compensation for cultural reasons (flex-time, vacation periods).
- ❑ Be aware of the conflict differences between expatriates and locals. Coach expats on how to address these issues with colleagues.
- ❑ Recognize and reward expat knowledge and skills when promoting global career opportunities, in presentations, in newsletters, with news releases, on project updates, and so on [20].

Career Paths and Reward Systems at Philips

Job rotation has always been the heart of Philips' philosophy of management development. It is seen as increasingly important in the firm's efforts to develop interdisciplinary skills and global perspectives. The candidates considered to have the most potential for tomorrow's top-management positions can be expected to be sent abroad for at least three or four years.

A recent variation on job rotation practice is the assignment of Philips managers to ventures with other companies. Those posted to these assignments have the opportunity to experience company cultures and practices different from their own. Transferring people in and out of these ventures contributes both to the individual's professional growth and to the expansion of the company's perspective as a whole. On-the-job training coupled with multicultural experience is the core of career development at Philips.

The following are the components Philips uses to rank its managers:

1. The *performance appraisal system* has become increasingly objective in an effort to assign demonstrable, job-related cri-

(Continued on next page)

teria to the evaluations. The emphasis on empirical and objective performance evaluation is spreading to include corporate staff functions that were previously thought to be difficult to evaluate in objective terms.

2. The *potential appraisal system* is more subjective because the outcomes are a combination of judgment and hypotheses about the future. However, it is the critical part of career planning and development for both the individual and the company.
3. The judgment of today's managers in identifying potential candidates for tomorrow's top-management positions is crucial, and it is a responsibility that is taken seriously. Responsibility for the management development program is therefore *spread throughout the entire organization,* with line managers shouldering the largest share, since they must perform the evaluations and appraisals.
4. Besides nominating those employees with high potential, appraisers of potential are required to identify two percent of management staff capable of rotation to other divisions. For the sake of credibility, they are obliged to show some consistency between judgments on performance and potential. This effectively reduces the temptation to cheat the system and promotes an *equitable flow of human resources.*
5. Because the company is large, the records must be centrally coordinated and tracked. This is the responsibility of the *corporate staff bureau,* which also develops the procedures and monitors the system. And very importantly, it maintains a companywide perspective on strategic planning and management requirements.
6. Because the corporate staff bureau function is considered so critically important to the company's future, the director of the bureau reports directly to the *president of the board of management.* Filling the top 120 positions of the company is the responsibility of the president, the board of management, and the director of the corporate staff bureau. Other management positions must be filled by the various organizations themselves [9, pp. 108–111].

Global People for the Global Company

A special kind of person—one with "glob-able" qualities and attributes—is needed for the global organization. One of the powers of a global company (through its reputation, opportunities, and worldwide reach) is its ability to attract and keep the best people, no matter their nationality. As we have seen in this chapter, the organization must have a systematic plan to recruit, select, train and develop, reward, and retain such people. In Chapter 6, we will explore the specific strategic steps the global company should undertake to optimize the capacities of these global human resources.

References

1. Ronen, S. "Training the International Assignee," in *Training and Career Development.* I. Goldstein (Ed.), San Francisco: Jossey-Bass, 1989.
2. Marquardt, M. and Engel, D. "HRD Competencies in a Shrinking World." *Training & Development,* May 1993, pp. 59–65.
3. Kohls, R. "Preparing Yourself for Work Overseas," in *The Global HRD Consultant's and Practitioner's Handbook.* A. Reynolds and L. Nadler (Eds.), Amherst, Mass.: HRD Press, 1993.
4. Mendenhall, M. and Oddou, G. "The Overseas Assignment: A Practical Look." *Business Horizons,* Sept.–Oct. 1988, pp. 78–84.
5. Miller, V. *Guidelines for International Trainers in Business and Industry.* Boston: International HRD Press, 1993.
6. Hofstede, G. *Cultures and Organizations.* London: McGraw-Hill, 1991.
7. Storti, C. *The Art of Crossing Cultures.* Yarmouth, Me.: Intercultural Press, 1989.
8. Evans, P., Doz, Y., and Laurent, A. (Eds.). *Human Resource Management in International Firms: Change, Globalization and Innovation.* New York: St. Martin's Press, 1990.
9. Van Houten, G. "Managing Human Resources in the International Firm," in *Human Resource Management in International Firms.* P. Evans, Y. Doz, and A. Laurent (Eds.), New York: St. Martin's Press, 1990.

10. Black, J., Gregersen, H., and Mendenhall, M. *Global Assignments: Successfully Expatriating and Repatriating International Managers*. San Francisco: Jossey-Bass, 1992.

11. Odenwald, S. *Global Training: How to Design Training for a Multinational Corporation*. Homewood, Ill.: Irwin Professional Publishing, 1993.

12. White, B. *World Class Training: How to Outdistance the Global Competition*. Dallas: Odenwald Press, 1992.

13. Dowling, P. and Schuler, R. *International Dimensions of Human Resource Management*. Boston: Kent Publishing, 1990.

14. Callahan, M. "Preparing the New Global Manager." *Training & Development Journal*, Vol. 43, No. 3, Mar. 1989, pp. 29–32.

15. Marquardt, M. and Engel, D. *Global Human Resource Development*. Englewood Cliffs, N.J.: Prentice Hall, 1993.

16. Boyacigiller, N. "The International Assignment Reconsidered," in *International Human Resource Management*. M. Mendenhall and G. Oddou (Eds.), Boston: PWS-Kent Publishing Company, 1991.

17. Morrison, T., Conaway, W., and Borden, G. *Kiss, Bow or Shake Hands*. Holbrook, Mass.: Bob Adams, 1994.

18. Business International Corporation. *Developing Effective Global Managers for the 1990s*. New York: BIC Press, 1991.

19. Tung, R. *The New Expatriates: Managing Human Resources Abroad*. New York: Ballinger Press, 1988.

20. Andersen Consulting. *Going Global in Financial Markets: Implications for Human Capital*. Washington, D.C.: Andersen Consulting, 1996.

21. Molner, D. E. and Loeww, G. M. "Global Assignments: Seven Keys to International HR Management." *HR Focus*, Vol. 74, No. 5, May 1997, pp. 11–12.

6

Strategies for Global Success

In his classic book *Total Global Strategy,* George Yip writes: "Turning a domestic, multinational, or international company into one worldwide business that has an integrated, global strategy presents one of the stiffest challenges in today's world." The question should not be "whether to have a global strategy" but "how global is our industry and how global should our business strategy be" [1, p. 1].

Developing a global strategy requires the ability to manage chaos. It involves however, more than creating a business strategy concerned with products, customers, geographic markets served, major sources of sustainable competitive advantage, functional strategy for each of the company's most important value-added activities, competitive posture including the selection of competitors to target, and investment strategies. Rather, global strategy focuses on how to integrate and manage resources for worldwide business leverage and competitive advantage, all ocurring within a global maelstrom of multicultural nuances and massive environmental changes. The global strategy, as opposed to the independent country strategies of a multinational firm, involves a number of cross-cultural alliances, includes a strategic rather than opportunistic selection of country targets, and makes determinations about the performances of business functions where they are most efficient. A global strategy should have no home-country bias and should recognize the need for a strong presence in the triad of Europe, Japan, and the United States [1].

Why Have Global Strategy?

Global strategy establishes the organization's long-term direction while setting specific performance objectives; it must formulate targeted global strategies in light of oftentimes conflicting internal and external circumstances and data.

Global strategy, as Moran, Harris, and Stripp note, is composed of:

> general principles that have remained fairly constant throughout history and are universally applicable. Strategy always involves long-term planning; defining objectives; analyzing one's own and the competitor's strength; understanding the geography of the land or environmental conditions; planning moves accordingly; assessing options and preparing contingency plans; organizing transport, supplies, and communication; anticipating the competitor's actions; and determining when and where to act. The general principles of strategy always include a central purpose, a set of objectives, an intelligence function with emphasis on analysis of internal and external strengths and weaknesses, a consideration of alternative actions, a strategic choice, and a means of coordination and control. Strategy considers the whole picture, determining when and where to act. Logistics organizes the internal resources and develops the lines of communication, supply, reinforcement, and retreat. Tactics occur at contact and determine the manner of execution and employment of resources. All of this is driven by policy, which is an outgrowth of individual and group philosophy [2, p. 34].

Global strategies should include ways to develop systems for linking and leveraging each country's or region's capabilities on a global scale and to move between global and local strategies in a flexible and timely fashion. Other key elements include:

- ❑ Seeking out best opportunities for each operation from throughout the world.
- ❑ Capitalizing on emerging markets by accessing the expertise of "glob-able" teams.
- ❑ Developing cadres of global experts in core competencies of the organization.

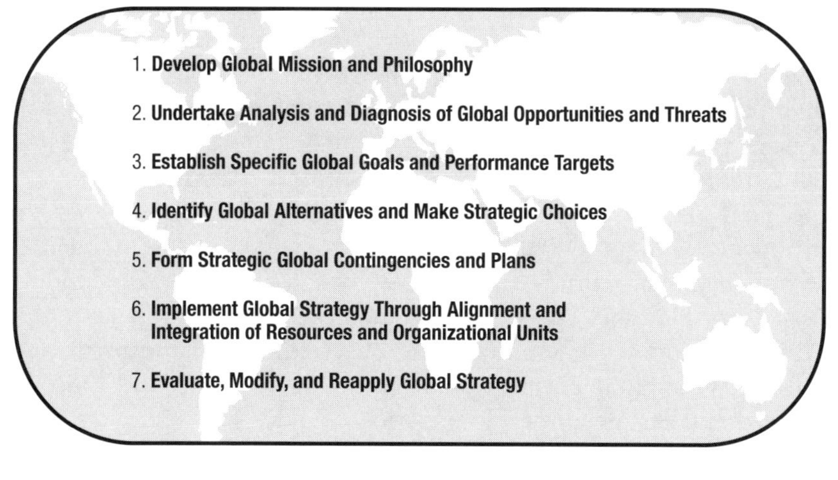

FIGURE 6-1. GLOBAL STRATEGIES.

❑ Learning and implementing the steps and strategies necessary to move a company from a domestic or international-multinational status to a global status.

The basic framework for developing a global strategy consists of seven steps: (1) developing a global mission and philosophy; (2) external and internal analyzing and diagnosing of global opportunities and threats; (3) establishing strategic objectives and performance targets; (4) finding strategic alternatives and making strategic choices; (5) developing a strategic global plan; (6) implementing and executing global strategy (leadership, personnel, logistics, and tactics); and (7) assessing and reformulating global strategy (see Figure 6-1).

Developing a Global Mission and Philosophy

The single most important task of global leaders is to give their employees a sense of direction, to define the organization's business and develop a strategic mission. Articulating this global mission compels leaders to think through the scope and mix of organizational and environmental issues, to reflect on what kind of organization they wish to create and on what markets they seek to penetrate.

The mission cannot be formulated until the leaders' philosophy is properly articulated. The corporate philosophy includes fundamental beliefs, concepts, and attitudes (that is, the corporate values—see Chapter 4). The statement of philosophy should express the basic purpose and values of the company. This includes ethical values, as well as philosophies and chosen practices in achieving them.

Kenichi Ohmae, a noted global leader and theorist, feels that the path to becoming a global company begins with the development of the proper global attitude and philosophy [3]. Two other noted globalists, Gary Hammel and C. K. Prahalad, believe the proper attitude is an obsession with winning. The obsession takes the form of a strategic intent that permeates the total organization and must be nurtured and sustained for a long period of time [4].

To establish a global mission statement, people in top management must draw upon their personal and corporate philosophies and evaluate global opportunities in light of existing corporate resources. The mission statement should "present a message that is so simple and compelling that employees are driven to follow it. Top management must articulate the mission in a written statement, which will be used by middle- and lower-level managers as a guide for action" [2, p. 45].

The following is Dow Chemical's formula for developing a simple global mission statement. Dow asks five key strategic questions:

1. What is the thrust or focus for future business development?
2. What is the scope of products and markets that will, and will not, be considered?
3. What is the future emphasis or priority and mix for products and markets that fall within the scope?
4. What key capabilities are required to make the strategic vision happen?
5. What does this vision imply for growth and return expectations?

How Leading Global Companies State Their Global Missions

MCI

MCI's mission is leadership in the global telecommunication service industry.

CIGNA

CIGNA strives to be a consistently profitable, borderless provider of insurance products and services, meeting the needs of select customer segments through well-trained, highly successful people.

WHIRLPOOL

Whirlpool's mission is to shape and lead the emerging global home-appliance industry.

External and Internal Analyzing and Diagnosing of Global Opportunities and Threats

The second step in developing a global strategy is conducting a comprehensive analysis and diagnosis of opportunities and challenges worldwide. The global marketplace and environment change ever faster, and companies must systematically and continually assess and understand the possible impact of those changes [5]. The environmental analysis includes both internal and external review of strengths, weaknesses, opportunities, and threats (commonly referred to as SWOT).

External. In tracking the global environment, strategists must pay particular attention to a variety of external factors, such as international economic indicators, national governments, legal structures, competitors, suppliers, technology, geography, and local markets.

Internal. Before a corporation can take advantage of possible global opportunities, it should first perform an internal audit. Factors to look at include financial strength, marketing and distribution systems, production and operations, personnel, and corporate resources.

Warner-Lambert's Look at the Future

"Bringing great products to market with maximum speed" is how Warner-Lambert states its mission. To bring its products to market at the earliest moment and do all in its power to encourage the products' rapid acceptance by consumers, the company must makes its best prediction of what the future will look like and where the best opportunities lie. Here are some of Warner-Lambert's predictions:

- As the world's population continues to grow older, more people will experience the diseases associated with aging. Much of Warner's research will target serious, chronic disorders, conditions that typically require lifelong therapy.
- So much demand exists for new pharmaceutical products that Warner expects to virtually double its pharmaceutical sales by the year 2000.
- The emerging economies of Asia and Eastern Europe will furnish Warner-Lambert with a major new marketing frontier.
- The managed health-care revolution that has swept over the medical care industry has permanently reshaped the pharmaceutical marketing landscape.

One of the key areas to look at is the core competence of the corporation, what Hammel and Prahalad call a company's ability "to build at a lower cost and faster than competitors" [4].

Core competencies revolve around the collective learning of the organization, especially how to coordinate diverse production skills and integrate multiple streams of technologies. The development of core competencies requires communication, involvement, and a deep commitment to working across organizational boundaries. The entire organization, from the chairman on down, must become involved.

Three criteria can be applied to determine the core competencies in an organization:

1. A core competence provides potential access to a wide variety of markets.
2. A core competence should make a significant contribution to the perceived customer benefits of the end product.
3. A core competence should be difficult for competitors to imitate.

Nortel's Core Competence

At Nortel, our vision of "A World of Networks" recognizes that customers want more than equipment. They want network solutions that give them competitive advantage in an era of unbridled competition. We believe that Nortel is unique in its ability to provide customers this advantage through a combination of our extensive global presence, broad product portfolio, and digital network leadership.

Establishing Specific Goals and Performance Targets

Based upon the general direction and philosophy provided by the mission statement and the results of the SWOT, the third step in developing a global strategy is the development of clear global objectives, that is, the desired outcomes to be achieved by the corporation within a specified time period. Specific performance targets are needed in all areas affecting the survival and success of an enterprise, and they are needed at all levels of management. The act of establishing formal objectives converts the general direction of an organization into clear targets to be achieved. It also guards against aimless activity, drift, confusion about what to accomplish, and loss of purpose.

Objectives should lay out what performance each managerial unit is supposed to achieve, what contributions different managerial units are expected to make in helping other units meet their objectives, and what contributions managers can expect from others in the organization.

Objectives should provide clear, unambiguous, measurable results; a deadline; and a specific assignment of accountability. They should, at a minimum, specify the following:

- ❑ The market position and competitive standing the organization aims to achieve.
- ❑ Annual profitability targets.
- ❑ Key financial and operating results to be gained through the organization's chosen activities.
- ❑ Other yardsticks by which strategic success will be measured.

Key objectives in the quest to become a world-class company include extremely high levels of quality levels, significantly reduced manufacturing cycle time, and an overarching dedication to serving the customer.

For global objectives to be useful, they should be close-ended. Open-ended objectives, which are objectives stated in very general terms, provide limited value because they cannot be measured and because it is not known when or if they can be achieved.

Identifying Global Alternatives and Making Strategic Choices

The next strategy step is to begin exploring alternative strategies and options. The firm should explore the best ways for dealing with corporate opportunities and threats (identified in Step 2) on a worldwide basis. The organization, in this step, seeks to examine its global market positions, facilities, and investments so as to focus on leveraging and linking opportunities. Some questions to ask at this stage include the following: Should we play just in the big markets? Should we standardize core products? Or is it best to concentrate on value-added activity in a few countries? Can we adopt a uniform market position? Would it be better to integrate competitive strategy across countries? Should we adopt the preemptive use of global strategy (that is, should we be the first competitor to make use of a particular element of global strategy—be it global market participation, global products, global activity location, or global marketing)?

Yip has identified five possible global, competitive moves:

1. **Cross-country Subsidization**—Using profits from one country in which a business participates to subsidize competitive actions in another country.
2. **Counterparry**—Defending against a competitive attack in one country by countering in another country.
3. **Globally Coordinated Sequence of Moves**—simultaneous or planned sequence in which competitive moves are made in different countries in the same business.
4. **Targeting of Global Competitors**—Identifying actual and potential global competitors and selecting an overall posture (attack, avoidance, cooperation, or acquisition) for each.
5. **Developing Country Competitor Plans**—Analyzing strengths, weaknesses, opportunities, and threats for each global competitor in each major country and developing a competitive plan or action for each country-competitor combination.

The key benefit of globally integrated competitive moves "lies in magnifying the resources available in any single country for competitive actions by leveraging the global resources of a business. So head-office managers can design competitive strategies that involve the power of multiple moves, while local managers can call on help beyond that available in just their own countries. Such an approach also helps managers to see country linkages so that they recognize the competitive interdependence of countries" [1, p. 177]. This taps the global power of linking and leveraging worldwide resources.

Sarkar and Cavusgil state that we "should no longer be asking what is the most efficient form of entry into a foreign market. Instead we need to focus on how the combinations of partnering strategy, relationship development, negotiation approaches, and long-term strategy of the firm impact . . . a firm's choice of markets and its extent of involvement in various cultural contexts"[6, pp. 844–845].

Moran, Harris, and Stripp [2, p. 51] have identified a number of possible strategic alternatives a company might consider in its march toward globalization:

- ❑ Strategic alliances
- ❑ Transnational ownership of equity securities

- ❑ Transnational management organization
- ❑ Wholly owned manufacturing branch plant or subsidiaries
- ❑ Consortium
- ❑ Joint ventures
- ❑ Cross-production agreements
- ❑ Turnkey operations
- ❑ Manufacturer's contracts
- ❑ Research consortium
- ❑ Outsourcing agreements
- ❑ Franchising
- ❑ Licensing with partial ownership
- ❑ Cross-licensing agreements
- ❑ Management of technical assistance contracts
- ❑ Cross-distribution agreements
- ❑ International barter and countertrade
- ❑ Foreign branch sales office
- ❑ Export directly to end user, foreign distributor, foreign sales agent
- ❑ Export indirectly through an export management company, through hiring an export agent, through selling to an export merchant, or through selling to a commission buying agent

Forming Strategic Global Contingencies and Plans

This step of the global strategy brings into play the critical issue of just how the targeted results (Step 3) are to be accomplished. Objectives are the "ends," and we are now exploring the "means" of achieving them. We now examine all the important entrepreneurial, competitive, and functional actions that are to be taken in pursuing organizational objectives to position the organization for sustained global success.

The strategic plan should address the following issues:

1. How to respond to the changing global conditions—changing global customers, emerging trends in the industry worldwide, new global competitors, and so on.
2. How to allocate resources throughout the organization's various business units, divisions, and functional departments on a global

scale (see Chapter 8 on global structures). This deals with making decisions that steer capital investment, learning, knowledge, and human resources behind the chosen strategic plan.

3. How to compete in each of the industries or countries in which the organization participates. This decision addresses how to develop customer appeal, to position the firm against rivals, to emphasize some products/services and de-emphasize others, and to meet specific competitive threats.
4. What actions and approaches to take globally and in each country, thereby to create a unified and more powerful global entity.

During this step of global strategizing, it is necessary to explore the following options and opportunities:

- ❑ Searching actively for innovative ways the organization can improve on what it is already doing.
- ❑ Ferreting out new opportunities for the organization to pursue.
- ❑ Developing ways to increase the firm's competitive strength and to put it in a stronger position to cope with competitive forces.
- ❑ Devising ways to build and maintain a competitive advantage.
- ❑ Deciding how to meet threatening external developments.
- ❑ Encouraging individuals throughout the organization to put forth innovative proposals, and championing those proposals that have promise.
- ❑ Directing resources away from areas of low or diminishing results toward areas of high or increasing results.
- ❑ Deciding when and how to diversify product and/or service lines.
- ❑ Choosing which products or services to abandon, which of the continuing ones to emphasize, and which new ones to enter or add.

Global Alliances

One possible aspect of any global strategy is the consideration of global alliances. Robert Radway notes that "in the new global marketplace, technological, financial, and other competitive challenges are helping to seal different kinds of strategic alliances that would not have been possible less than a decade ago." He goes on to add that:

> The rules of the game are not yet well understood, and cultural differences are preventing the successful integration of management strategies and teams in these new alliances. U.S. companies, in particular, are learning that key factors for success in these, be they joint ventures for manufacturing, research and development, financial consortia, or technology transfer, demand much more careful planning and training than has been required in the past [2, p. 298].

Partnerships and global alliances are very important because they provide a quick, efficient, and effective way for a company to absorb knowledge, stimulate innovation, and become an insider in new markets. Rossbeth Kanter notes that global organizations must have strong internal unity. Strength comes from "both excellence in each line of business and the combined power of the whole. Global competitiveness also involves watching, listening, and learning both outside and within the company. Openness to learning from foreign markets and external partners is often a key to success" [7].

Both Rover and British Telecom (BT) have seen the creation of global alliances as a powerful global integrator. Rover globalized with Honda from 1978 through 1994 and has done so with BMW since 1994. BT saw its future success as being able to exploit opportunities globally through partnerships, alliances, and joint ventures. The company has found that global contracts force people to work together, and thereby global contracts create a global mind-set. BT now has collaborative programs with several other telecommunication companies. Delco has also established several global alliances. Likewise, Whirlpool has initiated a global partnership with three universities—Indiana University, the University of Michigan, and INSEAD in Paris.

For many companies, the quickest way to gain global technological advantage is through strategic alliances between firms that work together under a cooperative agreement to attain some strategic objective. Corporations that want to gain access to advanced technology are often well-advised to enter into an alliance to offset the immense expense that research and development entails. Allies can share costs, establish a pool of joint resources, and create a synergistic effect in the problem-solving process.

The success of an alliance obviously depends upon the compatibility of the partners. Therefore, a firm should take the time to find a partner with a "cooperative business philosophy, a complementary

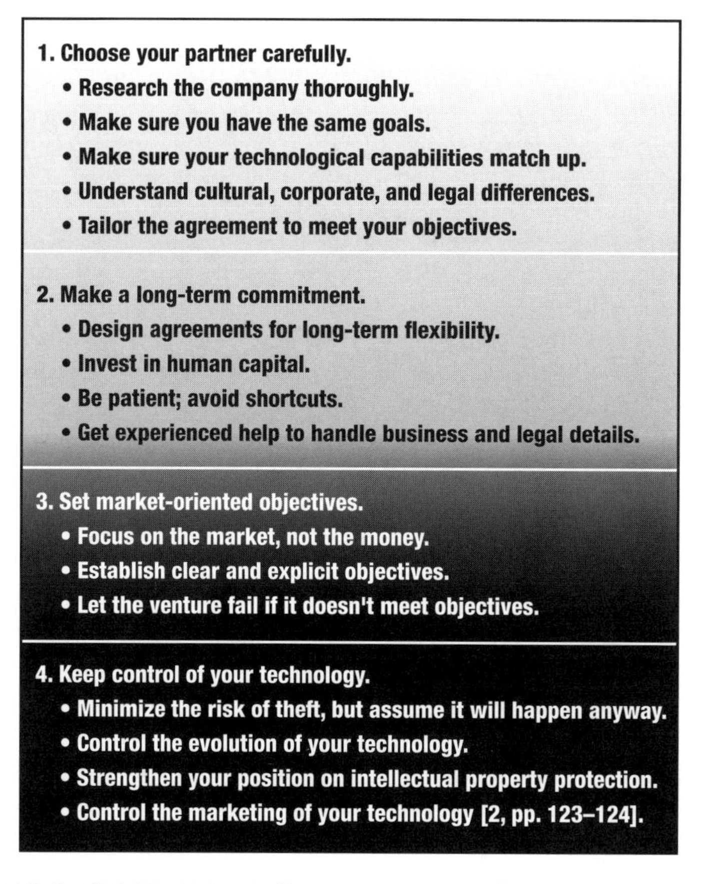
1. Choose your partner carefully.
    - Research the company thoroughly.
    - Make sure you have the same goals.
    - Make sure your technological capabilities match up.
    - Understand cultural, corporate, and legal differences.
    - Tailor the agreement to meet your objectives.
2. Make a long-term commitment.
    - Design agreements for long-term flexibility.
    - Invest in human capital.
    - Be patient; avoid shortcuts.
    - Get experienced help to handle business and legal details.
3. Set market-oriented objectives.
    - Focus on the market, not the money.
    - Establish clear and explicit objectives.
    - Let the venture fail if it doesn't meet objectives.
4. Keep control of your technology.
    - Minimize the risk of theft, but assume it will happen anyway.
    - Control the evolution of your technology.
    - Strengthen your position on intellectual property protection.
    - Control the marketing of your technology [2, pp. 123–124].

FIGURE 6-2. CHECKLIST FOR ESTABLISHING AN ALLIANCE PARTNERSHIP.

mission, compatible managerial capabilities, and the resources necessary to acquire and develop new technology" [2, p. 123].

Moran, Harris, and Stripp have developed a comprehensive checklist that can be helpful in establishing a strategic alliance (see Figure 6-2).

Percy Barnevik, former CEO of ABB, offers the following valuable advice relative to strategic alliances:

> Strategic alliances can be powerful tools for penetrating new markets, allowing one partner to build on the other's experience and achieve substantial savings by using the partner's distribution networks. When the product and market range are well defined and the partners have

> few conflicting interests, strategic alliances can help participants achieve short- and long-term success.
>
> Nevertheless, entering into strategic alliances can be dangerous as a general strategy for globalization. Acquiring and merging with companies in other countries, and going on to establish a common corporate culture and agenda is demanding, even with a common set of shareholders and board members and a single top management team. Add to this the challenges of optimizing the global structure by reallocating export markets, closing plants, and transferring production when national loyalties come into play. And keep in mind that these changes become even more difficult to effect when minority interests need to be protected or an equal partner needs to be placated. . . . Further, the rewards from a common global strategy—whether it is applied by equal partners in an alliance or by wholly owned companies in a group—are often shared unequally [7, pp. xvii–xviii].

Negotiating and Contracting with Global Partners

When negotiating with global partners, a number of cultural factors can add a tremendous amount of time and cost in preparing documents and getting final approval and acceptance.

1. **Establishing Trust and Rapport.** In the American culture, one may quickly get down to business and write up the contract. In most other cultures, the process of developing a trusting relationship between the two parties must occur first, and this may take weeks or even months. Attempts to bypass this step will lead to resentment and failure.

2. **Power Structure.** In societies in which there is a clear pyramidlike power structure, lower-level officials or managers will never make final decisions without the approval of the higher authorities. It is difficult for them to take risks or to do something new or untested. Only when the top person (who must first see hundreds of documents) has reviewed and signed off, can one go forward.

3. **Context.** In negotiating and signing agreements, low-context and high-context cultures differ significantly. In low-context cultures, such as in Switzerland and Germany, every detail must be agreed to and put in writing. High-context cultures, such as in Malaysia, may never

require a written contract. Good personal relationships and trust mean that a personal handshake may be all that is necessary.

4. **Communication.** The cultural context often makes it difficult for the global manager to obtain the level of communication necessary. For example, a subordinate who has the data needed may be a mere shadow in a meeting that includes his superiors, whereas he may have been very articulate outside the meeting. A senior official who is open and warm when negotiating alone may become extremely careful and formal when his colleagues are present.

5. **Language.** Negotiating and contracting become even more challenging when people must perform these actions in other than their primary language. The tone, nuance, or even the meaning of a message might be inadvertently lost through mistranslation. Roger Craig, in his book *The Fall of Japan,* argues forcefully that the Japanese government, although willing, was unable to accept the surrender terms of the Potsdam Conference because the wording would not have been, in the judgment of the Japanese, possible for the emperor to employ because it would deny his deity.

Implementing Global Strategy (Leadership, Personnel, Logistics, and Tactics)

Putting the strategy into place and getting individuals and organizational units worldwide to execute the global plan successfully involves:

- ❑ Building an organization capable of carrying out the strategic plan.
- ❑ Developing strategy-supportive budgets and programs.
- ❑ Instilling a strong organizationwide commitment both to organizational objectives and the chosen strategy.
- ❑ Linking the motivation and reward structure directly to achieving the targeted results.
- ❑ Creating an organization culture that is in tune with strategy in every success-creating aspect.
- ❑ Installing policies and procedures that facilitate strategy implementation.

- ❑ Developing an information and reporting system to track and control the progress of strategy implementation.
- ❑ Exerting the internal leadership needed to drive implementation forward and to keep improving how the strategy is being executed [8, p. 11].

Implementing and executing the global strategy also requires employees at all levels to answer the question "What is required of us to implement this part of the global plan, and how can we best get it done?" A number of fits are needed:

- ❑ A fit between strategy and the internal organizational structure
- ❑ A fit between strategy and organizational skills, technical know-how, and operating capabilities
- ❑ A fit between strategy and staff size and the allocation of budgets
- ❑ A fit between strategy and the organization's system of rewards and incentives
- ❑ A fit between strategy and internal policies, practices, and procedures
- ❑ A fit between strategy and the corporate culture

The stronger these fits, the more strategy-supportive the organization's way of doing things is. The sequence of actions and the speed of the implementation process are important aspects of uniting the whole organization behind strategy accomplishment. The enthusiasm, pride, and commitment of employees worldwide creates the crusade vital to carry out the chosen strategy and to achieve the targeted results.

Global startup, according to Hordes et al. [9], requires the following:

Instant Critical Mass—The ability to blanket the globe with a web of technology and human resource practices that provide a seamless execution of product, service, and information dissemination

Leveraging of Capability and Development of Knowledge Workers—The ability to generate relevant new knowledge, move it to the point of need, and apply it

Global Coordination—The ability of sharing information, aligning efforts, and allocating responsibilities among dispersed locations

Global Startup at JM Perry Corporation
(by Paul Wright, executive vice president and equity owner)

The JM Perry Corporation is a training and management consultancy founded in 1982. Located in Palo Alto, Calif., it now has twenty staff members and annual sales of $4 million. Services include executive coaching, conflict resolution, team building, and corporate communication.

Entering the global marketplace came as a result of a global client requesting our services in Europe. Immediately, we were faced with tactical implementation decisions with huge implications for our future. Should we open an office in Europe? Who should the ultimate service delivery team be? Do we put people on airplanes, or do we recruit locals with the language skills and knowledge of the culture? If we employ local people, will they be contractors or employees? How do we protect our brand?

The decisions we needed to make would, in essence, change the central character of our company. While answering these questions, we had to begin training **now**. Service companies—small and large—face the dilemma of having to sell services before staffing themselves.

We have learned two important lessons in our initial venture into encircling the globe:

1. Be clear about vision and mission. Don't fall into the trap of incremental decision making. For instance, we were advised that our business was "too American" and would not work in other cultures. We were close to making significant changes before realizing that we wanted to stay with what was appropriate for us (a decision that has led to better results for us).
2. Be sure your product or service, as well as the pricing, fits the markets you are considering. We chose to stay with a

(Continued on next page)

price and product-set targeted to senior leadership (again, with excellent results).

Ultimately, you want to have an enjoyable global journey and also be proud of what you have created.

Coordination on a global basis provides an enterprise with the flexibility also to respond to competitive threats, regardless of the origin of that threat. The truly global company can pick its battles and decide where and how to make a stand to force competitors to implement a defensive reaction in countries in which they are often least prepared to be responsive.

The CEO must be heavily involved in the globalization effort. She or he must develop direct contacts with employees around the world. The CEO must visit as many markets and subsidiaries as possible, conducting detailed meetings with middle managers, customers, and government officials. One of the CEO's primary tasks on the road is to encourage management teams to meet the challenges of globalization and to assure them that they will be rewarded for doing so [10].

According to McGrath and Houle, the integration and implementation of global strategy can begin in any one of the following five areas:

Product Development. By using global design teams to develop products once, and only once, for the global market, a company can eliminate costly redesigns every time it wants to enter a new market. These products can have variables to meet the needs of individual countries, as the cost of overdesigning some products is still lower than having to redesign them if the need arises. A good communication system is essential for the design teams so they can monitor local tastes, technical standards, changing government regulations, technology developments, and competitors' products.

Purchasing. Economies of scale in purchasing comes from consolidating raw material sources and paring down a company's supplier base. By purchasing on a global instead of a local basis, companies have the freedom to choose the best suppliers in the world, no matter where their operations are located. They also have a better chance of receiving lower unit costs and better delivery schedules because of the larger global contract.

Production. To take advantage of their larger capacity and geographic diversity, global manufacturers should streamline the flow of inventory between plants. Managers can begin restructuring production by analyzing how materials flow from plant to plant. Coordinating and simplifying materials flow requires two things: (1) balancing production *vertically* within the production pipeline, from component manufacturing to final assembly, and (2) balancing production *horizontally* between plants that manufacture the same or similar products. For vertical balancing, the tightest connection between component, subassembly, and final assembly plants comes from creating a global system analogous to single-plant, just-in-time inventory management. Horizontal balancing requires central coordination of plants that handle the same step in the manufacturing process by assigning production based on cost, plant capacity, technical capabilities, availability of material, and closeness to the customer.

Demand Management. A sophisticated global forecasting system is necessary for managers to set sales quotas, plan production schedules and inventory requirements, negotiate supplier contracts, and establish corporate revenue plans. Demand management teams can be used to make informed decisions on any necessary production changes if an original forecast fails to be accurate.

Order Fulfillment. To gain a global scale advantage in the area of order fulfillment, companies must "focus on coordinating customer orders with distribution at the global level. The result is more efficient order management, a decrease in total finished goods inventories, and quicker, more direct delivery. Ideally, orders are linked to the most appropriate factory, which then ships the product directly to the customer" [7, pp. 98–103].

Global Integration at Digital Equipment Corporation (DEC)

Although a pioneer in computer networking, Digital Equipment Corporation improved its communication system by creating an e-mail network that links its employees worldwide. DEC estimates that the use of this nework has contributed to a twofold reduction in product development time. The company has also been able to simplify its complex and unwieldy fulfillment system. The new process reduces the number of transactions, streamlines the distribution flow, considerably improves delivery time, and increases the accuracy of orders, as well as customer satisfaction.

Evaluating, Modifying, and Reapplying Global Strategy

The final step in the development of a global strategy is to evaluate the plan in its entirety to determine if it is working, and to develop provisions for allowing alterations or redevelopment based on feedback or new input.

Yip suggests that in measuring the effectiveness of globalization strategy the following aspects of the strategy should be examined:

- **Business Definition**—Are customer needs addressed, appropriate technologies used, customer segments served, correct products offered, and the best geographic scope used?
- **Strategic Thrust**—Are performance priorities in terms of market share, revenues, and profitability?
- **Financial Targets**—Are global, regional, and national targets being met? How do they correlate?
- **Sources of Competitive Advantage**—Have we located and leveraged our advantages in areas such as patents, research capability, product or service quality, customer relationships, unique manufacturing technology, global reputation, financial resources, cross-business synergy, customer service, distribution capability, and learning capability?

- ❑ **Strategy Elements**—Are the best strategies being employed in terms of technology, manufacturing, product line, pricing, selling approach, marketing, distribution, and customer service?
- ❑ **Value-Adding Activities**—Are we exploiting our strengths in research, development, procurement, production, marketing, distribution, and customer service?
- ❑ **Competitive Strategy**—Have we specified strategy versus each of our major competitors?

Among the globalization measures that a comprehensive global strategy addresses are:

1. **Global Market Participation**—Market share, market presence, global coverage
2. **Global Products and Services**—Mix standardization, content standardization
3. **Global Location of Activities**—Concentration of individual activity and of entire value chain
4. **Global Marketing**—Comparative marketing intensity, marketing uniformity
5. **Global Competitive Moves**—Multicountry competitive moves and counterparry moves
6. **Global Management Processes**—Global strategic information system, cross-country coordination, global strategic planning, global budgeting, global evaluation
7. **Market Drivers**—Common customer needs, global channels, transferable marketing, lead countries
8. **Cost Drivers**—Global scale economies, steep experience effects, sourcing efficiencies, favorable logistics, differences in country costs, high product development costs, fast-changing technology
9. **Government Drivers**—Tariffs, subsidies, nontariff barriers, compatible technical standards, common marketing regulations
10. **Competitive Drivers**—Exports, imports, competitors from different continents, globalized competitors
11. **Learning**—Knowledge-managed, speed and quality of learning [1]

Based on these analyses, as well as ongoing assessment of the success of the global strategy, the global strategic plan will probably require corrective adjustments and reformulations. Changing global conditions, the emergence of new opportunities or threats, a new corporate culture, and new learnings are all examples of what could necessitate reformulating the strategic plan and its implementation.

Successful Global Strategy at Whirlpool

Our consistent improvement in operating performance during the past three years has demonstrated the soundness of our long-term strategy to shape and lead the emerging global home-appliance industry, a strategy intended to carry Whirlpool well into the next century. The heart of the strategy remains our studied belief that the process and product technologies of the home-appliance industry are the same the world over. Of course, as we encourage and exploit these similarities, we will continue to respect the differences between national and regional markets in terms of consumer preferences for styling, features, and other characteristics. The global strategy is the path we have chosen to take us to the top one-quarter of large, publicly traded companies in terms of total return to shareholders.

Strategizing for Global Success

Developing a global business strategy is an overwhelming challenge in a world of tremendous competition, continuous change and chaos, massive amounts of information, and staggering political, social, and economic issues and options in each country and region of the world. Yet, as we have seen in this chapter, a number of global companies have enjoyed great global success because of their ability to systematically plan, implement, and reformulate a comprehensive global strategy. In Chapter 7, we will explore how each of the twelve operations of a global company is planned and managed for global success.

References

1. Yip, G. *Total Global Strategy*. Englewood Cliffs, N.J.: Prentice Hall, 1992.
2. Moran, R., Harris, P., and Stripp, W. *Developing the Global Organization*. Houston, Tex.: Gulf Publishing, 1993.
3. Ohmae, K. *The Borderless World*. New York: Harper, 1990.
4. Hammel, G. and Prahalad, C. K. *Competing for the Future*. Cambridge, Mass.: Harvard University Press, 1994.
5. Lussier, R., Baider, R., and Corman, J. "Measuring Global Practices: Global Strategic Planning Through Company Situational Analysis." *Business Horizon,* Vol. 37, No. 5, May 1994, pp. 56–63.
6. Sarkar, M. and Cavusgil, S. T. "Trends in International Business Thought and Literature: A Review of International Market Entry Mode Research: Integration and Synthesis." *International Executive,* Vol. 38, No. 6, Nov. 1996, pp. 825–847.
7. Kanter, R. (Ed.). *Global Strategies: Insights from the World's Leading Thinkers*. Cambridge, Mass.: Harvard Business Press, 1994.
8. Thompson, A. and Strickland, A. *Strategic Management: Concepts and Cases*. Homewood, Ill.: Irwin Professional Publishing, 1996.
9. Hordes, M. J., Clancy, A., and Baddaley, J. "A Primer for Global Start-ups." *Academy of Management Executive,* Vol. 9, No. 2, 1995, pp. 7–11.
10. Roth, K., Schweiger, D. M., and Morrison, A. J. "Global Strategy Implementation at the Business Unit Level: Operation Capabilities and Administrative Mechanisms." *Journal of International Business Studies,* Vol. 22, No. 3, pp. 369–402.

7

Globalizing Operations

Young and Nie in their book *Managing Global Operations* [1] designate "operations as being the very soul of the organization" and note that global manufacturing and global service firms have "similar challenges in going global." Global executives agree that all corporate operations, beginning with research and development (R&D) and continuing to customer service, need be globalized for the organization to integrate, link, leverage, and optimize its global powers. In this chapter we will look at how to globalize each of the twelve operations of the global company (see Figure 7-1).

Global Research and Development

Yip [2] emphasizes that the essence of a global strategy for R&D is that it be conducted to serve the entire global market rather than only individual countries. This has been the traditional weakness of most multinational companies that have historically run their R&D operations to stress serving either the home market or individual foreign markets rather than the global market as a whole.

Global R&D, at its best, operates in the following manner:

- It taps into sources of knowledge and information wherever those sources might be located in the world.
- It transmits that knowledge back to the central R&D, wherever that might be.
- It allocates priorities globally on the basis of strategic need rather than of proximity.

FIGURE 7-1. GLOBAL OPERATIONS.

- It is able to develop global products with the capability for customization for major national markets.

All these tasks have to be performed while balancing the need to achieve critical mass and economies of scale. A number of factors affect where R&D should be located and how it should be managed:

- Universal global customer needs make it less necessary to locate R&D in multiple countries, thus favoring concentration of R&D efforts to thereby achieve maximum scale benefits. The presence of global customers allows companies to place some of their R&D activities close to their most important global customers. The existence of these important lead countries (for example, the United States and Japan) requires companies to locate at least some of their R&D activities there. As a minimum, companies should locate a scanning function in lead countries to gather information on leading-edge developments. A classic example of locating in a lead country to tap into R&D resources is the strategy of Japanese computer and electronic companies opening laboratories to do basic research in the United States, partly to lure the most creative American computer scientists to work for them.

- R&D activities in most industries may need a large amount of expensive equipment and many scientists to work in close collaboration to achieve any significant results. The high cost of R&D makes the duplication of facilities (as multinational companies are wont to do) very expensive.
- Companies may find it necessary to locate in particular countries to understand better the technical specifications and regulations. For example, the drug approval process is so complex that having a local R&D presence can help companies deal with the local processes more successfully. Governments are also eager for technology to be transferred into their countries. A local R&D facility that operates as part of a global network can thus be used to enhance relations and bargaining power with host governments.
- The need to locate R&D in globally strategic countries and the spreading availability of R&D skills are encouraging companies to spread out their R&D efforts and to find creative ways to maintain a globally integrated network of R&D workers (for example, Texas Instruments researchers are located in countries in Asia, Europe, and the Americas).
- Finally, global companies may find acquisitions or mergers especially helpful in strengthen their global R&D, both as a way of obtaining technical expertise and as a way of enhancing the scale of R&D operations. PPG noted that in business units where technology is global (for example, paint coatings), employees in those units are more inclined to have global thinking. Whirlpool has corporate-run advanced technology centers located in all regions of the world, each focusing on a major product line. Other firms emphasize the importance of establishing R&D centers at locations only where the best global resources and research are readily available.

Global Manufacturing

The manufacturing strategy must (a) support the company's global business strategy and yet (b) be consistent across all facilities. To align these two strategies, global companies should analyze existing plants—including their locations, capacity, and the range of products they produce—and the ability and willingness of their managers to communicate with each other.

Global manufacturing has many benefits:

- Enhancement of customer relations in specific countries
- Gaining of access to local immobile factors of production and technological resources
- Reduction of transportation costs
- Avoidance of tariff and nontariff barriers
- Satisfying of some demands from, as well as gaining benefits from, local governments
- Becoming an insider within the local country (for example, Japanese plants move to Britain to get their vehicles certified as vehicles of European origin even though a high percentage of the vehicles' content is originally imported from Japan).
- Hedge against country-specific risks
- An ability to preempt competition
- Greater efficiency of scale than manufacturing in numerous countries; not operating below full capacity in multinational locations
- A higher level of learning and valuable experience
- Getting access to low-cost production factors.
- Using local technological resources.
- Gaining proximity to local markets.

The differences in country costs favor the use of global manufacturing by making it worthwhile to locate in specific countries because the company can exploit low labor costs, as well as reduce taxes. Within a global manufacturing network, there are opportunities to set transfer prices and subsidiary remittances so as to minimize total tax liability [3, pp. 127–128]. These advantages are gained through (a) the selective location of manufacturing facilities with either low or negotiated tax rates and (b) the transshipment of raw materials, as well as intermediate and final products.

Global Manufacturing Questions at Warner-Lambert

According to Larry Osborne, vice president of operations at Warner-Lambert, the company must correctly answer these questions to be a "global winner" in the year 2000:

- ❑ What levels of specification will achieve economies of scale without offsetting losses due to the costs of manufacturing complexity?
- ❑ What technology investments make the most sense in ensuring manufacturing flexibility and driving competitive points of difference?

A key to global manufacturing is flexible manufacturing, which interacts with both the use of globally standardized products and the use of geographically concentrated manufacturing. Flexible manufacturing allows more scope for producing customized variants of a core global product. A global company can therefore design a standardized global core that it then customizes in a centralized manufacturing facility for different national or regional markets.

It is much easier to produce a limited product line than a broader line in a factory. In today's global market, the product cycle is shorter than ever, and customers' tastes and demands change constantly. Thus a manufacturing configuration is needed that can adapt quickly to changing demand patterns. Machinery and equipment should be considered for purchase that can not only manufacture the current product but also be quickly and easily retooled for future changes in the product.

Product designs that are changing rapidly to meet changing market needs require a close linkage among marketers, designers, and manufacturing. So the stable product designs that dominate in the mature stage of the product life cycle should make it easier to use global manufacturing.

Manufacturing obviously interconnects with a large number of activities, including the development of product and process technology, the building of production capacity and plant facilities, the maintenance of the manufacturing information system, management of materials and inbound and outbound logistics, maintenance of quality and reliability standards, production planning, and the management of the actual production operations. Typically, most of these activities need to be performed in close proximity to each other so that location decisions tend to cover these activities as a package. Some specific characteristics of a company's manufacturing process may make it easier to shift from a situation of duplicated independent plants to one of an interdependent global network.

The importance of interconnecting these activities (designing for manufacturability, or DFM) can be seen by the different experiences of IBM and Gillette. To develop the IBM Pro-Printer, IBM put together a team of product designers, manufacturing managers, and marketing managers that produced a printer that met and exceeded customer requirements and was easy to manufacture. Gillette's sensor razor, however, which was developed without manufacturing input, proved costly and difficult to manufacture [1, p. 21]. New-product development must be aimed at the ultimate customer, so it is imperative that DFM teams receive some form of customer input. Firms competing in global markets must consider the wants and needs of all customer groups, the manufacturing capabilities of their plants, and the challenge of marketing across borders.

Flexible Manufacturing at Toshiba

Flexibility is the key word at Toshiba. Toshiba President Fumio Sato led a campaign to "make more products with the same equipment and people." Now Toshiba produces twenty varieties of laptop computers on the same assembly line and nine different word processors on another. Product life cycles are so short in the personal computer industry that such behavior is a competitive necessity. Similarly, Toyota installed flexible lines and was able to cut setup times for new models in half by using "intelligent pallets"—computer-controlled pallets that make adjustments for different models. In sum, shortened product life cycles increase the need for simultaneous or concurrent engineering. Software designers have even devised ways to facilitate the transfer of geometric data between computer-aided design (CAD) and computer-aided manufacturing (CAM) [1, p. 22].

Global Product Development

Companies should globally standardize products, with local variations, while at the same time establishing and maintaining world-class quality for all products and services. Cultural differences need to be identified in determining product specifications. Product strategies should specify the market needs that may be served by offering different products. Product strategies should deal with such matters as number and diversity of products, product innovations, product scope, and product design.

Three global product strategies are possible: (1) producing the same product for use worldwide, (2) modifying the product for different markets, and (3) designing and developing the product to meet the local needs.

One possible strategy for compromising between uniformity and diversion is to standardize some components while changing the end characteristics. For example, Coca-Cola exports its concentrate to its thousands of bottling plants all over the world. Carbonation, sugar, and color are added at local bottling plants. The amounts added may vary from one country to the next so as to conform with local preferences. This type of change has practically no cost because "standardization is achieved for the concentrate process and because the finished product cannot feasibly be exported" [4].

When designing products, global corporations should be sensitive to the various technical and environmental conditions of the consumer countries. Global companies need to recognize that the dream of universal products is often unachievable. A company selling in a multitude of cultures usually cannot sell the exact same product everywhere.

In designing a product for the global marketplace, Moran, Harris, and Stripp [4] suggest that companies consider some of the factors shown in Figure 7-2.

The best global products are usually those that are designed from the start rather than being merely adapted from national products. Designers of global products and services should try to maximize the size of the common global core while also providing for local tailoring around the core.

Managers need to continually examine how they are currently producing products and strive to find better ways for product develop-

Factors	Possible Product Change
• Level of technical skill	• Product simplification
• Level of labor cost	• Automation, manual labor
• Level of literacy	• Remarking; product simplification
• Level of income	• Quality and price change
• Interest rates	• Quality and price change
• Maintenance needs	• Change in tolerances
• Climatic differences	• Product adaptation
• Isolation (difficult to access)	• Product simplification; reliability improvement
• Differences in standards	• Recalibration; resizing
• Availability of other products	• Greater/lesser product integration
• Availability of materials	• Change in product structure/ fuel requirements
• Power availability	• Resizing
• Special conditions	• Product redesign or invention

FIGURE 7-2. FACTORS TO CONSIDER IN DESIGNING GLOBAL PRODUCTS.

ment. One basic approach to the improvement of product development is:

1. Flowchart or diagram the process.
2. Examine all the steps of the process.
3. Interview the processors to find out what they do and why they do it.
4. Streamline the process.

Creating global design teams is another crucial part of globalizing product development. If members of a product design team are located all over the world rather than clustered at a central site, each designer can monitor local tastes, technical standards, and changing government regulations. Designers in the field can also stay abreast of local technology developments and gain quicker access to competitors' products. Fundamental rethinking and radical redesign of products may sometimes be necessary to achieve dramatic improvements in critical, contemporary measures of performance, such as cost, quality, service, and speed.

Global Product Development at Beloit Corporation (by Pete Rosenberg, manager, corporate relations)

The most ambitious project to date at Beloit Corporation for going global is the development of international standards for future engineered products. As a global company, we need to provide metric equipment as our standard offering and to use engineering and manufacturing "centers of excellence." Global standardizing of products and processes generates greater value at lower cost, resulting in cycle time improvements. The S2000 program involves selecting the best designs from Beloit's global design bases and converting them, where necessary, to the new metric design standards. These designs will then be available for repeated worldwide use. This is really key to cutting costs and reducing delivery time within engineering, purchasing, and manufacturing. It is a huge step toward becoming a single global company.

Basic elements of the new global program include:

- ❑ Reducing variety or selections of both purchased materials and manufactured products.
- ❑ Establishing standard engineered products.
- ❑ Integrating the common use of components across product lines.
- ❑ Developing common worldwide, unified engineering processes, systems, and techniques.
- ❑ Developing readily available application materials and specifications.
- ❑ Developing product pricing structures.
- ❑ Implementing a "standards" distribution and retrieval system for ease of use.

In the process of determining metric sizes for our standard materials, we've had trouble finding suppliers who stock those sizes. But that is changing, as our main supplier has promised to start stocking metric sizes.

Standardizing our raw materials increases both savings and flexibility by:

- ❑ Simplifying the ordering of material.
- ❑ Reducing the amount of inventory required.
- ❑ Creating the capability to manufacture products at any of the company's global facilities, regardless of where the engineering takes place.

Another major global focus of the Beloit Corporation was to create one ordering system from the previous five. We can now communicate instantaneously and worldwide with our engineering and manufacturing systems.

Our previous separate systems caused several problems: (1) they crippled our ability to share engineering information internally; (2) customers didn't like to get Beloit drawings and documentation that look completely different from each other; and (3) now that manufacturing facilities are specializing in the machine selections they build, customers do not want to get and interpret five different sets of engineering information.

Technology now makes it possible for all of Beloit PMG Engineering to gain access to information on all the BelCadd systems and the IBM system in Beloit. The worldwide teams have adopted the Beloit-Wisconsin engineering ordering system as the new world standard because it is the most comprehensive. They are now outlining a plan for training engineering personnel worldwide to use this system.

Global Product and Service Quality

In the highly competitive global marketplace, the quality of product and service is necessary to attract customers. And quality must be offered on a global scale, in each and every location in which the product or service is delivered. Uniformity is key to any global organization's measurement approach. Operations managers must coordinate quality and productivity measurement systems so that they offer valid comparisons from plant to plant. Global quality-control officials must be able to measure quality via a variety of tools: control charts, fishbone diagrams, Pareto diagrams, run charts, scatter diagrams, and frequency histograms.

David Garvin has identified eight dimensions for global quality:

1. **Conformance**—Ability to meet customer specifications
2. **Aesthetics**—Physical appearance of the product or the physical surroundings and ambiance of the service (for example, Lexus 400, AT&T Slimline phone, Four Seasons Hotels)
3. **Perceived quality**—What customer thinks of product or service quality
4. **Reliability**—The ability to meet expected performance time after time (such as Federal Express)
5. **Durability**—The product's ability to withstand stress and to last (for example, Samsonite)
6. **Performance**—The product's ability to do whatever the customer requires
7. **Features**—The bells-and-whistles items attached to the product that may increase the product's desirability. These may be standard items that come with the product or additional options, but the customer perceives that the value of the product increases with added features
8. **Serviceability**—The ability to repair a product, correct a service solution, or in general receive needed customer service {5}

ISO 9000 Series, Malcolm Baldridge, and Demming Awards—Global Standards of Excellence

In Europe, the quality requirements established by the International Organization for Standardization (ISO) are quickly becoming the benchmark against which all companies' products are measured. The certificate awarded to companies by this organization shows customers how a company tests products, trains employees, keeps records, and fixes defects; the certificate is an accepted seal of quality approval. The ISO 9000 series consists of five categories:

1. ISO 9000—Quality Management and Quality Assurance Standards—Guidelines for Selection and Use
2. ISO 9001—Quality Systems—For Design/Development Production, Installation and Servicing
3. ISO 9002—Quality Systems—For Final Inspection
4. ISO 9003—Quality Systems for Final Testing
5. ISO 9004—Quality Management and Quality Systems Elements—Guidelines

Another standard recognized globally is the Malcolm Baldridge Award, which is scored according to leadership (10 percent), information and analysis (7 percent), strategic quality planning (8 percent), human resource utilization (15 percent), quality assurance of products and services (14 percent), quality results (18 percent), and customer satisfaction (30 percent). The predecessor to ISO and Baldridge is the Demming Awards, which are awarded to the top quality companies of Japan.

Many global companies have made quality an important step in building toward global status. Whirlpool, for example, has created its Whirlpool Excellence System (WES) to determine and measure quality throughout the organization according to global standards. The global system is based on the criteria of the various global standards and has been essential to integrating new joint-venture partners into the Whirlpool system.

Global Finance, Purchasing, and Procurement

Global financing refers to a company's ability to (a) seek and acquire, on a worldwide basis, money at the lowest cost, (b) hedge when necessary to protect currency risk, (c) invest in local currency, and (d) list shares on various foreign exchanges. To maximize their global reach, global companies:

- ❑ Invest with financial institutions that have expertise and success on a global scale.
- ❑ Learn about the currency conditions and regulations of countries and regions in which the companies operate.
- ❑ Understand the tax policies and systems to determine the best environments in which to invest.

A globally centralized and integrated approach to purchasing can ensure that the business has access to the best possible materials and components, as well as the best possible prices. Whether to incur the costs and additional management requirements of global purchasing depends on the specific potential benefits. For example, Singer Furniture found its own offshore sourcing inefficient and unable to exploit the potential for sourcing economies. So it contracted with another company, IMX, to be its exclusive agent for overseas purchasing. In turn, IMX uses its own global network to find low-cost sourcing opportunities that lower the purchasing and shipping costs of Singer goods. Similar activities occur within the automotive industry where the European Ford Secot sources components from fifteen different countries [3, pp. 125–126].

The many challenges for the manager of global finance and purchasing include the following:

- ❑ Identifying international risks
- ❑ Working in multiple currencies
- ❑ International project finance
- ❑ International tax issues
- ❑ Coping with multiple accounting issues
- ❑ Risks (commercial, country, customer, supplier, and exchanges)

Global companies must also be cognizant of the issue of ethics in global buying. They cannot be naive to the potential for graft and corruption surrounding buyer-seller relationships. What we might call bribery in the United States is considered no more than the cost of doing business in other countries. Unfortunately, many global bids are won and/or projects obtained by the company with the most to offer in financial or other incentives to buyers [1, p. 61].

Global Materials Management, Inventory Systems, and Sourcing

Materials Management

The Japanese proved to the world that the best solution to materials management was to design a "pull" system, one that responds to meet customer orders (rather than one that builds inventory) and thus minimizes inventory investment. Materials managers perform the balancing act of trying to provide materials while minimizing their materials investments.

Globalization requires the logistics function to be coordinated on a global scale with ongoing dialogue between the regional or national offices. Whirlpool's global process of moving products from manufacturing to the customer demonstrates the need for world-class logistics functions that are coordinated on a global scale.

Inventory Systems

Global inventory management must answer these key questions:

- ❑ Do we have a consortium of suppliers with the ability to deliver materials just in time?
- ❑ Do we have the capital to invest, or the need to purchase software for inventory management?
- ❑ Can inventory be shared across plants/regions/countries?
- ❑ Do we have the software capabilities to access inventory information from a centralized data base?

Global firms can improve their materials management by networking inventory systems, connecting via electronic data interchange, and sharing a data base of information [1, p. 81].

Sourcing

Global managers must decide whether they intend to source materials from a selected few vendors or offer the business to many sources. Sourcing selection should be based on the factors of price, quality, delivery dependability, and service.

Many global businesses are now following the example of Japanese and Korean buyers by reducing their vendor relationships. Advantages of single sourcing include reduction in paperwork, fewer trucks to receive products from, the possibility of long-term relationships, lower prices, and most importantly, higher quality.

Global Marketing, Advertising, and Pricing

Global marketing and advertising policies include the following:

1. Appropriate customization and differentiation
2. Global product strategies
3. Global pricing
4. Global and local distribution channels
5. Culture-based advertising
6. World-class standards for quality and service
7. Global sales and promotion strategies
8. Global customer education

Let's examine these issues in more detail.

Global Marketing

The debate about whether marketing should be a global, standardized, unified, single-product approach or a multilocal, global-market segmentation approach has been raging for a number of years. The answer may be both—depending on the firm's resources and the target markets. Or it may depend on whether global managers see a heterogeneous world with customer preferences being very diverse or if they see a homogeneous world where television, trade, and travel have narrowed the range of customer preferences.

Most global leaders now favor the marketing of global products but provide regional discretion if economies of scale are not affected. When possible, global companies should attempt to develop global brands, use core global marketing practices and themes, and simultaneously introduce new global products worldwide. It is important to involve marketing people from country and regional offices to assure culturally appropriate input.

Marketing penetration can be built by directly entering a country or developing a marketing alliance. The countries chosen for entry and investment should be determined on the basis of global strategic importance, as well as on the basis of stand-alone attractiveness. Although alliances and joint ventures can provide a quicker and easier way to build global market participation, they also can weaken the potential for a fully integrated global strategy.

Global Advertising

Global advertising seeks to effectively communicate information and persuade customers on a worldwide basis to purchase a product or service. To advertise across various cultures, it is important to understand the local cultural values and buying patterns. Factors such as language, religion, family life, history, economics, and politics all have an impact on how to advertise in a particular culture. Some cultures prefer certain modes of advertising (for example, billboards in Russia, and newspapers and television in the United States). Millions of dollars have been foolishly wasted and potential customers have been insulted because advertisers either advertised as if in their home countries or missed the cultural clues of the local culture [6].

When possible, the use of global advertising can save money on commercial production costs and can allow corporations to retain greater control over the message and content of advertisements than was previously possible. However, organizations must be conscious of problems posed by the global standardization of advertising (such as, translation, legality, credibility or image, and media availability) before launching advertisements in diverse cultures.

Moran, Harris, and Stripp list eight factors to consider when determining whether a product should be globally advertised:

1. **Type of Product**—If it has universal selling points, such as razor blades and automobile tires do
2. **Homogeneity of Markets**—Similarity of customer characteristics
3. **Availability of Media**—To advertise using the same media or a variety of media
4. **Availability of Global Advertising Agencies in Market Segment**
5. **Absence of Government Restrictions**—Certain products (such as pork in Islamic countries) may be prohibited by law
6. **Government Tariffs**—Costs for artwork or other advertising materials
7. **Trade Codes, Ethical Practices, and Industry Agreements**—Whether to use certain media or resources
8. **Company itself**—Whether global or not [4]

Advertising Blunders—Literal Translations

Body by Fisher = "Corpse by Fisher" in Flemish
Come Alive with Pepsi = "Pepsi brings your ancestors back from the grave" in Chinese
Rendezvous lounges of U.S. airline = "Rooms for making love" in Portuguese
Nova automobile = "No go" in Spanish
Low tar in cigarette = "Low asphalt" in Japanese
Computer software = "Computer underwear" in Polish
Hydraulic rams = "Wet sheep" in Arabic

Global Pricing

Two of the most important objectives in price setting are (a) maintaining the loyalty of the middlemen and distributors and (b) enhancing the image of the firm and its products. Many companies have made mistakes in these areas, resulting in permanent damage in various regions. A good example of this is Proctor & Gamble's performance in Japan. The company refused to listen to cultural advice that warned against discount pricing and as a result lost the support of both wholesalers and small retailers after the company's image was damaged.

Pricing strategies should be guided by the following:

- ❑ Overall market-share strategy
- ❑ Competitor prices
- ❑ Desired market segment
- ❑ Importance of brand equity
- ❑ Volume
- ❑ Shipping costs
- ❑ Distribution resources

Global Marketing—The Coca-Cola Story

Of all American companies, Coca-Cola comes closest to following a purely global marketing strategy. The firm's marketing strategy is built on a few standardized world markets rather than on many customized markets. The corporation offers globally standardized products that are advanced, functional, reliable, and above all, relatively low-priced. The corporation does not completely reject product customization and differentiation but adjusts to differences in product preferences only after exhausting all efforts to retain standardization.

According to Moran, Harris, and Stripp [4, pp. 185–186]:

> On its path toward becoming a global corporation, Coca-Cola faced a lot of pitfalls and learned a great deal. Based on its experiences, Coca-Cola has developed the following rules for success in the global marketplace:
>
> 1. Successful global companies must develop single and relentless strategies for attacking and conquering new markets. Companies that want to globalize should take a pragmatic approach. Management should do whatever it takes to globalize, countering excuses and reasons for not globalizing. . . .
> 2. A company that wants to go global must have or build or buy a powerful trademark. The best example is Coca-Cola. In an international survey, Coca-Cola was the most well-known, most highly respected, and most powerful brand name in the world. IBM finished second.
> 3. Effective global marketing requires a highly coordinated, global distribution system. Coke's success is tied to the efforts of more than 1,000 bottling partners and multitudes of salespersons who work long, hard hours to sell Coke products. In Australia, one father-and-son sales team drives 7,000 kilometers (4,340 miles) through the Outback every week to deliver Coke to isolated pockets of consumers. In the Philippines, one seventy-four-year-old salesman sells Coke for twelve hours every day, refusing to leave the mar-

(Continued on next page)

ketplace until he has sold at least fifty cases. Dedication like this results in global success.

4. Global companies should live by the simple code "Think Globally, Act Locally." You don't necessarily need a global product to be a global competitor. It is more important to have a global state of mind.
5. Global companies should tailor their messages to the local market. Before introducing its "You Can't Beat the Feeling" campaign, Coca-Cola determined that the message had wide universal appeal. However, the message was adapted and localized in many countries. In Japan, the theme became "I Feel Coke"; in Italy, "Unique Sensation"; in Chile, "The Feeling of Life."
6. The global marketing department must be extremely careful with translations and cultural differences. When Coke reentered China in 1979, it discovered that the literal representation of Coca-Cola in Chinese characters meant "Bite the Wax Tadpole." Coke engaged an Oriental language specialist to experiment with alternatives. The final choice was four Mandarin characters sounding very similar to the name *Coca-Cola* but meaning "Can Happy, Mouth Happy."
7. Global companies should adjust their products for local tastes. For example, Germans prefer a tart orange taste, while Italians prefer a sweet orange taste. Coca-Cola adjusts the sweetness of Fanta orange soda in those markets. In some markets, local fruit is used to make Fanta.
8. Global companies should concentrate on a central theme, idea, or symbol to bind together their business systems, brands, and consumers. Advertising and marketing is designed to encourage consumers to associate Coke with their best feelings and memories, such as their friends and families, moments of joy and laughter, and sporting events and musical concerts. The worldwide system is designed to ensure that wherever consumers travel, they will find one friendly point of reference—a can of Coke.

Global Distribution

Distribution (that is, the channel that products travel between manufacturing and being available to the customer) is much more complex at the global level. Global companies must choose methods of distribution to various countries from the point of production, as well as the method of distribution within the country of sale. Several functions must be performed as goods go through this channel:

- ❑ Transfer of title (buying and selling)
- ❑ The physical movement of the products (transportation)
- ❑ Storage (warehousing)

Every country's distribution system has unique aspects based on the history and culture of the country. European distribution systems "vary dramatically from country to country, region to region, and city to city. The same is true in the Pacific Basin, South America, and the Middle East. Often, foreign distribution systems are so archaic that even established corporations find it difficult to distribute their new products" [4, p. 211].

Global firms have two options when selecting a distribution system: (1) they can use indigenous channels of distribution, or (2) they can develop a global distribution system.

Indigenous Channels of Distribution

A number of situations exist in which indigenous channels of distribution may be the most effective:

- ❑ Sometimes it is easier for the local businesses to be more aggressive in their approaches.
- ❑ Indigenous companies are also likely to have more contacts throughout the market area.
- ❑ Government regulations may favor distribution through indigenous firms.
- ❑ Local channels may also have pre-existing local headquarters, branch offices, and warehouses, as well as a local sales force.
- ❑ Local distributors can provide knowledge of local business practices and market demand.

❑ In countries that restrict the entry of imported products, the use of local distributors sometimes provides a means of market access.

The following questions should be addressed if the global company seeks to utilize a local distributor:

1. Does the distributor have the physical facilities, financial strength, and organizational resources to import, warehouse, collect payment, and offer credit?
2. Does the distributor have a good relationship with government agencies?
3. Will the distributor consider new products?
4. How effective is the personnel of the distributor?
5. What is the reputation of the distributor?
6. Is communication, both technologically and in person, easy and effective [4, p. 214]?

Once indigenous distributors are selected, the global company should establish a program of regular contact and training to ensure that the distributors' sales forces have solid technical expertise in the product line. Distributors must be kept current regarding new products, new potential markets, and new sales techniques. To keep the alliance on solid ground, corporations should carefully select distributors, carry out positive support and training programs for them, and continually monitor their performance.

Global Channel of Distribution

A global firm may want to use its own distribution system within one, many, or all countries because a strong competitive advantage is possible with the quality and reliability of an effective global distribution system. A globally-operated distribution system is especially important if the product line is technologically sophisticated. Likewise, high sales and service standards may dictate the global approach.

In creating an effective global distribution system, a global company should adhere to these seven steps:

1. Find out what customers want, including service, convenience, delivery, choice, repair, technical help, and so on.
2. Find out about costs and feasibility for the company, support systems, and suppliers.
3. Determine management's objectives and the ideal global distribution system for the corporation's product line.
4. Compare options.
5. Review assumptions by bringing in lawyers, political consultants, and distribution experts to challenge the assumptions.
6. Confront the gap between the present system and the ideal, and develop a plan to rectify the difference.
7. Implement the plan [4, pp. 215–216].

It is important to recognize the importance that changes in government policies and/or politics can have in redefining the optimal configuration of a global distribution system. For example, in Europe the removal of border controls is allowing distribution managers to redraw the maps that show the time required from their distribution centers to various delivery points. Maps that had been contorted by the time taken for trucks to pass frontier controls now show smooth, concentric circles instead. As a result, distribution centers can be consolidated and centralized, like manufacturing sites.

Yip emphasizes that "operating creatively about the global value-added chain can produce highly effective global distribution." For example, Benetton, from a single computerized warehouse in Treviso, Italy, ships its products all over the world, directly to the independent, but contractually tied, retail stores that sell its clothing. This distribution centralization is made possible by Benetton's use of just-in-time ordering. Benetton makes no garment until it is ordered by one of its stores.

Global Sales and Services

Global sales requires clear communication, necessary to persuade customers to buy a certain product or service. A deep understanding of the local culture is absolutely essential to understand how to sell to and service customers in the global marketplace. Through an understanding of the cultural aspects of social and business etiquette, history, folklore, religion, sports, customs, and current events, as well as practical matters such as currency used and sites for sales, a company can build a sales plan that works.

In most cultures, the most important ingredient for sales success is the existence of a good personal relationship with the customer. Trust will sell more in most countries than will product quality, pricing, and contracts. Likewise, most global customers are uncomfortable with the Americans' pressure tactics, which are seen as too brash, arrogant, and untrustworthy. Moran, Harris, and Stripp have identified fifteen dos and don'ts for selling overseas (see Figure 7-3).

A worldwide service network can be an important competitive advantage for global companies. A product that cannot offer service in every country in which it is sold is asking for trouble when a problem occurs. Globally standardized services can bring not just the benefit of cost savings but also the benefits of improved quality and customer preference.

The quality of customer service is oftentimes as critical as the quality of the product itself, because future customers can be either gained

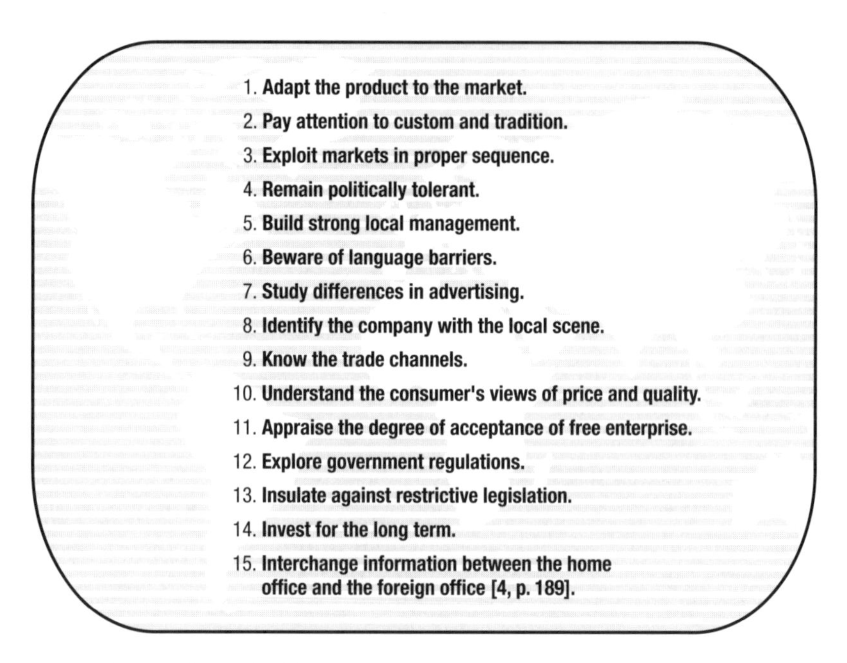

FIGURE 7-3. 15 DOS AND DON'TS FOR SELLING ABROAD.

or lost through customer service or lack thereof. American Express, Federal Express, Nordstrom, Honda, and Mercedes are all known for their customer service networks across the world [1].

Providing a global, uniform standard of service provides assurance to global customers. However, it is important to recognize that differences in local customs affect what customers may expect in different countries. For example, in Japan, medical-equipment company sales representatives wash the cars of the doctors they call on and may even collect their children from school.

Governmental or regional standards of service are also beginning to emerge. For example, most European and a growing number of Asian buyers are demanding that products be certified with the ISO 9000 stamp of quality.

Many global companies now have the ability to respond to customer service needs around the world from remote sites. Although service must usually be performed locally, some aspects, such as information and communication systems, can be centralized or relocated. For example, AT&T now provides telephone support to its U.S. customers from Ireland. This points out another value for customer service in global companies to be both centralized and decentralized.

World-Class Technology

Global companies should attempt to ensure that every manufacturing or service unit has unique, state-of-the-art process technology. They should keep abreast of and have a mastery of all possible process technologies that either are in use or show potential in the production of a product or service. Relative to products, global firms must sell the technology that customers want. Managers should stay current in new layouts and equipment that might increase productivity, quality, and profitability.

Global technologies in plants include the following:

- ❑ CAD and CAM
- ❑ Expert systems
- ❑ Robotics
- ❑ Flexible manufacturing systems
- ❑ Computer numerically controlled machine tools

- ❑ Electronic data interchange
- ❑ Automated materials-handling systems
- ❑ Office automation, communication technology, and software packages
- ❑ Satellite technology
- ❑ Modems and groupware
- ❑ LANs/WANs
- ❑ Business application packages (spreadsheets, project management, and so on)

When selecting technology, global companies need to consider the aspects of cost, speed, quality (durability, reliability, features, performance, and conformance), space, potential for obsolescence, experience of machine manufacturer, maintenance costs, customer service, dependability, and ease of use.

The use of information technology in manufacturing may differ from region to region. U.S. companies are concerned with integrating the information of materials flow into manufacturing. Japanese companies focus on process information, while European companies tend to emphasize sales information in manufacturing planning. It is essential for global leaders to stay updated on new technology via trade shows, benchmarking tours, scientific periodicals, and general business publications [1].

A cultural issue to consider when introducing technology is its capability to lessen the importance of a person's work or eliminate it altogether, thus causing a "loss of face," a very painful issue in many cultures, particularly Asian.

Federal Express—Using Information Technology to Globalize Global Customers

Federal Express delivers nearly three million packages in 210 countries each day. FedEx is not simply pushing globalization for itself but also for hundreds of other companies around the world, "not just because it is adding planes and routes, but because it is using information technology to reengineer its clients' worldwide supply and distribution systems. In the process, global sourcing and sales are becoming an ever more integral part of these companies' way of operating" [7, p. 21].

Jeffrey Garten, dean of the Yale School of Management, observes that FedEx has "become the global logistical backbone for many of its corporate customers." It manages the worldwide inventory, warehousing, distribution, and customs clearance of many emerging global organizations—thanks to FedEx's state-of-the-art technology. The company can help its clients "assemble and make products with near-perfect precision by securing supplies from Penang to Peoria in the most reliable and cost-effective way, while squeezing unnecessary mass out of expensive inventories."

Federal Express can perform these functions because it can "electronically track where any shipment is at any given moment, and it can guarantee on-time delivery." For many global companies, FedEx can handle their entire global supply systems.

The core of FedEx's global strategy is to use information technology to help global customers take advantage of the global marketplace. One of its customers, National Semiconductor, has facilities in the United States, Europe, and Asia and has used FedEx to manage its global warehousing and distribution systems, reducing National's logistical costs by nearly 60 percent in the last three years. Dell Computers has been able to eliminate its costly distribution infrastructure by relying on FedEx to coordinate the assembly of computers in Malaysia with shipping to customers in Japan and Taiwan.

Federal Express illustrates, according to Garten, that global companies are creating a globalization that "is now truly irreversible" [7, p. 28].

Global Telecommunication and Information Systems

Global companies realize the importance of building a global communication and information-sharing reporting format for each regional and/or country-specific business unit. Thus, any inventory of requisite global capabilities should include an effective, comprehensive communication and information processing system. In fact, because achieving global advantage depends on quick and accurate communication between far-flung plants, global companies should make the purchase and utilization of computer and communication equipment a corporate priority.

Operational requirements for global companies include (1) global data access, to allow corporate managers desktop, on-line access to corporate statistics, and (2) global consolidated reporting for planning, controlling, and budgeting. All forms of information technology should be utilized, including the Internet, the company intranet, commercial on-line services, teleconferencing, and electronic mail.

Information systems must be able to report operating results to a central base and then throughout appropriate parts of the organization. Mechanisms should be in place for vertical and lateral communication to occur across all borders and business units.

The global integrating mechanisms should include an integrated system of divisions support systems (DSS), expert systems, and executive information systems. The global management system must be able to support the operational, tactical, and strategic decision making of global companies in their attempt to integrate organizational decision making across functional fields, planning horizons, and national boundaries.

Connecting globally is greatly enhanced by using identical desktop computer software and information systems in all parts of world. This capacity must be complemented, however, by encouraging and training people throughout the organization to understand and apply the power of information technology.

It is important to develop a globalization communication plan that respects and appreciates cultural differences and one in which there is an appreciation of the difficulty and challenges of communicating across borders and cultures. To accommodate language differences, global firms should search for tools (such as portable computers and voice mail) that have translation abilities, or they should employ translators when needed.

Digital Equipment Corporation (DEC), a pioneer in computer networking, improved its communication system by creating an e-mail network that links its employees worldwide. DEC estimates that the use of this has contributed to a twofold reduction in product development time. Marriott, National Semiconductor, and Honeywell are other examples of global companies that have extensive worldwide communication, including elaborate videoconferencing capabilities.

Global Administration

In carrying out administrative operations, the global manager needs to consider a multitude of factors that may be unique to each country yet be ready to globalize as many of them as possible.

Cultural Nuances

Every cultural group perceives management, authority, and power differently. Expectations regarding the administrator's style and level of involvement, as well as the tasks to be performed, vary dramatically from Sweden with its collegiality to Singapore with its strong, clear authority. Moreover, the dynamics of an American managing Japanese, Germans, or a multinational, multicultural team are much more complex than those involved when Americans manage only other Americans.

Political and Economic Systems

The responsibilities of the administrator, as well as the manner in which he or she carries out those responsibilities, depend a great deal on the political and economic system within the country. Marketing a product, for example, is dramatically different in a country with a small private sector versus in a country with a strong capitalist base.

Geographic Distance

Even with global telecommunication technology, it is much more difficult to administer, communicate, and interact with people and organizations thousands of miles away. The skills of the global administrator have to be all the more developed and tested.

Resource Limitations

In many developing countries, the administrator will simply be unable to secure the supplies, materials, facilities, or even the local workers needed for the various technical or even administrative tasks.

Government Regulations

Some governments regulate almost every aspect of an employee's work, detailing the who, what, when, and how of the training. Other governments are similar to that of the United States, where very little is prescribed to the administrator.

Financial Approvals

Particularly in developing countries and in the public sector, the handling of financial matters can be time-consuming and frustrating. Approvals for programs may be put on hold for months; staff may return to the United States because of payment delays; equipment and materials may be repossessed because the government bureaucracy has delayed payments to the organization. The local organization and/or the local workers may move elsewhere. Strong planning and political skills, as well as patience, are obviously critical.

Headquarters-Field Differences

Representing the importance, difficulties, and needs of the business unit within the organization from a distance and across cultures can be a trying experience. Headquarters may not appreciate the problems of incorporating the headquarters programs into another culture or may not be aware of the obstacles of local labor strikes, government regulations, and religious holidays. The local manager must therefore serve as a bridge between the local reality and the needs of the top management.

Working with Government Ministries

Among the many groups with which the administrator must work in other countries are various government ministries, which must be closely consulted before, during, and after sometimes arbitrary points. In much of Asia, Africa, Europe, and Latin America, the Ministry of Labor closely regulates items such as the following:

- ❑ Labor union representation or affiliation
- ❑ Equal pay and work opportunities
- ❑ Safety regulations
- ❑ Welfare of employees, including their families
- ❑ Work permits for trainees and non-nationals
- ❑ Selection and certification procedures for apprentices
- ❑ Trainee pay scales
- ❑ Worker seniority (retirement, upgrading, layoff, tenure, and so on)
- ❑ Dismissals (in many countries, such as Egypt and Indonesia, it is illegal for a foreign corporation to fire or lay off a local employee)
- ❑ Examinations and evaluations for skill accomplishment
- ❑ Occupational classification and related pay scales
- ❑ Social security, medical care, housing, and transportation
- ❑ Supervisory and administrative procedures
- ❑ On-the-job upgrading

Most European countries have some form of mandatory standardized skills and achievement testing system to qualify workers for occupational status and related pay scales. Usually the Ministry of Labor establishes the standards and administers the test.

Global administrators must study labor-management work contracts and national legislation that may stipulate training clauses regarding work hours, wages, program length and scope, and trainee/skilled-worker ratios. They should, for example, be cognizant of these regulations when developing job training standards for occupations covered by such regulations.

The structure of educational and training systems in the countries where the enterprise is operating may be very different. Many countries (such as Switzerland, New Zealand, and Germany) have a strong technical/vocational program at the secondary education level. Only a small percentage of students who continue education after age fifteen go on to an academic, college-bound track. The others receive strong apprenticeship-type programs. Most countries, except for the United States, have national manpower plans, in which present and future skills needs are identified and reported. National training centers then provide training in these areas.

Also, if working with the public sector or with public funds, one should become acquainted with the funding and administrative arrangements of the government. For example, a general system of government funding is used in countries as diverse as Belgium, Italy, Japan, Singapore, and Brazil. In Singapore and France, as examples, a certain percentage of corporation revenues are taxed for training purposes. A corporation may use/reclaim these taxes for training; what is not used is put in the general fund for government training programs.

It is important to develop a collaborative relationship with government officials because they often have a very important role in the development and utilization of the local workforce. They also are invaluable in coordinating training operations between employers and training organizations [8].

Labor Unions

Labor unions, in most countries, have much more power than in the United States. Globalization may be strongly opposed because it may be seen as destroying jobs and diminishing the role and importance of the labor unions.

Miscellaneous Responsibilities

Finally, the global administrators have a large number of additional and complex responsibilities, because they may have to oversee and coordinate areas such as the following:

- ❑ Immigration and travel details
- ❑ Work permits
- ❑ Compensation for local, third-country nationals (TCN) and U.S. staff
- ❑ Allowances (pay differentials)
- ❑ Housing
- ❑ Health care
- ❑ Insurance
- ❑ Recreation
- ❑ The family needs of personnel
- ❑ Schooling
- ❑ Safety and security

Globalizing All the Company's Operations

Every one of the twelve operations described in this chapter—from initial research and development to final sales and service—should be globalized, and as soon as possible. Operations that continue to function in a domestic, international, or multinational fashion will impede the effectiveness of operations that have been globalized. An important complementary component to the globalization of operations is the globalization of the corporate structure, the topic of the next chapter.

References

1. Young, S. and Nie, W. *Managing Global Operations—Cultural and Technical Success Factors.* Westport, Conn.: Quorum Books, 1996.

2. Yip, G. "Global Strategy in a World of Nations." *Sloan Management Review,* Vol. 31, No. 1, pp. 29–41.

3. Yip, G. *Total Global Strategy.* Englewood Cliffs, N.J.: Prentice Hall, 1992.

4. Moran, R., Harris, P., and Stripp, W. *Developing the Global Organization.* Houston, Tex.: Gulf Publishing, 1993.

5. Garvin, D. "Competing on the Eight Dimensions of Quality." *Harvard Business Review,* Vol. 67, No. 6, Nov.–Dec. 1987, pp. 101–109.
6. Ricks, D. A. *Blunders in International Business.* Cambridge, Mass.: Blackwell Publishers, 1993.
7. Garten, J. "Why the Global Economy Is Here to Stay." *Business Week,* Mar. 23, 1998, p. 21.
8. Marquardt, M. and Engel, D. *Global Human Resource Development.* Englewood Cliffs, N.J.: Prentice Hall, 1993.

8

Globalizing Structures

Structure casts a powerful directive on an organization's life and people. Structure determines the degree of internal control, the manner in which people work, the locus of power, lines of communication, the decision-making process, and how knowledge is managed in the organization. As Rossbeth Kanter notes, "In the future, organizations will be ruled by communication instead of bureaucracy, and hierarchies will be replaced by more peer-oriented relationships across borders. . . . globalization (and its structure) is more than just international operations, but a way of thinking and responding to all possibilities" [1]. Dunning concurs by stating, "Economic globalization both changes the spatial dimension of multinational enterprises and creates a need for more flexible production and marketing systems, and new forms of organization" [2, p. 202].

To globalize the structure of the organization, companies must reengineer and improve the ways they:

- ❑ Arrange the organizational departments, hierarchy, and the infrastructure itself.
- ❑ Acquire, store, analyze, transfer, and utilize knowledge.
- ❑ Determine physical aspects of location, facilities, and layout.

Let's examine each of these three aspects of global structuring.

FIGURE 8-1. GLOBAL STRUCTURES.

Global Integration of Functions, Operations, and Units

Global Integration

Global organizations must transform their present international or multinational business units into global ones so that there is a true worldwide integration of organizational functions and activities. Structures should optimize the presence of worldwide operations while allowing for local diversity. The business dimension of global linking and leveraging is more important than and must therefore be stronger than geographic or functional dimensions. An integrated global strategy means integration across businesses within each country, as well as integration within each business across countries.

Global restructuring can occur in two ways:

1. One of the most effective ways to develop and implement a global strategy is to centralize authority so that all units of the same business around the world report to a common global sector head. An example of this form of global integration is the General Electric Canadian lighting business. Previously, senior managers needed to compete at headquarters with all other GE Canadian businesses for resources; now they go to the global lighting business head to seek funds. Surprisingly, this step is undertaken by few companies who remain tied to country-based organization (that is, multinational or international).
2. Another way of centralizing global authority is to have global heads of individual functions or value-adding activities. These heads either can have direct line authority over the function or can have a stafflike coordination responsibility (see Philips example below).

Global Production Centers at Philips

NV Philips' Gloeilampenfabrieken Multinational (Philips), a Dutch-based electronics company, began as a small electric-lamp producer in Eindhoven, Holland, in 1891. The organization has since grown into the fourth largest electronics company in the world, operating in more than sixty countries and employing 344,000 people around the world. It is also one of the most diversified electronics companies, with a product scope that includes lighting, small and major domestic appliances, and consumer electronics (audio/video products, telecommunication/data systems, electronic components, medical equipment and systems, scientific instruments, and software).

Philips' global strategy began with the establishment of global production centers. The manufacturing facilities were renovated and then assigned worldwide production of product lines. Worker productivity doubled within ten years through factory

(Continued on next page)

modernization, reallocation, and workforce reduction through consolidation and transfer of factories.

A consolidation of responsibility in the product divisions was instituted. Traditionally each product division had a commercial and a technical director. With the advent of a global strategy, lines of authority and accountability were defined more clearly. Effectiveness of decisionmaking and communication of goals were improved to minimize the product-development-to-market time lag. Defending the territorial conflicts between technical and commercial managers was eliminated.

All product divisions now operate under a single managing director, assisted by directors with a range of commercial, technical, and financial expertise. This change reinforces a shift from a previously geographically oriented structure to one that is more product-oriented, with its centralized product management team. A second major change was the integration of several divisions, following the trend of integrated product systems and the general convergence of electronics technologies.

The flexibility of this system allows for rapid response to changing situations and has been easily transformed into a global system. Philips has combined global strategies, restructuring, the balance of centralization and decentralization, global management development, and human resource management into a successful globalization process [3, pp. 104–105].

Seamless, Boundaryless, and Holistic

A global organization should feature a fluid, boundaryless structure that has only modest respect for divisional barriers. Boundaries inhibit the flow of communication and knowledge, which are so critical to global organizations. Boundaries also keep individuals and groups isolated and tend to reinforce preconceptions, distrust, and bias across functions and across cultures. Global companies should streamline wherever and whenever possible, allowing optimal flow of communication, cultural ideas, differences, and energies. The goal should be to establish the borderless, one-company structure as the way to do business.

When top leaders are able to build a corporate culture that is focused on maximizing the globality of the organization, they are able to build capabilities that cross all boundaries—time, vertical, horizontal, external, and geographic. They create a holistic, systematic view of organizational life with all its systems, processes, and relationships. There is an integration, an intimacy, a closeness between management, employees, customers, competitors, and communities throughout the world. All these factors make it possible for the global enterprise to better understand and appreciate the changing needs and successes of people in and out of the organization.

Global Structuring of Parke-Davis/Warner-Lambert (by Robert Hoffman, director of organizational development)

Warner-Lambert is a diversified manufacturer of pharmaceutical, consumer health care, and confectionery products. In 1997, the company employed almost 38,000 colleagues (approximately 25,000 outside the United States and Puerto Rico), maintained 75 production plants worldwide, and had its products sold in nearly 150 countries. During the last several years, the company has globalized and consolidated each of its core business operations and streamlined its management structure through a series of evolutionary moves.

In one of its critical business units—namely the $2.5 billion Parke-Davis pharmaceutical business—the operating structure and reporting relationships have changed in response to the changing global business environment. Intense competition, more complex and demanding regulatory requirements in Europe and the United States, and increasing consumer awareness and vigilance were just some of the environmental factors that influenced the management of Parke-Davis to "de-layer" the global management structure recently. This was especially true in Parke-Davis's marketing and operations areas.

In previous years, for example, all the different heads of Parke-Davis's various European operations reported to a European regional president, who in turn reported to the president of

(Continued on next page)

worldwide pharmaceutical operations in the United States. This structure evolved with the elimination of the European regional president's position; all European affiliate heads now report directly to the president of worldwide pharmaceutical operations. These European affiliate heads—five in all—now have direct access to the president's office, along with the five other affiliate heads from other countries around the world. This means that the president of worldwide pharmaceutical operations has almost fifteen direct reports, which include the positions already mentioned plus people who lead various staff functions (manufacturing, product planning, human resources, finance) based in the company's U.S. headquarters.

This global restructuring was vital to the success of the global launch of a key product in Parke-Davis's portfolio. The product—Lipitor—was introduced to the market in record time. Undoubtedly, the structure allowed each of the affiliate heads an opportunity to provide input directly into matter concerning the product's introduction and to work together to coordinate activities to make the introduction a success.

The flat, global reporting structure means that there are regular, worldwide staff meetings, increased dialogue between managers in the United States and other countries, and the natural opportunity to question decisions and engage in healthy business debate. This means managers have more opportunity to directly influence decisions that affect them, which is very empowering. That empowerment creates tension in the organization. Our willingness and ability to successfully manage that tension has led to increased collaboration and better business results.

Streamlined and Non-bureaucratic

Rigid, tall hierarchies with unbreachable, impregnable departmental silos are disastrous to global firms, as they prevent the necessary free, fast, and unimpeded flow of information essential to being globally competitive. In this undesirable type of hierarchy, power and authority do not flow to the point of greatest impact, and thus they hurt the organization's ability to quickly and effectively interact with customers, employees, and partners. To maximize the flow of communication and to increase collaboration across business units and across boundaries, a flat, streamlined structure with team collaboration and few modes of control works best.

Global powerhouse General Electric's company literature says GE believes that success "requires a hatred of bureaucracy and all that goes with it." Royal Bank of Canada believes that an organization should centralize paper but decentralize people. Staff should extricate out silly forms and policies that gridlock and strangle learning. Fewer boundaries and fewer bureaucracies allow the lifeblood of knowledge to flow quickly and freely throughout the organization.

Hewlett-Packard, an innovative company that had become a lumbering dinosaur, decided to undo its growing bureaucracy, which had become so encumbered that three dozen committees oversaw every decision, delaying new products and crushing learning, speed, and innovation. Employees were urged to rethink every process from product development to distribution. The new, lean, sleek global structure is now called a gazelle by industry leaders.

Asea Brown Boveri

Imagine a company where the organization chart looks like a steep-sided pyramid like this one:

Businesses	8
Business Areas	65
Independently Incorporated Companies	1,300
Autonomous Profit Centers	5,000
Multifunction High-Performance Teams	50,000

Asea Brown Boveri (ABB) has been described by management guru Tom Peters as "the most novel industrial-firm structure since Alfred Sloan built modern GM in the 1920s." Why? Because this $30-billion-in-sales-per-year firm with its nearly 200,000 employees is streamlined into units of no more than 50

(Continued on next page)

people. This isn't simply a curiosity in the museum of business ideas that didn't work. ABB is both extraordinarily different and highly successful.

The 8 businesses are divided into 65 business areas, and these into 1,300 independently incorporated companies with an average size of 200 people, and these into about 5,000 autonomous profit centers with an average size of 50 people. The profit centers are reorganized into 10-person, multifunction, high-performance teams, for a total of 50,000 work units. Most centers have their own profit-and-loss statements, balance sheets, and assets and serve external customers directly.

ABB functions as a matrix organization composed of individual profit centers, plants, and companies within a country on one hand and within business areas (such as, hydropower plants, financing, electric metering) on the other. The company headquarters in Zurich is very small. The management of ABB is distributed within the smaller companies themselves because they are closer to the local marketplaces.

ABB displays an unusual willingness to make changes. For example, one of the business areas was initially based in Sweden because the chief of the area was located there with his company. The business area's base later moved to Germany and then again to the United States. Now that's flexibility. Each of the moves was based on improved strategic location for the area's core business. It is an ABB strategy to keep the bases small so that they will remain responsive to their units.

The real advantage of business areas doesn't come from economies of scale, such as the combined purchasing power. A more powerful force is the global coordination between elements. There is a process of continuous expertise transfer. People at ABB talk of an atmosphere of trust. Sharing grows within the business-area businesses located all around the world.

ABB companies try to develop and use expert power in their hierarchyless organization to optimize expertise. Most ABB experts can be shifted to work teams, manufacturing cells, clusters, projects, or groups. At least 80 percent of experts at the division, group, sector, or corporate level can be inserted into these self-contained operating units.

ABB's philosophy is to think globally and act locally. Each company has one member of senior management who oversees progress in his or her own units and serves as a liaison with the central team. The central team meets one day each quarter to share experiences. The formal gatherings are important, but ABB people think greater value comes from the information exchange throughout the year that results from the relationships established. The system works best when a functional manager in one country feels compelled to telephone or fax the manager with the same responsibilities in another country. The motivation behind the contact can be either a problem or an idea.

There are also other ABB forums for information exchange and learning transfer. For example, a business-area management board meets quarterly, or more often, to chart global strategies. The sixty-five business-area chiefs have responsibility for the global strategies of their own businesses. They arrange job shifts for key people to transfer and leverage knowledge gained in one company and country to another.

Business-area staff with specialty areas of responsibility travel constantly, confer with local unit management, and support ABB's learning and coordination goals. Functional coordination teams, composed of members who are experts in various operations, meet twice a year to work on marketing, production, quality, and other issues.

The chief of ABB's Power Transformers business area has described his business area as a collection of local businesses with intense global coordination. Their key to competitiveness is not based on volume efficiencies but tight operations. They focus on reducing delivery time, increasing flexibility in design and production, enhancing customer focus, and creating a culture of trust and exchange.

Utilization of Global Project Teams As Key to Organization Implementation

More and more of the work of the future in global organizations will be done by project teams, because project teams are better able than individuals or functional units to respond to and serve the needs and interests of customers. The life of a project team may be indeterminate or just a few hours. Dynamic, short-lived project configurations will be commonplace. It will not be unusual for employees to work with four to five projects teams in a year—but any one employee may never work with the same configuration of colleagues. The smaller size, the quickness, and the accountability of project teams all encourage global speed.

Global structure will thus be built more and more around global teams. They will become "the heart of the globalization process" [4]. As companies spread their operations around the world, global teams will be used to both launch and manage the global programs.

A global team is a work group composed of multinational members whose activities span multiple countries. Two key factors affect the team's composition, operations, and performance.

1. **Task Complexity and Importance**—Global teams are extremely valuable for projects that are highly complex and have considerable impact on company objectives. Such teams are usually geographically dispersed with members on different continents in some cases.
2. **Multicultural Dynamic**—To obtain a maximum contribution from each of its members, the team must be adept at handling a variety of cross-cultural issues. A multinational team, in contrast with team members from a single culture, entails differences among members in language, interpersonal styles, and so on. Effective global teams directly confront the multicultural issues that inevitably arise in the group and search for ways to resolve them. Three separate cultures are operating simultaneously in global teams: national culture, corporate culture, and occupational culture.

When creating global teams, the following guidelines should be applied:

❑ Establish leadership teams with representatives from all locations.
❑ Conduct intercultural team-building with multicultural groups.
❑ Engage in group-dynamic activities that enhance the ability to understand cultural diversity.
❑ Carefully blend the talents of the global team.

The members of global teams have significant opportunities to build global business competence. Bartlett and Ghoshal [5] encourage the use of project teams for the purpose of achieving global efficiency, developing regional or worldwide cost advantages, and helping to standardize designs and operations. Global teams help their firms become global corporations that can act both big (efficiently) and small (responsively) while learning how to adapt continuously.

Slevin and Pinto [6] have identified ten factors that contribute to a successful global team:

1. Clear project mission
2. Top-management support
3. Well-developed project schedule and plans
4. Agreement by clients on project purpose and procedures
5. Necessary and competent personnel
6. Required technology available
7. Active involvement of clients in project schedule and implementation
8. Close monitoring and feedback
9. Interorganizational communication
10. Quick and effective troubleshooting

A number of global companies have used project teams with much success. Fuji Xerox sent fifteen of its most-experienced Tokyo engineers to a Xerox facility in Webster, N.Y. For the next five years, the Japanese engineers worked with a group of American engineers to develop the "world copier"—a copier that can be used worldwide and that has been a huge success in the global marketplace.

Eastman Kodak formed a team to launch its latest consumer product, the photo compact disk. The group of experts, based in London, developed a strategy for the simultaneous introduction of the photo CD in several European countries. The photo CD has been Kodak's most successful multicountry product introduction in this decade.

Each support function in Kellogg—information technology, human resources, nutrition, and so on—has a steering committee to bring ideas to the Center Management Board. British Telecom has Teams Across Frontiers for running development events that are designed to bridge cultural, linguistic, and physical barriers across BT's global communication division. Whirlpool employs a global executive committee that oversees the global initiatives of the organization [7].

Global Networking

Effective global organizations realize the critical need to collaborate, share, and synergize with resources both inside and outside the company. The network structure—which may include global alliances, informal ties among teams that work across functions, and new ways for employees to share information—uses a variety of connecting tools, such as management information systems and videoconferences. Such tools enable a company to operate in a form and style that is much more fluid, flexible, and adaptable to local environments.

According to noted global management theorist Ram Charan, a traditional corporate structure—no matter how de-cluttered or delayered—cannot muster the speed, flexibility, and focus needed in today's highly competitive marketplace. Networks are faster, smarter, and more flexible than reorganizations and downsizings. A network, in effect, creates a small company inside a large company that enables both organizations to achieve global success.

Structure and Systems for Managing Knowledge

The structure and systems employed by organizations to manage knowledge has quickly emerged as the single most important discriminator between success and failure in this intensely competitive global economy. Nonaka and Takeuchi, authors of *The Knowledge-Creating Company* [8], confidently predict that a company's ability to create, store, and disseminate knowledge will become absolutely crucial for staying ahead of the competition in terms of global quality, speed, innovation, and price. Only by developing and implementing systems and mechanisms to assemble, package, promote, and distribute the fruits of its thinking will a company be able to transform knowledge into corporate power.

Thomas Stewart, in his classic *Intellectual Capital: The New Wealth of Organizations,* writes, "Simply put, knowledge has become more important for organizations than financial resources, market position, technology, or any other company asset" [9]. Knowledge is now seen as the main resource needed for performing work in an organization because all the organization's traditions, culture, technology, operations, systems, and procedures are based on knowledge.

Globally successful organizations recognize that, indeed, only one asset grows more valuable as it is used—the knowledge skills of people. Unlike machinery that gradually wears out, materials that become depleted, patents and copyrights that grow obsolete, and trademarks that lose their ability to comfort, the knowledge and insights that come from the learning of employees actually increase in value when used and practiced.

Yet, in most companies the use of technology to manage their knowledge is totally uncharted territory. Managing know-how may be different from managing cash or buildings, but managing the intellectual investments of a company needs to be treated every bit as attentively.

Worldwide, organizationwide knowledge is needed by global companies for several reasons: (a) to increase the abilities of employees to improve products and services, thereby providing quality service to clients and consumers; (b) to update products and services; (c) to change systems and structures; and (d) to communicate solutions to problems. The ability to manage knowledge (and learning how to manage that knowledge) becomes a primary task of every worker in every global company.

Global organizations therefore need to learn how to manage the mechanics of knowledge, just as in the industrial era they learned how to manage the mechanics of production. Let's discuss the steps and strategies for managing and structuring knowledge.

Global System for Managing and Structuring Knowledge

A cohesive knowledge-management system involves five stages as knowledge transitions from the source to the user: (1) knowledge

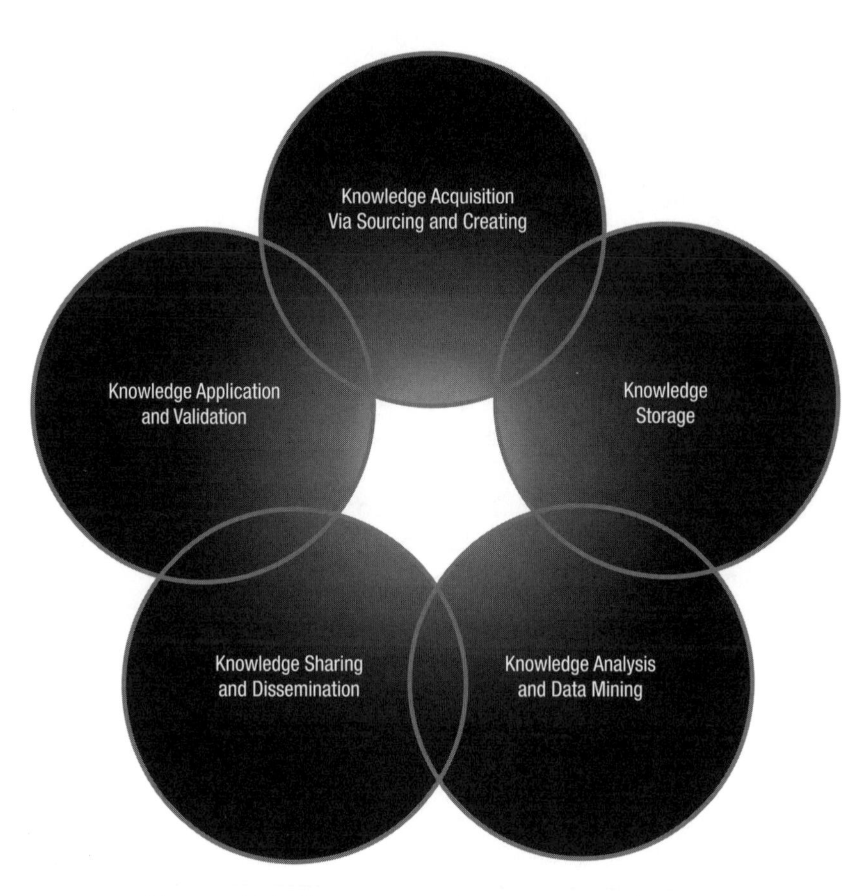

FIGURE 8-2. KNOWLEDGE MANAGEMENT SYSTEM.

acquisition via sourcing and creating, (2) knowledge storage, (3) knowledge analysis and data mining, (4) knowledge sharing and dissemination, and (5) knowledge application and validation (see figure 8-2).

Knowledge Acquisition Via Sourcing and Creating

An increasingly overwhelming volume of knowledge from a multitude of sources all over the world is required for global companies to adequately perform their work. And only through the careful application of sophisticated technology can needed knowledge be gathered. In determining the appropriate technology for knowledge acquisition, it is important to consider how the data/information will be later retrieved by different groups of workers for performing their job tasks. Functional and effective knowledge storage systems (as we will note in the following section) should be categorized around the following elements:

- ❑ Learning needs
- ❑ Work objective
- ❑ User expertise
- ❑ Function/use of information
- ❑ Location (where and how the information is stored)

Organizations acquire information and build their knowledge bases by sourcing information from internal sources, sourcing from external sources, and creating new knowledge.

Internal Collection of Knowledge

One of the major complaints of workers is that so much of their knowledge is never tapped by the organization. Often, companies are startled to learn how much intellectual capital is present in the brains of their own employees, which is what Nonaka and Takeuchi [8] call tacit knowledge. Tacit sources of knowledge include individual employees' expertise, memories, beliefs, and assumptions, all of which can be of high value to the organization. These tacit sources are usually difficult to communicate or explain but will result in tremendous benefit to companies.

External Collection of Knowledge

The pace of change is so rapid today that no single organization can ever gain control of or dominate all effective operating practices and good ideas. To be a global marketplace leader, an organization must look outward for constant improvement and new ideas. The old school of thought, which held to the if-it-wasn't-invented-here-then-it-can't-be-any-good theory, is a curse in today's high-velocity markets. Organizations don't need to invent what other companies have learned to do well. Today's rallying cry for companies is, "Acquire, adapt, and advance!" Companies can "rope in" information externally through a large number of methods:

- ❑ Benchmarking from other organizations
- ❑ Attending conferences
- ❑ Hiring consultants
- ❑ Reading print materials, such as newspapers and journals
- ❑ Viewing television, video, and film
- ❑ Monitoring economic, social, and technological trends
- ❑ Collecting data from customers, competitors, and resources
- ❑ Hiring new staff
- ❑ Collaborating with other organizations, building alliances, and forming joint ventures
- ❑ Utilizing the Internet and commercial on-line services
- ❑ Sharing ideas through "chat rooms" and e-mail

CREATING KNOWLEDGE

Knowledge can also be created through a number of different processes "ranging from ingenious innovation to painstaking and elaborate research." It can also come from the "uncanny ability people have to see new connections and combine previously known knowledge elements through complex inductive reasoning" [10]. The knowledge created through problem-solving, experimentation, and demonstration projects can oftentimes be the most valuable form of knowledge for organizations.

Knowledge Storage

A knowledge storage system enables an organization to contain and retain knowledge so that it becomes company property and does not go home at night or leave the organization when the employee leaves. Unfortunately, knowledge (also referred to as intellectual capital), though far more important than physical material, is usually scattered, hard to find, and liable to disappear without a trace because it is not stored. Storage is obviously important, but what knowledge should be stored? Stewart [9] proposes five general categories of knowledge that should be stored:

Corporate Yellow Pages—Capabilities of employees, consultants, and advisors of the organization (for example, who speaks Thai, who knows JavaScript, who has worked with Client A)

Lessons Learned—Checklists of what went right or wrong that might be applied to other projects (so the company can leverage what has been learned in the past rather than losing the recipes)

Competitor and Supplier Intelligence—Continuously updated company profiles and news from commercial and public sources and wire services; call reports from salespeople; attendees' notes from conferences and conventions; an in-house directory of experts; news about regulations

Company Experiences and Policies—Process maps and work flows, plans, procedures, principles and guidelines, standards, policies, performance measures, shareholder and customer profiles, products and services (including features, functionality, pricing, sales, and repair)

Company Products and Processes—Technologies, inventions, data, publications and processes; strategies and cultures, structures, and systems, as well as organizational routines and procedures that work

How Knowledge Should Be Stored for Global Companies

Knowledge is only clumsy data unless it is coded and stored in a way that makes sense to individuals and the organization. Too many organizations remain overwhelmed and inundated with vast amounts of data that clutter up the information highway. An organization cannot learn from the information if it is irretrievable, distorted, fragmented, or inaccurate.

To determine what data can be used, the organization must decide what is of value and then code the data based on learning needs, as well as on organizational operations.

The knowledge stored should be easily accessible across functional boundaries. It should be structured and organized so the users can find concise information in a quick fashion. Store the knowledge not only by topical categories but also based on learning needs of staff, organizational goals for continuous improvement, and user expertise. Finally, the knowledge stored should be updated so it remains accurate and valid.

In addition, the knowledge acquired should be stored in a way that it would be easy:

- ❑ For workers to decide which of their co-workers may have the knowledge needed for a particular activity.
- ❑ For workers to decide which of their co-workers would be interested in a lesson learned.
- ❑ For a worker to submit a lesson learned to the corporate memory (there should be a well-defined criteria for deciding if something is a lesson learned, deciding how it should be formulated, and deciding where it should be stored).

Challenges in Storing Knowledge for Global Companies

It is important to remember that knowledge storage involves technical processes (records, data bases) and human processes (collective and individual memory, consensus). As organizations become physically and geographically more spread out, as well as more specialized and decentralized, the organizations' storage systems and memories can become fragmented, and corporate benefits of the knowledge can be lost. And as work becomes more computer-oriented, the information needs of different organizational specialisms become potentially available across functional boundaries. Networked information technology must be utilized so that fragmented information can be reinterpreted and readily exchanged internally and externally [11].

Given the fact that new technology is increasingly able to store and provide more information to the organization's members, consideration must be given to the potential of data deluge or information overload. The amount of information stored should not exceed the organization's capacity to adequately process the data.

Knowledge Analysis and Data Mining

During the past thirty years, organizations have become skilled at capturing and storing large amounts of operational data. Unfortunately, until recently, we have not seen corresponding advances in techniques to analyze this data or to reconstruct, validate, and inventory this critical resource. Manual analyses with report and query tools remain the norm, but this approach fails as the volume and dimensionality of the data increases. New approaches and tools are therefore needed to analyze very large data bases and interpret their contents.

The latest development in analytical tools is data mining. Data mining enables organizations to find meaning in their data. By discovering new patterns or fitting models to the data, employees can store and later extract information to better develop strategies and answer complex business questions. Software is being developed that can analyze huge volumes of data and identify hidden patterns within that data. Whereas OLAP (on-line analytical process) can answer the questions managers ask, data mining software answers the questions managers didn't even think of!

There are several data mining tasks (classification, regression, clustering, summarization, dependency modeling, and change and deviation detection), as well as data mining methods such as:

- ❑ Decision trees and rules
- ❑ Nonlinear regression and classification methods
- ❑ Example-based methods
- ❑ Probabilistic graphical dependency models
- ❑ Relational learning methods and use of intelligent agents

Data Mining Tools

A number of data-mining tools are being developed for navigating data, for discovering patterns and creating new strategies, and for identifying underlying statistical and quantitative methods of visualization. Platforms to support these tools, techniques to prepare the data, and the ways to quantify the results are also emerging. For example, visualization products include AVS/Express, SGI MineSet, and Visible Decisions Discovery. To integrate data-mining products, DataMind and IBM's Intelligent Miner are extremely helpful.

American Management Systems (AMS) Analyses Data for United Kingdom Bank

AMS and a banking client in the UK sought to analyze more than 267,000 records of 132,000 customers to find correlations among customer behavior, demographics, and profitability. To

(Continued on next page)

look at these large volumes of data across 152 business dimensions, AMS used sophisticated statistical and visualization techniques. These included scatter-plot matrices and parallel-coordinate plots in conjunction with brushing, cutting, and high-dimension rotation.

Applying these techniques provided analysts with new perspectives on their data. They rotated and twisted a multidimensional image to search for relationships among groups of data in order to discover new patterns or trends. In this case, AMS was able to find correlations between channel usage (such as checks, branch visits, ATM site visits), age, and occupation to help the bank quickly zero in on the most profitable segments of bank customers. High-payoff uses also included credit card scoring, risk analysis, product profitability analysis, and retail site planning.

Knowledge Sharing and Dissemination

The sharing and transfer of knowledge is the sharing and transfer of power—a corporate capability indispensable for corporate success. Simply stated, knowledge needs to be disseminated accurately and quickly throughout the company and throughout the world to wherever it is needed.

The retrieval of knowledge may be either controlled (by the memory or records of individuals or groups) or automatic (for example, when situations trigger memories, ways of doing things, and so on). Weick [12] warns that as a result of the transformational nature of the storage and retrieval process, the normal integration of human memory, the impact of perceptual filters, and the loss of supporting rationales, information that is retrieved from organizational memory may bear little resemblance to what was originally stored. It is therefore very important for an organization to develop its corporate memory and its design processes in a manner to ensure accurate and timely knowledge retrieval.

Just-in-time access of required information leads to extension of an individual's long-term memory and reduces the working-load memory. The corporate knowledge base consolidates information into a central location, thus liberating an individual's working memory from such menial data as resource location. This creates the conditions for the rapid sharing of knowledge and sustained, collective knowledge growth. Lead times between learning and knowledge application are shortened systematically. Human capital will also become more productive through structured, easily accessible, and intelligent work process.

Ways of Sharing Knowledge

Global knowledge sharing requires rapid and extensive movement of information and knowledge, which can be distributed through a variety of non-technological and technological methods.

Non-technological Modes of Transferring Knowledge

There are many effective ways of transferring knowledge that do not require technology:

- ❑ Individual written communication (memos, reports, letters, open-access bulletin boards)
- ❑ Training (internal consultants, formal courses, on-the-job training)
- ❑ Internal conferences
- ❑ Briefings
- ❑ Internal publications (video, print, audio)
- ❑ Tours (especially in large, multidivisional organizations with multiple sites that are tailored for different audiences and needs)
- ❑ Job rotation/transfer
- ❑ Mentoring

Technological Modes of Transferring Knowledge

A comprehensive, wide-scale transfer of knowledge on a global scale, however, can only occur through the intelligent use of technology, such that the knowledge can be available anywhere, anytime, and in any form. Information communication software, including electronic mail, bulletin boards, and conferencing, allows for interactions between members, both person-to-person and among dispersed groups. It also provides an electronic learning environment where all members have equal access to data and are able to communicate freely.

If all the organization's personal computers are networked through the mainframe with relevant external systems, any person can take part in gathering and transferring knowledge. Remote access to national and global knowledge networks can be made available within the organization at any time. Sharing information on a virtual real-time basis and encouraging wider access to information involves:

- Creating on-line data bases that can be used across functional boundaries.
- Hooking into on-line data bases and electronic bulletin boards external to the organization, such as those of universities and other learning centers.
- Installing an electronic mail culture where its use is widespread.
- Using electronic data interchange to create comprehensive electronic network systems.

Newer search engines now allow for searches of all files located on a LAN or WAN using search criteria found in many web browsers. Current groupware offers the incorporation of expert systems or decision support systems into a standard graphical user interface and gives individuals access to knowledge that has been imported into the expert system from the external environment, as well as captures knowledge that exists within the organization (congenital and experiential).

Knowledge Application and Validation

Stewart notes that systematic application of "intellectual capital creates growth in shareholder value" [9]. This is accomplished through the continuous recycling and creative utilization of the organization's rich knowledge and experience. (Only as knowledge is applied can it be tested for value to the organization. The following example of Hewlett-Packard's ability to provide customer service through diagnosis and troubleshooting demonstrates the power of knowledge application and validation.)

Hewlett-Packard created an electronic network to manage and distribute knowledge to keep up with customers' demands for speedy service on a global scale. HP's customer response network supports 200 technical support staff members, mostly engineers, whose job is to keep customers' computer systems up and running. These systems are the customers' central nervous systems: If they go down, they must be fixed fast. When a client reports a problem, the electronic messages go automatically to one of four hubs around the world, depending on the time of day. Operators get a description of the problem and its urgency, type the information into a data base, and zap the findings into one of twenty-seven centers, where it might be picked up by a team specializing in that area. The data base is shared by all the centers and is "live"—that is, whenever an employee works in a file, it is instantly updated so that every employee has identical information about each job at all times. If the first center can't solve a problem quickly, the problem follows the sun—from California to Australia, across Asia to Europe, and back to the United States. HP managers are involved in moving the work around the network, so it is seamless.

A well-developed knowledge system allows a company to put its best people on the front line while still keeping their expertise available to the entire organization. Charles Paulk, chief information officer of Andersen Consulting, notes that, because of Knowledge Xchange, "When one of our consultants shows up, the client gets the best of the firm, not just the best of that consultant." Among the benefits of Andersen's knowledge management system, Paulk lists the following:

1. Savings—Andersen saves millions in FedEx bills alone
2. Ability to more easily tap into colleagues' knowledge
3. Helps Andersen work globally
4. Maps corporate brainpower
5. Allows coping with growth and staff turnover; the faster that newcomers can learn what the institution knows, the faster they can contribute to its success [11]

Knowledge Management Critical to Global Success for Price Waterhouse

Price Waterhouse, a global consulting firm headquartered in New York City, estimates that up to 99 percent of its revenue is generated from knowledge-based professional services and knowledge-based products. Its 56,000 employees, located in more than 400 offices worldwide, spend up to 80 hours a year creating and sharing knowledge.

Why is knowledge management so critical to Price Waterhouse? The driving forces include the following:

1. The geographic dispersion and need to serve global clients requires a timely coordination and sharing of information between the different subsidiaries.
2. Information about tax policies, legislation, banking, financial requirement, and so forth changes so rapidly that it needs to be quickly captured and disseminated.
3. Employee turnover of 15 to 25 percent per year necessitates systems to capture this knowledge before it is lost.
4. It is important to discover and constantly share best practices throughout the firm.
5. Employees must know about former projects and projects conducted in other parts of the clients' organizations.
6. The tendency to have "islands of knowledge activity" creates inefficiencies and duplication.

KNOWLEDGE MANAGEMENT RESOURCES

To meet the growing demands for acquiring, analyzing, and storing knowledge, Price Waterhouse has created a variety of knowledge management resources:

- KnowledgeView—PW's best-practices program (discussed below)
- Change integration—A business line for change management and reengineering (which represents 40 percent of PW's consulting business)

- ❑ Information technology—External knowledge support for PW clients
- ❑ Advanced Systems Engineering Centers—Include six software centers in the United States and two in Europe
- ❑ Information specialists
- ❑ Centers of Excellence
- ❑ Industry-related knowledge (such as knowledge of the petroleum industry) and process-related knowledge (for example, knowledge about supply chain management)

KnowledgeView

KnowledgeView, PW's proprietary best-practices repository of information, has been gathered from more than 2,200 companies worldwide and contains more than 4,500 entries, with references to more than 350 internal and external benchmarking studies. The goal of KnowledgeView is to support the firm's core competency of being business advisors: including the accumulation, analysis, creation, and dissemination of value-added information and knowledge that PW professionals can use to improve business performance of clients, and ultimately increase the value of PW's services.

KnowledgeView is Lotus Notes-based rather than CD-ROM-based, thereby allowing daily information updates, as well as the capacity to access and share knowledge instantaneously on a worldwide basis. The data bases in KnowledgeView incorporate the following information:

- ❑ Best practices as identified in PW and non-PW programs
- ❑ Benchmarking studies from internal and external sources
- ❑ Expert opinions synthesized by industry or process subject-matter experts
- ❑ Abstracts of books and articles on business improvement
- ❑ PW staff biographies with resumes data base according to country, industry, skill, language, and so on
- ❑ Views and forecasts of PW's own experts on important topics

(Continued on next page)

KnowledgeView is classified according to industry, process, enabler, topic, and measurement so that PW consultants can target and find the knowledge for which they are searching. An important feature of KnowledgeView is the format used for containing the information. For example, in the best-practices data base, the format is established to answer the following questions:

- ❑ What caused the change?
- ❑ What old process needed improvement?
- ❑ What is the new process?
- ❑ What is the new performance, and how is it measured?
- ❑ What were the lessons learned?
- ❑ What are the future directions?

KnowledgeView is maintained and updated at four Knowledge Centers, located in Dallas, London, Sydney, and Sao Paulo. Through these regional centers, local staff members have more immediate access points, as well as help in stimulating knowledge sharing. In 1996, Price Waterhouse received the Best Practices Award from *PC Week* magazine for its KnowledgeView technology.

Location and Layout of Facilities

Two of the most important and basic factors for achieving global operations success are (a) the choice of appropriate facility locations and (b) determination of the facilities' layout [13]. Where should a company locate its facilities and headquarters? How do we lay out the production process within the plant? What cultural aspects should we be conscious of? Do we assemble everything in one location, or is it advantageous to pass the various stages of assembly across the globe?

Facility Location

In most manufacturing industries, labor costs have been outweighed by market access, quality control, timely delivery, and responsiveness to customers as determinants of global competitiveness. Therefore, global site selections may need to hinge on the cooperation, flexibility, and trainability of the labor force rather than on cost [14]. Thus, manufacturing should not be dependent only on the factor of the country with the cheapest labor. Global companies should also consider:

- Maintaining a presence in an area that has many of the company's customers
- Establishing a portfolio of plants to hedge against exchange rate fluctuations or political instability, thereby enabling a speedy shift, if and when necessary, to production in the other plants.
- Real-estate costs and growth in value
- Customer and workforce demographics and availability
- Quality of the workforce and quality of the output. Poor quality can take away all the cost advantages of outsourcing to a low-cost plant.
- Market potential
- Transportation
- Cost of raw materials
- Taxes
- Political and social stability

Thus the final decision to determine site locations is based on a multitude of quantitative, qualitative, cost-benefit, and cultural factors.

Facility Layout

Facility layout includes product (assembly line) and process (job shops) layouts. Product layout is exemplified by the assembly line, which typically moves a product through a sequential series of steps to complete production. Global companies need to consider the cultural aspects, as well as psychological and sociological aspects, on the worker. The team approach, for example, used by Volvo involves seven to ten hourly workers assembled to work on one car per shift and meets the Swedish cultural need for ownership. In cultures with less desire for ownership, such an approach would not work.

Internal plant layout can be a source of efficiency or inefficiency. A well-designed layout can minimize cycle time and help get the product to the customer faster. The quality, size, and location of employees' offices is also important. The status of the manager, in many cultures, is based on the importance of the office building where he is working or on the quality of the hotel at which he is staying.

Feng Shui

On a recent trip to Singapore, I noted that the entrance of the Hyatt Hotel had been modified, with the large glass doors now turned 30 degrees from the previous position. Upon inquiry, I was told that the owners wished more luck for the building. Upon consultation with a *feng shui* expert, the owners were given the new, best direction that the doors should face.

Feng shui is based on the premise that people and events are affected by the environment. The two Chinese words—meaning "wind" and "water," respectively—are shorthand for acknowledging the power of nature and the importance of living in harmony with it.

Figure 8-3, known as *ba-gua* ("eight-sided"), shows the many elements of *feng shui*. Each direction governs a different aspect of life and has a color, natural element, and number, which when combined can create enhancements that engender success in any part of life [15]. How one decorates an office, chooses color, selects business phone numbers (8s are lucky), locates the manager's office (should be farthest from the main door), or arranges the lighting can affect the *chi*, or "energy," valuable for global success.

The use of *feng shui* is common, especially in Chinese cultures. For example, the forty-seven-story headquarters of the Hong Kong and Shanghai Banking Corporation building, one of the most technologically advanced skyscrapers in the world, was sited and constructed according to strict *feng shui* principles. Escalators are situated to disperse *chi* and wealth evenly throughout the structure. The building faces the sea, with Victoria's Peak at its back—"imbuing the corporation with the benefit of those highly auspicious land formations. The

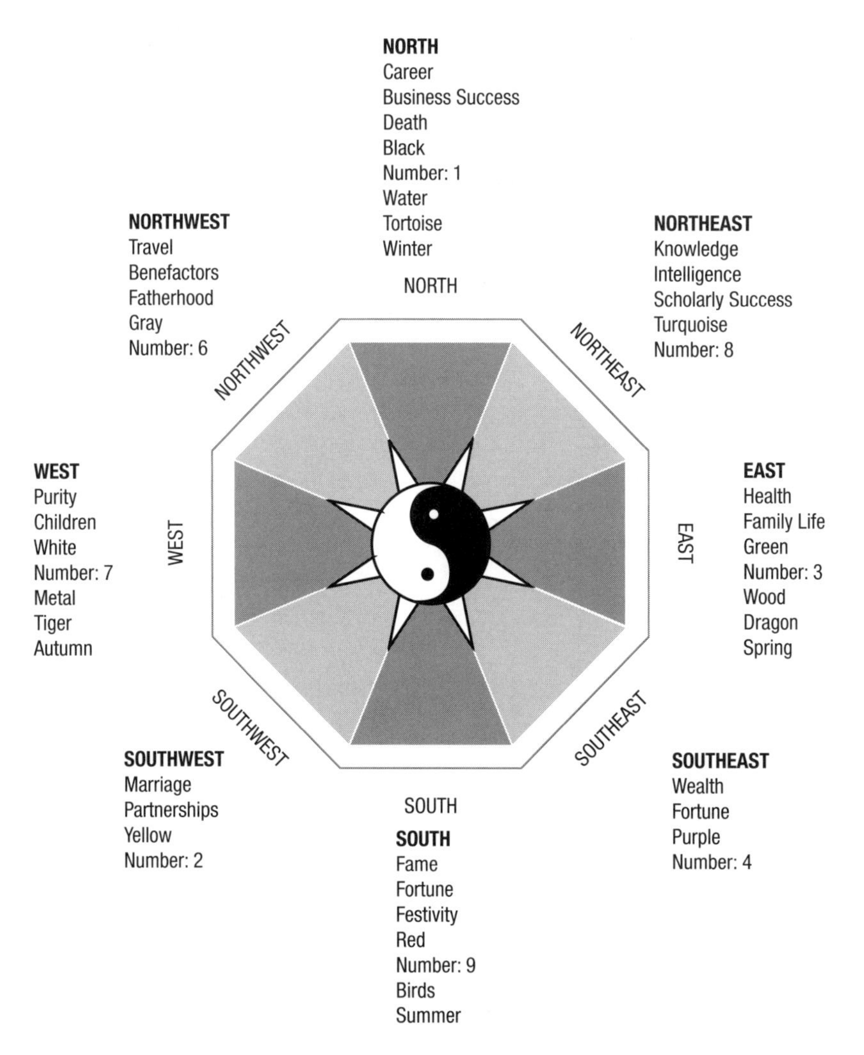

FIGURE 8-3. FENG SHUI BA-GUA.

mountain provides support and protection for the firm's business ventures, while the ocean invites wealth to flow into the building. . . . Even Donald Trump consults a *feng shui* master before embarking on a new building project" [15, p. 29].

Using Global Structure for Power and Success

Although form should follow function, the opposite is often the case. As a result, the form or structure of many organizations prevents them from being as effective on a global basis as they need to be. Rigid national or functional boundaries, bulky size, disjointedness of projects and tasks, bureaucratic restrictions, poor knowledge management, and insensitivity to global strategies and cultural nuances all help to kill rather than nourish globalization.

The desired structural characteristics of a global organization should emit flexibility, openness, freedom, and opportunity. Boundaries should be highly permeable, which maximizes the flow of communication and information, which opens the organization to greater worldwide learning and easier management of its experiences and knowledge. The firm's global structure should be based on learning needs, as well as performance needs.

A driving structuring principle is to put the necessary freedom, support, and resources in the hands of the people who need them. As tasks, needs, and people change, the structure changes so that customers and employees alike can optimally respond and grow. As we shall see in Chapter 9, whatever best allows and supports global learning and worldwide access to knowledge is a key for gaining and maintaining global success.

References

1. Kanter, R. (Ed.). *Global Strategies: Insights from the World's Leading Thinkers.* Cambridge, Mass.: Harvard Business Press, 1994.
2. Dunning, J. H. *The Globalization of Business: The Challenge of the 1990s.* London: Routledge, 1993.
3. Van Houten, G. "Managing Human Resources in the International Firm," in *Human Resource Management in International Firms.* P. Evans, Y. Doz, and A. Laurent (Eds.), New York: St. Martin's Press, 1990.
4. Snow, C. et al. "Use Transnational Teams to Globalize Your Company." *Organization Dynamics,* Spring 1996, pp. 50–66.

5. Bartlett, C. and Ghoshal, S. *Managing Across Borders: The Transnational Solution.* Boston: Harvard Business School Press, 1989.
6. Slevin, D. and Pinto, J. "Balancing Strategy and Tactics in Project Implementation." *Sloan Management Review,* Vol. 29, No. 1, Fall 1987, pp. 33–41.
7. Marquardt, M. and Snyder, N. "How Companies Go Global—The Role of Global Integrators and the Global Mindset." *International Journal of Training and Development,* Vol. 1, No. 2, 1997, pp. 104–117.
8. Nonaka, I. And Takeuchi, H. *The Knowledge-Creating Company.* New York: Oxford University Press, 1995.
9. Stewart, T. *Intellectual Capital: The New Wealth of Organizations.* New York: Doubleday, 1997.
10. Wiig, K. "Role of Knowledge-Based Systems in Support of Knowledge Management," in *Knowledge Management in Its Integrative Elements.* J. Liebowitz and L. Wilcox (Eds.), Boca Raton, Fla.: CRC Press, 1997.
11. Marquardt, M. *Technology-Based Learning.* Boca Raton, Fla.: St. Lucie Press, 1998.
12. Weick, K. "The Nontraditional Quality of Organizational Learning." *Organizational Science,* Vol. 2, No. 1, pp. 116–124.
13. Young, S. and Nie, W. *Managing Global Operations—Cultural and Technical Success Factors.* Westport, Conn.: Quorum Books, 1996.
14. Yip, G. *Total Global Strategy.* Englewood Cliffs, N.J.: Prentice Hall, 1992.
15. Lagatree, K. "Ancient Chinese Wisdom for the Modern Workplace." *Training & Development,* Jan. 1997, pp. 26–29.

9

Globalizing Learning

The decade of the 1990s has seen the emergence of knowledge as a company's most valuable asset and learning as a company's most important competency. CEOs and shareholders are now seeing knowledge as the "new organizational wealth" [1] and learning as the key to global success. Managing and measuring knowledge-based assets (especially learning capability) are become an important part of the balance sheet and annual reports of companies such as Skandia and WM-Data.

It has therefore become just as imperative for global leaders to examine the quality and quantity of learning in their organizations as it is to examine the organizational categories discussed in previous chapters (corporate culture, human resources, strategies, operations, and structure.)

Learning is a theme that has been interwoven throughout the chapters of this book. In Chapters 1 and 2 we noted how learning had accelerated globalization, as well as served as a key global driver. Chapter 3 illustrated how learning was a key "glue" in the *Global-Success* Model. Chapter 4 described the importance of continuous learning in the global corporate culture and how the cultural heroes (that is, the leaders) needed to be models of learning, as well to play a critical role in managing the learning of the organization. In Chapter 5, the role of learning before, during, and after overseas assignments was discussed, while in Chapter 6 we saw how critical learning is in the development and implementation of global strategies. In Chapter

7, learning was shown as being critical in developing and improving various operations, such as marketing, manufacturing, and product development. In Chapter 8 we examined the importance of creating a global structure that supports and enhances global learning and knowledge management.

In this chapter we will focus on three critical areas where learning and globalization must overlap and interplay: (1) creation of a global learning organization, (2) globalization of the design, delivery, and evaluation of learning programs and (3) globalization of learning materials (see Figure 9-1).

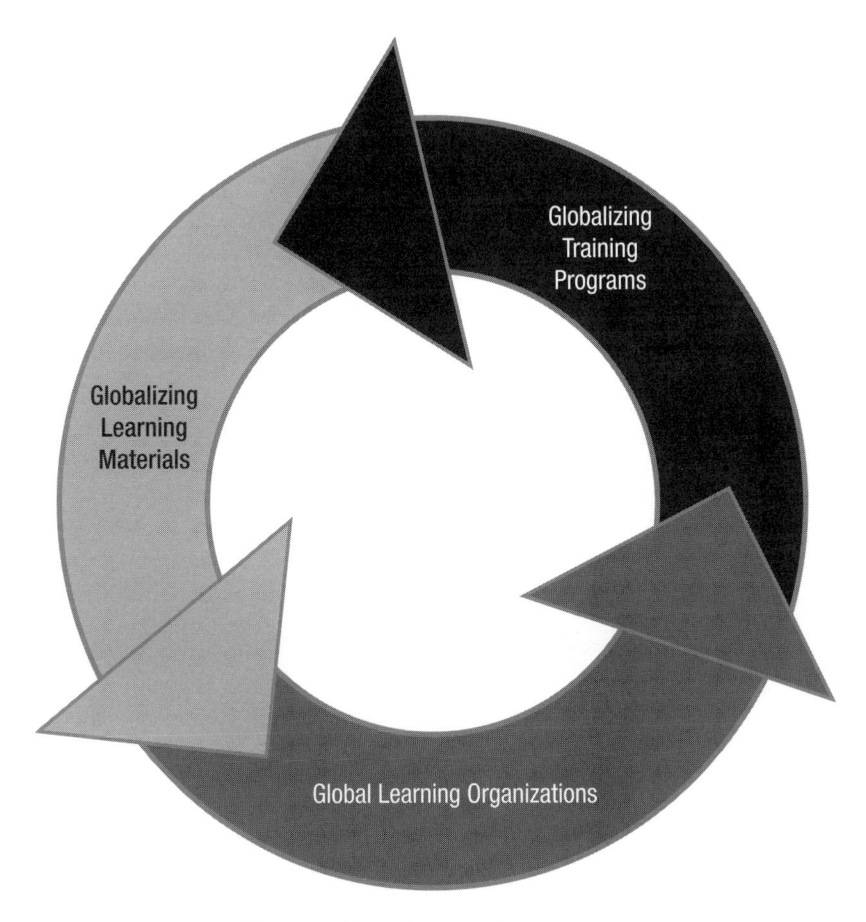

FIGURE 9-1. GLOBAL LEARNING.

Creating a Global Learning Organization

As we noted in Chapter 4, an important global corporate value is to make learning an all-encompassing value, where learning is continuous and ubiquitous, and is seen as critical for global success. In this section, we will expand this value to show how to create a global learning organization.

Learning organizations have a number of important dimensions and characteristics:

- ❑ Learning is accomplished by the organizational system as a whole, almost as if the organization were a single brain.
- ❑ Organizational members recognize the critical importance of ongoing organizationwide learning for the organization's current, as well as future, success.
- ❑ Learning is a continuous, strategically used process—integrated with and running parallel to work.
- ❑ There is a focus on creativity and generative learning.
- ❑ Systems thinking is fundamental.
- ❑ People have continuous access to information and data resources that are important to the company's success.
- ❑ A corporate climate exists that encourages, rewards, and accelerates individual and group learning.
- ❑ Workers network in an innovative, communitylike manner inside and outside the organization.
- ❑ Change is embraced, and unexpected surprises and even failures are viewed as opportunities to learn.
- ❑ Everyone is driven by a desire for quality and continuous improvement.
- ❑ Activities are characterized by aspiration, reflection, and conceptualization.
- ❑ Well-developed core competencies serve as a taking-off point for new products and services.
- ❑ The learning organization's ability to continuously adapt, renew, and revitalize itself in response to the changing environment is present [2, 3].

Research into the practices of successful global learning organizations indicate the presence of five closely interrelated subsystems that interface and complement one another (see Figure 9-2).

1. **Learning Subsystem**—Levels of learning (individual, group, and organizationwide), skills of learning, and types of learning
2. **Organization Subsystem**—Vision, culture, structure, and strategy of the organization
3. **People Subsystem**—Employees, leaders, customers, partners, and the community
4. **Knowledge Subsystem**—Acquisition, creation, storage, and transfer of knowledge
5. **Technology Subsystem**—Technology-based learning and technology-based management of knowledge

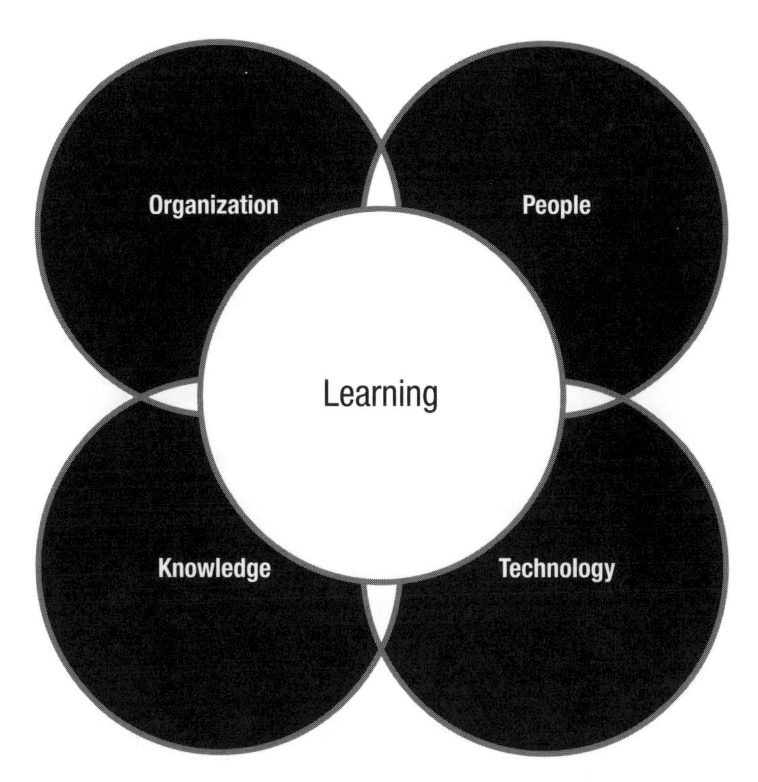

FIGURE 9-2. LEARNING ORGANIZATION MODEL.

Each of these subsystems needs to be developed and applied in a way that incorporates the cultural and global values and practices of the firm. Six key steps in creating a global learning organization include the following:

Intertwine and Align Organizationwide Learning with Business and Personal Success

Probably the most important strategy in inspiring and motivating the entire organization to quickly and emphatically move toward becoming a learning organization is to link increased learning with increased global success, to show that learning is the only source of sustainable strategic global advantage for the company.

Businesses know that, in the long run, strategic and competitive advantages lie with organizations that develop core competencies that will enable them to create new products or services swiftly and thus adapt to rapidly changing opportunities and different cultural environments. These core competencies, indeed, represent the collective learning of the organization.

Stephen Gill [4] recommends that global leaders link learning events and outcomes clearly and explicitly to business needs and strategic goals by undertaking the following actions:

- ❑ Map out the relationship between strategic goals and areas such as job behaviors, job skills, job-success indicators, and the global business objectives.
- ❑ Design prelearning activities, learning-event activities, and post-learning activities that are integrated into key business processes.
- ❑ Create an iterative process of delivery, feedback, and redesign for achieving timely learning and effective change as business goals shift.

Build Learning into All Operations and Activities

Learning organizations quickly and deliberately plan and structure learning into all organizational processes—global manufacturing, marketing, finance, and so on. And once firms begin to learn how to incorporate genuine learning processes in the fabric of practical work settings, they see dramatic results.

An example is at Ford Motor, where a car-development learning laboratory uses a computer simulator and related tools to aid systems thinking, as well as using methods to enhance reflection and conversation. The laboratory helped a development team assemble a manufacturing prototype at full line speed—a first at Ford. The prototype allowed advanced testing of assembly processes and was voted the highest quality ever by Ford's manufacturing organization. With the exception of minor adjustments, the vehicle was completed a record ten months early!

The value chain (values added at each stage) of any organization should include a domain of integrated learning. This means thinking of the value chain as an integrated learning system. When thinking about each major step of the work process, beginning with strategic planning and through customer service, think of how learning experiments could be constantly engaged. Thus structures and processes to achieve outcomes may be simultaneously viewed as operational tasks and learning exercises.

Therefore organizations must fundamentally redesign work so that producing and learning are inextricably intertwined. Organizational work can be seen like practice fields that involve redesigning work settings to incorporate the continual movement between performance and practice that is characteristic of how teams learn in sports and artists in the performing arts. Saturn has established such a setting at its Worker Development Center, a learning laboratory adjacent to the assembly line that includes a complete mock-up of the assembly process.

If learning comes through planning and experience, it follows that the more one can plan guided experiences, the more one will learn. Until organizing for production at any stage of the value chain is also seen as a learning experiment, as well as a production activity, learning will come slowly. Managers need to learn to act like applied research scientists at the same time they deliver goods and services.

By systematically and intentionally building learning capacity through the integration of learning and producing, global organizations are also building their performance capabilities.

Make Staffing Personnel Policies and Practices Relate to Becoming a Learning Organization

One of the most efficient ways to introduce an organization to and immerse an organization with learning and learners is through learning-rewarding personnel policies. Global learning organizations recruit and hire people worldwide who continually learn and who enjoy expanding and exploring their potential. Staff members who are dedicated learners and who enhance learning in people around them are promoted to supervisory positions. Non-learners are encouraged to learn or to seek employment elsewhere.

Recognize and Reward Learning

"That which gets rewarded gets done" is a valid maxim everywhere in the world and gets attention in global learning organizations. Learners, especially learning teams, get promoted, receive bonuses, and are recognized and lauded. New ideas that lead to better services or products provide a "royalty" for their originators. People who collect and transfer knowledge from internal or external sources are commended. Performance appraisals look at learning acquired and distributed as much as other actions of the individual. Teamwork is encouraged, and the ability to build and motivate teams and team learning is highly rewarded.

Measure and Broadcast Impact and Benefits of Learning

Companies hoping to become learning organizations should develop a variety of ways of measuring learning. Focusing only on the typical measure of output (cost or price) ignores learning that affects other competitive values, like quality, delivery, or new-product introductions.

One of the most innovative and valuable tools to measure learning is the half-life curve, developed by Analog Devices, a leading global learning organization. A half-life curve measures the time it takes to achieve a 50 percent improvement in a specified performance measure. Companies that take less time to improve must logically be learning faster than their peers; and in the long run, their short learning cycles will be translated into superior performance.

Generate a Large Number of Learning Opportunities

Generally, the more opportunities for learning that exist and/or are created, the more learning occurs, and the better it is. Learning organizations build into their employees both the desire and opportunity to learn. Action-reflective learning is a regular part of day-to-day corporate activity.

Renowned specialists from inside and outside the organization are tapped either in person or through media such as video, audio, electronic mail, and teleconferencing. Learning forums are designed with explicit learning goals in mind. Strategic reviews and planning are seen as golden corporatewide learning opportunities. As people examine the changing competitive environment and the company's product portfolio, technology, and market position, learning is expected. Systems audits provide another opportunity for learning. Other learning opportunities include:

- ❑ Internal benchmarking reports, which identify and compare best-in-class activities within the organization.
- ❑ Study missions, which are dispatched to leading organizations worldwide to better understand their performance and distinctive skills.
- ❑ Jamborees or symposiums, which bring together customers, suppliers, outside experts, or internal groups from around the world to share ideas and learn from one another.

Most organizations now recognize that up to 90 percent of all learning occurs while a person is on the job. It is therefore highly leveraging for managers and workers to not only appreciate the learning that they are accruing but also to create ongoing learning opportunities, as well as to build into the company a learning-reflecting mentality.

Globalization and Acculturization of Training Programs

Global companies should strive to transform all their training programs into ones that will be effective globally and yet be culturally sensitive to local situations. A useful tool to accomplish this adapta-

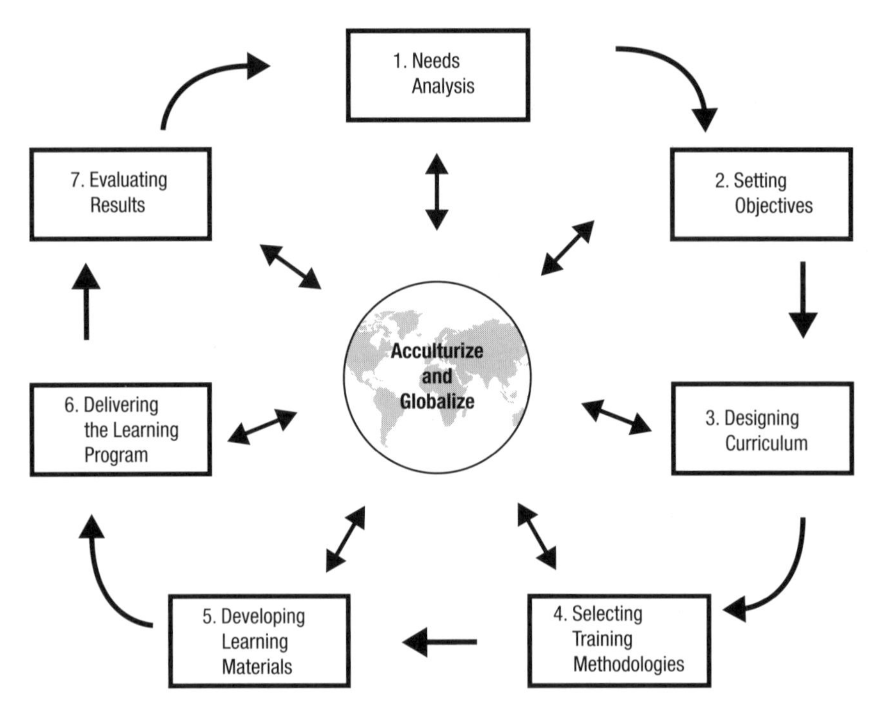

FIGURE 9-3. GLOBAL TRAINING MODEL.

tion is the Global Training Model. The Global Training Model contains seven steps, each of which is modified via acculturization and globalization (Figure 9-2).

Acculturization is the change necessary to convey the learning program (including content, methodology, objectives, and so on) across cultural boundaries; to use a computer term, it means the change necessary to assure that the training program is user friendly. An acculturized training program will include as few roadblocks to the learner as possible. The objective for the global trainer is to ensure not only that learning occurs but that it is appropriate for the cultural milieu in which it takes place. The cultural adaptation is crucial. It is as important to success as is language translation (where that is necessary). Without this acculturization, much less learning will occur [5].

Because an "outside" foreign person will have difficulty in fully understanding and appreciating the nuances of another's culture, it is important and highly beneficial to involve local people in the acculturization aspect of each step in the Global Training Model.

Globalization of the training programs represents the changes made to standardize for worldwide use as many processes, procedures, and materials as possible of each stage of the Global Training Model.

Let us examine the acculturization and globalization aspects that might be applied at each step.

Needs Analysis

An important element of needs assessment is the identification of the gaps, weaknesses, and limitations among the individuals to be trained. In many cultures, it is difficult for the learner to admit such a need or to allow the needs analyst access to such information. It may cause a person to "lose face" if he or she were to admit some degree of incompetence and weakness, especially in front of other people. Therefore, the expert training professional should already have this information. The possession of such information is presumed to be why the trainer is in the authoritative position he or she occupies. It is taken as a sign of the trainers' incompetence if they have to ask you what they should already know.

Another difficulty is that in cultures that place a high value on agreement and politeness, the learners will attempt to guess what the trainer may be looking for and attempt to give that type of response. The global HRD practitioner must, accordingly, strike a delicate balance between discovering and predetermining the learning needs.

For these and other reasons (language, unfamiliar organizational environment, different educational system, cultural and corporate customs and rituals), it is critical for global trainers to devote much more time and attention to conducting needs assessments and analyses when they are in other cultural settings.

Setting Objectives

In establishing training objectives, American trainers are encouraged to set clear-cut, competency-based objectives that the learner will be able to demonstrate at the end of the program. Objectives should include exactly what the person will do (performance), under what circumstance he or she will be able to do it (condition), and the degree of performance desired (quality).

For many cultural groups, such clearly defined objectives may be seen as:

- ❑ **Presumptuous**—The learners may wonder how the trainer can know beforehand what the learners will be able to do and/or what only God/Allah knows.
- ❑ **Threatening**—If the learners are unable to do this, they will have failed! Therefore training designs that begin by asking for expectations or personal goals are unlikely to be met with comfortable or enthusiastic responses.
- ❑ **Foreordained**—If God/Allah wills them to have these competencies, it will happen with or without their efforts.

Another cultural fact is that for many learners, the primary and only objective is the acquisition of a certificate, not the learning, because in their culture, credentials are much more important than competency for career advancement.

For trainees in many cultures, the building of relationships and the development of friendship is of equal or higher importance than learning. A key training objective is the opportunity to practice and apply the learning together, both during and after the training.

Another factor when establishing goals in other countries is the importance of standards and testing requirements that have been established by labor ministries and the specific regulations that cover the various occupations and jobs. Global trainers need to incorporate these cultural and national elements into their thinking as they establish training objectives.

Designing Curriculum

In developing the curriculum, it is important to study the cultural learning styles to determine how the trainees learn best and what structure and sequence they expect from the training. These styles are influenced by various cultural factors and differ from country to country, and even from locality to locality.

However, some fundamental differences do exist between the learning style of Americans and that of the rest of the world. Americans (and Northern Europeans) have a cultural system, learning style, and reasoning preference that tends towards the inductive task and problem-centered approach to learning (that is, they move from specifics to generalization). Most of the world has a strong preference for deductive and topic-centered reasoning (moving from generalizations to specifics). Most of the world rarely applies factual data in the multiple ways that people in the inductive cultures do every day of their lives.

In developing a curriculum for deductive cultures, where trainees respond slowly in moving from generalization to specifics, a deductive approach and topic-centered structure should be used at the initial stages. After a period of time, an inductive, experiential approach can be used and will be better appreciated and more successful in generating learning.

Another aspect of curriculum development is the scheduling of time allotted to various content areas and activities. Some useful suggestions:

- ❑ Do not schedule too tightly; most groups want considerable time for discussion and exploring.
- ❑ Take into account the values, styles, and attitudes of the learners; do not limit team activities to fifteen minutes when the cultural perception of agreement is harmony and consensus, and not majority-rule.
- ❑ Bilingual programs need much more time than monolingual ones.
- ❑ If English is the trainees' second language, schedule more frequent breaks to allow rest for the trainees, who are attempting to comprehend and speak in English.
- ❑ Allow time for socializing and building relationships.

Many global trainers, in comparing curriculum designs of French, Germans, and Americans, find that Germans feel quite comfortable with training developed in the United States because American curricula are highly structured, have a tight logical flow, and employ the rapid pace enjoyed by Germans. The French, on the other hand, prefer a slower pace and find American training lessons too cursory. The French enjoy discussing and arguing the merits of a subject. A one-day program in the United States would generally need to be designed to last two days in France.

Selecting Training Methodologies

More than one hundred different training methodologies are available to global HRD practitioners, ranging from the didactic, trainer-directed, knowledge-focused methodologies to the experimental, learner-centered, and skill-focused ones.

Many American trainers emphasize the importance of experimental learning, adhering to the adult learning theories of Knowles, Bradford, and others. This process-oriented learning is seen as more effective and enjoyable.

For people of most cultures, however, these self-directed learning methodologies can be uncomfortable and run counter to cultural mores. Participants from Asian and Arab cultures especially feel much more relaxed learning by rote and prefer to observe the instructor demonstrating a skill rather than risk being seen as foolish through risk-taking and learn-by-doing methodologies.

Cultures that expect their instructors to (a) teach with authority and power and (b) to be experts with absolute truths will obviously prefer more teacher-centered training methods. Cultures that are more egalitarian and participative and that seek less structure will prefer more learner-centered training methods.

Depending on the culture, specific methodologies may be effective or ineffective. In Asian countries, for example, experienced global trainers discourage the use of role playing and structure experiences because people in these cultures find it difficult to place themselves in the shoes of others or to confront each other because of the high cultural value placed on conflict avoidance and authority relationships. In addition, risk taking through role playing, in countries like Japan and Korea, is taboo because no one wants to be a fool or stand out.

Games can also be ineffective because Asians separate game playing from the serious business of learning. In Asia, the best participative training methodologies are small-group discussions and case studies carried out between participants of similar age and status, which should then be followed by a report of results gained by each small group to the total group by representatives of each group. Why? Because this allows the representatives to discuss the process freely without any individual member having to take personal responsibility or accolades for the group's efforts.

Structured experiences, such as Star Power (a game in which power is randomly distributed and enforced), or role plays that reverse the normal power positions can become uncomfortable for participants from many cultures. Asians attach great value to their positions and status differences. Exercises that strip them of these trappings tend to cause embarrassment, confusion, and "loss of face" for all participants, and thus reduce learning.

The use of interactive video as a training strategy is not appreciated in countries like Japan (where it was invented) and other collectivist societies because it is a method that focuses on the individual. Japanese prefer to learn and work in teams.

Some global trainers discourage the use of debate and extensive verbal methodologies in China and Japan because they conflict with at least three cultural beliefs by:

1. Placing human-centered hierarchy over propositional truth.
2. Overemphasizing definition and distinction in cultures where the languages create a world view more given toward imagery and ambiguity.
3. Valuing oral communication more than meditation, reflection, and thought.

In a similar vein, the use of the case analysis in Arab countries may be ineffective because the Arab culture encourages verbal comments by only the leader or manager of the group and not the individual participants.

In Saudi Arabia and other Gulf countries, paper exercises and games are thought to be activities for schoolchildren; the preferred methodology for learning is group discussions.

Germans tend to prefer methodologies that are orderly, systematic, detailed, and analytical (case analysis), while the French seek lively, witty activities (such as brainstorming).

Because the eventual utilization of experimental methodologies is so critical to developing certain skills and competencies, it is best to perhaps begin more formally, through lecturing and modeling. Only after gaining the confidence and comfort of the learners should the trainer begin employing more learner-centered methodologies.

Developing Learning Materials

During this step of the training design, all the necessary learning materials are written, adapted, and/or produced. This includes workbooks, handouts, instructor guides, audiotapes and videotapes, and computer software. These materials provide the content to enable the learners to achieve the training objectives. (We will examine this step in the Globalization and Acculturization of Learning Materials section, later in this chapter).

Delivering the Learning Program

When delivering or presenting a global learning program, there are a number of fundamental dos and taboos relative to (a) language, (b) culture in general, (c) culture in specific, (d) activities, (e) groupings, (f) scheduling, and (g) administration and coordination.

Language

- ❑ If you are unable to speak the local language, try to at least learn some of the basic phrases (good morning, thank you). The trainees will be pleased with your interest in their language.
- ❑ Be sure to learn and use the culture's body language and nonverbal cues. For example, in India and some Arab countries, the shaking of the head from left to right does not mean "no" but rather, "Keep talking. I'm listening to you." And the American gesture meaning "OK" has another, obscene meaning in Brazil and Greece. Also, never shake hands with a Muslim woman wearing the traditional costume.
- ❑ If the training program is being conducted in English and English is not the first language of the participants, be sure to carefully assess their language ability and respond accordingly. Do not assume they understand you or the training materials. Be sensitive to their difficulties in comprehending the program. Avoid colloquialisms or jargon unless you carefully define and explain them.
- ❑ Concentrate on speaking slowly and clearly. Remember that the American accent may be difficult to understand for Indians, East Africans, and others who speak British dialects.

- ❑ Use visuals as often as possible. Overhead transparencies, graphics, and pictures will make it easier for the learners to follow you.
- ❑ To ensure understanding, reinforce key points and ask the participants to restate them.
- ❑ Plan for the fact that the training program will take longer.
- ❑ Encourage participants to speak, and give them reinforcement when they do. This will help them become more comfortable in using their non-native language.
- ❑ Distribute training materials in advance when appropriate. This will allow participants time to prepare and gain a better understanding if the materials are not in their local language.
- ❑ Be patient and listen carefully. Respect their efforts to convey learning and feelings in another language (and therefore in another cultural context).

Culture—General Guidelines

- ❑ At the beginning, address the issue of cultural differences. Ask their indulgence for any blunders you might make. Encourage them to provide cultural feedback to you.
- ❑ Explain your expectations—of yourself as a trainer, of the trainees, and of the interactions between you and them. Try to be specific about behavior rules—how you wish to be addressed, how you will address them, and your expectations.
- ❑ Be sensitive to the local educational system and cultural habits for learning. Be careful in ascribing motivation or meaning to behavior even when it seems familiar. For example, behaviors that we associate with timidity might actually reflect assertiveness on the local cultural scale.
- ❑ Realize that the trainees in many cultures may be reluctant to raise questions. Therefore create a climate and expectation that trainees can ask questions without fear of offending the trainer or appearing foolish if they make mistakes.
- ❑ Remain comfortable with occasional silences. The silence may be related to the cultural behavior of learners, or it may be that they are taking time to translate and/or think in English, two time-consuming processes.

❑ Recognize that participants may tend to base their responses on what they think you want rather than what they actually believe or feel.

Culture—Specific Guidelines

Each culture has some specific cultural expectations regarding the manner in which a trainer presents the training program. Let's look at a few cultural nuances:

JAPAN

The good trainer should begin in a humble vein and show his respect for the learners by honoring them in some small way. He must be dressed conservatively. Sincerity is important. Japanese prefer a more indirect approach but with a careful exploration of inner meanings. The trainer should avoid exaggerations and be prepared to give specific information. He should speak to the group as a group and not identify particular participants or subgroups.

FRANCE

In France, trainers have to prove themselves. Opinions have to be supported with facts and numbers. Because the French separate a person's public and private life, the trainer should be reserved about mentioning the latter. Political jokes are widely used. The use of hard-sell techniques will turn off French trainees. They prefer gentle persuasion.

CHINA

Never acknowledge another person's emotions in China because you would embarrass that person with such a public acknowledgment of feelings.

GREAT BRITAIN

The British see American trainers as too forward, too informal, and too open. They, like many other groups, are often ill-at-ease with what they perceive as the too-quick informality and familiarity of Americans.

DIFFERENT QUESTIONING STYLES OF GERMANS, SWEDES, AND AMERICANS

The types of questions the participants ask can often be predicted by different cultures. Germans, for example, focus on technical questions. Americans favor practical questions, to explore how things work in practice. Swedish groups ask more theoretical questions that seek to define the implications of strategies.

Activities and Methodologies

As mentioned above, the global trainer in some cultures should be prepared to begin training in a more formal, didactic manner, by lecturing and answering questions. The trainer can then gradually shift to more learner-centered strategies as the participants become more comfortable and willing to participate in inductive, experimental activities.

Problem solving, for example, might be introduced deductively in traditional, didactic ways with the instructor identifying the problem and encouraging support of the solution. In subsequent sessions, the introduction of the problem might be followed by questions and answers that help ensure that all understand the problem and even the solution. With good facilitation, this might evolve into group discussion of the problem and its aspects (financial, personnel, raw materials, plant equipment). From this might spring small-group discussions of each aspect of the problem by those in charge of that aspect, with small groups reporting back to the whole group. Such incremental steps taken over a long period might lead to a processing of small-group reports, to shared inputs, and even aspects of group problem-solving itself.

As global trainers begin to use more experiential methodologies, they should search in advance for the participants who may be most comfortable and successful with those methodologies. For example, in looking for a volunteer to critique a role play, one should designate the most senior person as the observer because that person traditionally may be the one who is allowed (or who knows how in that culture) to critique the performance of subordinates.

Global trainers should allow flexibility and time. Distribute role-play materials in advance to allow the trainees time to become familiar with the roles and perhaps even rehearse the situation. Give them the option to role play or simply to discuss it if they are uncomfortable.

Groupings

As the trainer is conducting a learning activity, a number of occasions will arise on which the trainer will need to put people into small groups. In the United States, trainers often do this at random (that is, they count off into groups of three, draw numbers, and so on). In other countries, this random approach could result in some uncomfortable, ineffective, and even offensive groupings, especially at the early stages of the training program when cultural patterns are still strong and the participants have not yet become comfortable with foreign approaches.

In creating groups, global trainers must be aware of the cultural significance, if any, of mixing by gender, status, age, and/or ethnic group. In many cultures, for example, learning would be next to impossible with groups of mixed gender. In Asia, young people in a group will hesitate to speak out if older people are in the group. In many cultures, people's status in the community or group continues to determine the degree to which they can state their opinions. Mixing people from cultures with a history of antipathy will usually be counterproductive.

Schedule frequent breaks, especially if participants are learning in a non-native language. Don't rush them, or you will only wind up wasting time later restating and explaining information that you thought had been covered.

It is wise to allow participants, while working in small groups, to be allowed to discuss the case or problem in their own language and to prepare a flipchart summary, also in their native language. When presenting to the trainer and the whole group, the group spokesperson can then translate the summary into the common language.

Scheduling

Three aspects of scheduling are extremely important for the global trainer to take into account in determining the day-to-day activities: (1) time, (2) meals, and (3) events.

TIME

Different cultures have widely differing perspectives regarding the use of time. In the United States, time is very important. "Time is money" and "Don't waste time" are dictums we hear from early childhood onward. Time is seen by Americans as a precious resource they can and should control. This attitude is less prevalent in many other societies, especially in Latin America and the Middle East, where time is not only not worshipped, it is downright ignored. In these regions of the world, relationships are more important than promptness; and fully understanding and discussing an interesting point is more important than staying on schedule.

When training in another culture, there may be a number of differing expectations regarding the 9 a.m. start. In some cultural settings, when the schedule indicates 9 a.m. as the starting time, it may mean that no one arrives until then, and the true starting time will be 10 a.m. Other cultures take the 9 a.m. as absolute, and if the instructor is a few minutes late, participants feel he is not taking them or his responsibilities seriously.

In these situations, it is critical for the instructor to determine and make clear to everyone which cultural definition of time will be employed—his or the group's—and then *stick* to it. On the second day, the trainees will arrive at 9 a.m. if you start at 9 a.m. and are serious about it.

MEALS

In allocating time for meals, remember that different societies have different customs regarding the amount of time set aside for the meals. In most countries, it typically takes about one hour for lunch. However, in France, they expect two hours; in Spain, they take two to three hours but then are willing to work until 8 p.m. Remember the important social and group interaction values that eating provides for various cultures. If eating times cannot be compressed, try to build some learning activities into these longer eating times.

There are a large number of considerations in determining the food to be served at training programs. The Hindus do not eat beef; the Muslims do not consume pork or alcohol. Indonesians and most Asians expect rice with their meals. Meridian International Center in

Washington, D.C., which trains thousands of leaders annually from all over the world, found chicken to be the most globally accepted food.

Events

It is important to allow time for formal events in the training program. Ceremonial time for awarding certificates, listening to short speeches from outside dignitaries, and other such formalities show the importance of the program and encourage greater group motivation, participation, and learning.

Administration and Coordination of Training Team

An obvious first priority is to be sure that an appropriate team of HRD people has been assembled to carry out the training or consulting assignment. The skills and competencies of the team members should complement one another. They should be able to effectively work with each other and to learn from each other. They should have the administrative support (typing, translation, transportation) necessary so they can focus on their learning functions.

Materials

Locating and securing materials and supplies can be an adventure in some developing countries. HRD administrators may need to have trainers bring such resources with them or have the resources sent from headquarters. David Lassiter, who has worked throughout the world with the Peace Corps, recommends these precautions:

- ❑ Take basic training supplies (paper, pens, markers) with you.
- ❑ Find out where you can purchase or borrow necessary materials.
- ❑ Check the audiovisual equipment; be sure it is the correct voltage, and take along extra bulbs for backup because replacements may be unavailable in the country or village to which you are travelling.

Training Venue

Selecting the training site and facilities is important. The venue, surroundings, and technology can enhance or diminish the status and receptivity toward the training.

Trainee Accommodations

In managing the learning program, the global HRD administrator may also need to arrange for living accommodations for the trainees. In societies where power is the basis for clear and great distances among people and where hierarchical status differences are present, it is important to provide, if possible, different facilities (or floors or rooms) for people of different status levels. Mixing them together can alienate all the trainees, both those of high and low status.

Ceremonies

A valuable role that the manager of the learner program can perform is to arrange for senior-level people from within or outside the organization to be present or speak at the opening or closing ceremonies of the training program. The providing of certificates or plaques for program completion is also important throughout the world. These gestures indicate the importance and prestige of the learning program to the learners, as well as to the instructors. The appreciation of the learners will also result in a higher level of learning transference and application.

Evaluating Results

Evaluation seeks to measure the reactions and learning of the trainees and the quality of the training itself, including course design, the instructor, and materials. The evaluation should also identify ways of revising and improving the training program.

There are significant cultural differences as to who evaluates, what is evaluated, and how and when evaluation is done. In the United States, in addition to evaluating the learners' progress, the trainer generally seeks feedback from the trainees on how well he is doing. The trainees are encouraged to identify ways in which the learning can be improved, as well as changes that might be made. Americans are generally comfortable in providing information about how they are doing and how the instructor is doing, particularly if it can be done anonymously.

However, people from most other cultures would not be comfortable to evaluate the learning program, even if done anonymously. Any suggestions and criticisms might imply a lack of confidence of the authority-expert trainer. Therefore they will respond with only positive comments. And if critical evaluation is offered by the trainer, there will often be a significant deterioration or even a cessation of performance by the trainees.

Our sense of evaluation is based upon U.S. values of frankness and openness, whereas many other cultures more highly value hiding one's feelings and thoughts and not prying into the feelings and thoughts of others. Experienced global HRD practitioners suggest the following strategies in designing the evaluation component:

- ❑ Appoint a steering committee to meet at the end of each day. Trainees would be encouraged to give feedback and suggestions to this committee, which would then forward these comments to the trainer.
- ❑ Designate a person (be sure the group sees him or her as a leader because of position, age, status, and so on) to whom individuals can provide feedback on the progress of the program at any time.
- ❑ Utilize the training team members who are from the local culture in gathering the data.
- ❑ Design the evaluation instrument to focus more on the positive—ask for suggestions for improving what is going well.
- ❑ Plan to spend time following up with some trainees individually.
- ❑ Show that learning has indeed occurred by allowing participants to demonstrate the competencies they have developed.

To evaluate the competency attained by a trainee versus what is required for a given position, it is necessary to develop a culturally reliable data base of norms for that position and culture. For example, let's consider measuring the warmth, approachability, and friendliness of a salesperson. If we were to measure an Italian salesperson against English norms, that person would be rated as uncontrollably emotional. A German salesperson measured against French norms might be judged humorless and cold.

In developing evaluation measures, Wilson Learning, for example, developed fifteen different data bases that enabled it to measure German behavior against German norms, French behavior against French norms, and so forth. Wilson Learning tests about 500 people in each culture to develop such a cultural data base.

Another aspect of evaluation that Wilson Learning has analyzed and developed is the comparative value of a culture's rating system relative to other cultures. For example, there is a great reluctance among the Japanese to ever rate anyone at the top end of the scale because the Japanese simply do not deal in superlatives the way Americans do. To compensate, Wilson decided that in Japan a rating of 4 equaled 7 in the United States. Likewise, a 10 in Indonesia might equal a 7 in the United States.

Globalization and Acculturization of Learning Materials

The process of creating new materials or adapting already developed materials for use in other cultures is not a simple task. Global companies must not only translate materials but also must be sure to carefully transpose them all to a totally new environment in a way that gains acceptance in the local culture.

Materials developers should assume cultural differences rather than similarities. They should treat each cultural environment as different and requiring culturally appropriate learning materials that will not be seen as offensive to, or be resisted by, the learners.

Developing Global Learning Materials at Motorola

Motorola is a leading global corporation in the design of learning programs that are acculturized so that knowledge and skills can be transferred promptly and effectively in the local culture. Motorola found that globalizing all its training materials was a great impetus for building global thinking and action within the company. Motorola applied the following eight-step plan to assure that training materials would work in another culture:

1. Local instructors and a translator, ideally someone who is bicultural, observe a pilot program and/or examine written training materials.

(Continued on next page)

2. The educational designer then debriefs the observation with the translator, curriculum writer, and local instructors.
3. Together they examine the structure, sequence, and materials.
4. They identify stories, metaphors, experiences, and examples in this culture that might fit the new training program.
5. The educational designer and curriculum writer make changes in the training materials.
6. The local instructors are trained to use the materials.
7. Materials are printed only after the designer, translator, and native-language trainers are satisfied.
8. The language and content of the training materials are tested with a pilot group.

You should also consider a number of culturally specific guidelines as you develop training materials:

- ❑ Avoid culturally inappropriate pictures or scenarios—for example, photos of women in Arab cultures.
- ❑ Use plenty of graphics, visuals, and demonstrations if the trainees are learning in a second language.
- ❑ Provide many handouts and instructional materials; these are highly valued and even displayed in many cultures.
- ❑ Beware of corporate ethnocentrism in which the company must be presented exactly the same all over the world.

In many cultures, especially Asia where a high value is placed on clear and specific instructions, training materials must be well-organized and unambiguous. The materials should include written examples for all worksheets that participants are required to complete, explicit written instructions for any exercise, and sections that completely and accurately summarize all lectures. Without these specific instructions, participants may become agitated by the lack of direction and, often covertly, blame the trainer for any negative outcomes resulting from the training experience.

Adapting of Existing Training Materials

In adapting training, one should avoid using training materials that represent American culture or imply that the American way is the best or only way. If too American-focused, these materials may not tell the trainees how to apply the knowledge and skills in their own environments.

Illustrating concepts with examples that are familiar and acceptable to the trainees makes learning much more productive and enjoyable. Exercises should be tailored to the local culture, for example, through the use of local names, titles, and situations whenever possible. One should modify the situations, change case studies, and rewrite applications when taking training materials to another culture.

The degree of adaptation required depends on what is being taught. The more technical the topic, the less need for change. For example, if you want to teach someone to operate a particular machine, there will be need for little adaptation. On other topics, however, such as communication and supervisory skills, the amount of training material to be adapted will be considerable.

Translation

Translation is more than translating word for word the content from one language to another. To the extent possible, the values and local applicability must also be translated. Translating instructional materials is a difficult process, especially when it involves formulating new words to conform to good language usage, cultural meaning, and the learning objectives of the training program.

It is important to remember that there are words that are not directly translatable to another language. For example, the English word *no* has no translation into Thai. Similarly, the many *you*s of Thai cannot be translated into English. There is also not an automatic interchangeability of technical terms. For example, no Arabic words exist that mean "metal tubing" or "jet propulsion."

It is crucial therefore to study the language—vocabulary and terminology. Gaining both agreement with the local people on terminology and a glossary will help in preparing training manuals and workbooks. An excellent source for terminology is the International Labor

Office, which has published a series of glossaries for technical and vocational training in a number of different languages.

A final aspect of translation is the level of language skills, written and oral, of the trainees. Training materials should be prepared according to their language capabilities.

Computer Software

Computer-based learning (CBL) is increasingly being used in global training. Global CBL specialists realize that the necessity for computer courseware to be acculturized is even higher than other training materials because it is not an oral medium that can be acculturized on the run by an instructor. Learning through CBL systems depends on the written and graphic communication between a program and a learner.

According to Angus Reynolds [6], there are a number of areas to consider in adapting computer programs to other cultures:

Space. Some languages require more printed space than others to convey the same information. For example, German requires approximately 30 percent more space than English. Extra space must therefore be reserved simply to provide sufficient room for the new language.

Format. When the target language does not lend itself to an acceptable presentation within the available space format, problems can arise. For example, Arabic is written from right to left, and therefore the graphic should go on the left of the text rather than the right, as it does in English.

Simplicity. Although creativity is valuable for making a program interesting and effective, it is important to keep a lesson reasonably simple so that it can be more easily adaptable.

Clarity. An explanation or narrative that is obscure in English will be just as obscure in Indonesian or Swahili.

Standardization. Standards protect against practices that make adaptation difficult. Specify the size of the borders, and specify locations where certain information will always appear on the learner's display.

Cultural Relevance. Use narratives and examples that fit the culture and environment. Baseball, for example, is not understood in most parts of the world.

Jargon. Jargon does not lend itself to translation, and employing current slang in training materials or presentation is usually neither necessary nor effective.

Acronyms. Acronyms create confusion. What is easily pronounced or understood in English may be unfathomable in another language.

Humor. Humor is always potentially dangerous because it can leave the learner wondering what the point is or, worse, insulted. It is also difficult to translate.

Videotape

The video content must fit the culture and be sensitive to local customs and behavior. What do you do if you are producing a video that you plan on utilizing in two or more cultures? Do you dub in the local language, use subtitles, or reshoot all or part of the video? It depends on two factors: (a) the norm for the culture you are working in and (b) the skills you are trying to teach.

Based on the cultural norm, for example, in France you would generally dub (French are accustomed to watching American movies), while in Scandinavian countries you would use English subtitles (that is the custom there).

If you are developing a video about interpersonal skills, you would reshoot the entire video because this skill is so cultural. The topic of business etiquette would also need to be reshot because of unique cultural differences. For example, Americans talk business during a coffee break, while French are there to drink coffee.

Global Learning—Essential for Creating and Maintaining Global Success

Learning across borders and across the organization is critical for global companies. According to noted global theorists Kevin Barham and Marion Devine, "The future is not just about global competition, but about global learning"[7, p. 37]. Global companies need therefore to become global learning organizations, as well as to globalize their training programs and learning materials. Learning is necessary for both building a global company, and for maintaining global success.

References

1. Sveiby, K. *The New Organizational Wealth*. San Francisco: Barret-Koehler, 1997.
2. Marquardt, M. *Building the Learning Organization*. New York: McGraw-Hill, 1996.
3. Marquardt, M. and Reynolds, A. *The Global Learning Organization*. Burr Ridge, Ill.: Irwin Publishing, 1994.
4. Gill, S. "Shifting Gears for High Performance." *Training & Development*, May 1995, pp. 25–31.
5. Marquardt, M. *How to Globalize Your Training*. Alexandria, Va.: ASTD Press, 1997.
6. Reynolds, A. (Ed.). *Technology Transfer: A Project Guide for International HRD*. Boston: International HRD, 1984.
7. Barham, K. and Devine, M. *The Quest for the International Manager*. London: Business International Press, 1991.

10

Global Steps Toward Global Success

Globalizing an organization is a challenge that demands an understanding of and a commitment to mobilizing all six of the organizational components explored and illustrated throughout this book, namely, corporate culture, people, strategies, operations, structure, and learning. It is a difficult and daunting task, but certainly there is no task more important for assuring the survival and success of your organization. As General Electric CEO Jack Welch succinctly stated, companies either "globalize or they die."

Taking the specific steps to build a global organization requires a firm commitment and a well-orchestrated plan on the part of many people in the organization. Maintaining this new, higher level of global power is an equally demanding challenge, one that requires a serious determination not to fall back down the globalization curve. (Witness how most of the "excellent companies" cited in Peters and Waterman's *Search for Excellence* either dropped from their high ratings or disappeared altogether because they did not know how to maintain or sustain excellence.) To sustain globality will also require constant vigilance and continuous growth.

Steps in Building the Global Organization

The external pressures forcing a company to globalize are great. However, the obstacles created by culture, politics, and distance (as described in Chapter 2) are not easily overcome. Producing any significant organization transformation is difficult —too many organizations fail and drift back to an earlier stage in some or all parts of the globalization process. In Chapters 4 through 9, we delineated the various ways a company could globalize each of the six global components. In this chapter, we will look at how to put the entire package together—how to systematically integrate these six dimensions and thereby globalize the corporation. We have identified sixteen steps to guide this globalization process (see Figure 10-1).

1. **Establish a strong sense of urgency about becoming a global organization.**
2. **Commit to becoming a global organization.**
3. **Form a powerful coalition pushing for becoming a global organization.**
4. **Assess the organization's global readiness and capability.**
5. **Create and communicate the vision of the global organization.**
6. **Develop a global corporate culture and mind-set.**
7. **Develop global leaders and global teams.**
8. **Connect globalization with all business operations.**
9. **Demonstrate and practice globality.**
10. **Remove obstacles that prevent the company from becoming a global organization.**
11. **Select and develop "glob-able" people.**
12. **Transform the structures.**
13. **Globalize all learning.**
14. **Create short-term successes along the globalization journey.**
15. **Consolidate progress achieved and push for continued movement toward global status.**
16. **Anchor globalization throughout the corporation's culture.**

FIGURE 10-1. 16 STEPS TO ACHIEVING GLOBAL ADVANTAGE.

Establish a Strong Sense of Urgency About Becoming a Global Organization

Globalizing is indeed urgent. Survival in the global marketplace requires the company to globalize in all six dimensions. Leadership needs to establish this urgency throughout the organization. The pressures to globalize that emerge from demanding global customers and powerful global competitors will not allow much time to dawdle in the multinational, international, or domestic stages. Therefore organizations need to quickly get on the track to globalization through a variety of integrated, complementary actions and in all units of the company.

Research has shown that most successful change efforts begin when individuals or groups within the organization look seriously at the company's competitive situation, market position, technological trends, and/or financial performance and realize that a great crisis or opportunity looms. This first step is essential because getting a transformation program started requires a strong realization of urgency on the part of many individuals. Unlike other organizational transformation efforts, top leadership must quickly jump to the forefront when attempting to go global.

Most companies never get their globalization efforts off the ground because they fail at this first phase. What are some of the reasons for these failures?

- ❑ Executives underestimate how hard it can be to drive people out of their comfort zones, especially zones built with cultural cocoons.
- ❑ Leaders lack patience to handle this resistance or inertia.
- ❑ Top leadership becomes paralyzed by the downside possibilities of the significant impending changes; for example, top leaders may fear senior employees will become defensive, key people will refuse to take global assignments, morale will drop, events will spin out of control, short-term business results will be jeopardized, and so on.
- ❑ Managers are afraid to take the risks involved in creating the new global corporate culture, strategies, and structures.

A key tactic at this point is to make remaining at the status quo seem more dangerous than launching into the unknown. Until the urgency rate is pumped high enough, the transformation process cannot succeed. The alarming demise of companies that are unable to take the leap into globalization should provide sufficient warning and impetus.

Commit to Becoming a Global Organization

Top management must make a determined and clear commitment to becoming a global company, recognizing that business survival and success depends on globalization. Obstacles and resistance should not be allowed to deter the firm resolve to move forward toward global status.

This commitment must be based not only on the urgency of the task but also on the many benefits that will accrue to the organization, to employees, and to shareholders. There needs to be a belief that global companies will be exciting and fulfilling places in which to work and learn.

Global leaders such as Jack Welch of General Electric and Jorma Ollila of Nokia demonstrate continuously in their meetings with boards and staff, as well as in the corporate annual reports, their enthusiastic belief in and commitment to globalization as a requirement for global success.

Form a Powerful Coalition Pushing for Becoming a Global Organization

Recognizing the importance and necessity of moving past the international or multinational status to global status may at first originate with a small number of people within the organization. But to globalize the organization and its culture requires a critical mass of individuals truly committed to this goal.

John Kotter, a Harvard professor who has had extensive experience in assisting organizations in major change efforts, notes that:

> In successful transformations, the chairman or president or division general manager, plus another 5 or 15 or 50 people, come together and develop a shared commitment. . . . In my experience, this group never includes all the company's most senior executives because some people just won't buy in, at least not at first. But in most successful cases, the coalition is always pretty powerful—in terms of titles, information, expertise, reputations, and relationships [1, p. 62].

The core of the group may be a number of senior managers, but it should also include board members, representatives from key customers or partners, and whatever other stakeholders one can mobilize. Get as many people as you can to take a rapid, active role in pushing for global status.

The coalition needs to develop a shared sense of urgency about globalization and to create a maximum level of trust and communication. Off-site retreats are especially valuable at this stage.

Organizations that fail in this step of the organizational transformation process have usually (a) underestimated the difficulties of producing change and the critical importance of a powerful guiding coalition or (b) not developed the ability to work in teams. A globalization effort that does not have a powerful enough guiding coalition may make some apparent progress for a while, but sooner or later, the other important issues emerge and slow down the change. And time is not much of a luxury if you want to go global before all your competitors do.

Assess the Organization's Global Readiness and Capability

As in most change efforts, a critical early step is to assess the present readiness and capability of the organization to go global, to identify existing internal strengths and weaknesses, as well as external threats and opportunities. Although many organizations may informally or haphazardly assess some aspect of their globalization efforts, the top companies recognize the importance of undertaking a more comprehensive, systematic examination of their global capability and readiness.

The *GlobalSuccess* Capability and Readiness Profile, found in the Appendix, has been used by a number of organizations seeking to go global. The instrument examines each of the six organizational components (global corporate culture, global human resources, global strategy, global operations, global structure, and global learning).

For those seeking further information about the use of the *GlobalSuccess* Capability and Readiness Profile, contact Global Learning Associates, 1688 Moorings Drive, Reston, Va. 20190 USA (fax: 703-437-3725; e-mail: mjmq@aol.com).

Create and Communicate the Vision of the Global Organization

As we noted in Chapter 4, one of the first and most important steps of globalization is to change the corporate culture, that is, to change the vision and purpose of what the company is all about and thereby the mind-set, values, and activities necessary to achieve that vision.

A successful transformation to global status requires a vision of the future that is clear, exciting, significant, and meaningful so as to appeal to employees and other stakeholders. Without this vision, the transformation effort can easily dissolve into a list of confusing and incompatible programs and projects that can take the organization in the wrong direction or nowhere at all.

Kotter cites a useful rule of thumb: "If you can't communicate the vision to someone in five minutes or less and get a reaction that signifies both understanding and interest, you are not yet done with this phase of the transformation process"[1, p. 63].

Develop a Global Corporate Culture and Mind-set

David Whitwam, CEO of Whirlpool, declared that the key to globalizing the organization was to get everyone in the organization to think and act globally, not just a few [2]. Developing a global mind-set in which people have the ability (a) to exchange ideas and implement activities easily across cultural and personal borders, (b) to accept other cultural perspectives, and (c) to break down natural provincial ways of thinking is essential.

People with global mind-sets seek to continually expand their knowledge, to develop a high conceptual capacity to deal with the complexity of global organizations, to be extremely flexible, to strive to be sensitive to cultural diversity, to be able to intuit decisions with inadequate information, and to have a strong capacity for reflection. With a global corporate culture, organizations are better able to balance global and local needs and to operate cross-functionally, cross-divisionally, and cross-culturally around the world.

Develop Global Leaders and Global Teams

It is important to identify key present and future global leaders for the organization and then develop and guide them to handle the six key leadership activities of global leaders identified by Rhinesmith [3], namely:

1. Managing competitiveness by allocating and aligning resources.
2. Managing complexity by determining what must go right.
3. Managing adaptability by trusting process over structure.
4. Managing teams by valuing diversity.
5. Managing uncertainty by thriving in times of unpredictable change.
6. Managing learning by growing successfully as individuals.

Global leaders should seek to develop a variety of "glob-able" competencies, such as:

1. The ability to describe clearly the forces behind the globalization of business.
2. The ability to recognize and connect global market trends, technological innovation, and business strategy.
3. The ability to outline issues essential to effective strategic alliances.
4. The ability to frame day-to-day management issues, problems, and goals in a global context.
5. The ability to think and plan beyond historical, cultural, and political boundaries, structures, systems, and processes.
6. The ability to create and effectively lead worldwide business teams.
7. The ability to help the company adopt a functional global organization structure.

Global leaders are best developed through participation in global teams, especially teams that use action learning to solve global problems. As companies spread their operations around the world, global teams can be used to both launch and manage the global programs. When creating global teams, the following guidelines should be applied:

- ❑ Establish leadership teams with representatives from all locations.
- ❑ Conduct intercultural team-building with multicultural groups.
- ❑ Engage in group dynamic activities that enhance the ability to understand cultural diversity.
- ❑ Carefully blend the talents of the global team members.

Connect Globalization with All Business Operations

The next step is to link clearly and explicitly all strategies and operations toward the company's vision and strategy of globality. Strategic planning, manufacturing, marketing, distribution, R&D, customer service, administration, policy and procedures, and technology acquisition should all be undertaken with a mentality bent toward how each of these functions can contribute to further globalization of the enterprise.

At regular intervals, these activities should be examined and assessed to determine the degree to which they have been globalized and the degree to which they have contributed to the globalization of the entire organization.

Demonstrate and Practice Globality

Transformation into a global company will not happen until leaders begin acting and thinking like global leaders. Their new global mind-set should be evident in the ways they operate and guide others.

To get the company to buy into globalization, the leading proponents should incorporate the vision into their hour-by-hour activities. For example, in routine discussions about a business problem, they should talk about how proposed solutions will fit or not fit into this new global vision; during performance appraisal sessions, they should reward according to how the employee's behavior helps or undermines his or her efforts in becoming a global employee; in routine meetings with employees, they should tie their answers back to the globalization efforts within and outside the company.

Corporate leaders should use every existing communication channel to broadcast the vision. Boring and unread company newsletters should be turned into collections of lively articles about the global activities in the company (such as the newsletters at companies like Honeywell and National Semiconductor). Leaders should turn ritualistic and tedious quarterly management meetings into exciting discussions of the transformation into a global enterprise (as Whirlpool and Beloit Corporation regularly do). And, most importantly, they should "walk the talk" of a global leader—work with global teams, plan global programs, and thereby consciously attempt to become a living symbol of the new corporate global culture.

Develop an integrated, strategically driven global training program. Replace the old management courses with courses that focus on global issues and global skills. Sylvia Odenwald, in her excellent book *Global Training* [4], lists learning categories (executive development, cultural awareness, multicultural communication, country-specific training, and language) and suppliers for each of these categories.

Remove Obstacles That Prevent the Company from Becoming a Global Organization

Successful transformations begin to involve growing numbers of people as the change process progresses. Global transformation requires not only the positive steps identified above; change also requires the removal of obstacles. Six major obstacles are the main culprits in hindering the globalization process:

- ❑ **Bureaucracy,** where policies, regulations, forms, and busy work become more important than change
- ❑ **Competitiveness,** which emphasizes individualism rather than teamwork and collaboration
- ❑ **Control,** which may provide a high for those in control but is always a low for learning and trying new ways to globalize
- ❑ **Poor communication,** as a result of the filters, conscious and unconscious biases, narrow listening, and delays
- ❑ **Poor leaders,** who neither preach nor practice global behavior and are most concerned about protecting their turf
- ❑ **Rigid hierarchy,** which forces people and ideas to go up and down narrow silos

In the early stages of becoming a global organization, few companies may have the momentum, power, or time to get rid of all obstacles. But the big barriers must be confronted and moved. Action on them is important, both to empower others and to maintain the credibility of the globalization effort as a whole.

Select and Develop "Glob-able" People

According to global management guru Kenichi Ohmae, rule No. 1 in globalization is "Globalize people, globalize personnel." Because the process of globalization can take a long time, Ohmae emphasizes that companies should develop "glob-able" people early. The No. 1 priority is people. Ohmae writes, "You may have strategy, you may have visions, but unless you have global people, you can't deliver" [5, p. 28].

Companies now recognize that the ability to compete globally will depend on the quality and level of global training in their organizations. For organizations seeking to compete in globalized markets, world-class global HRD will be very important. Successful global corporations recognize that global training and development have several benefits, including:

- ❑ Improved ability to identify viable business opportunities.
- ❑ Reduced waste of resources on ill-conceived ventures.
- ❑ Increased competitiveness around the world.
- ❑ Higher job satisfaction and retention of overseas staff.
- ❑ Less business lost because of insensitivity to cultural norms.
- ❑ Improved effectiveness in diverse business environments.

It is therefore important that the company develop a systematic training/development strategy that includes:

- ❑ Connection of business goals to training.
- ❑ Creation of a global training mission.
- ❑ Examination of internal and external factors and resources related to global training.
- ❑ Identification of training goals and objectives.
- ❑ Identification of action steps to accomplish learning needs of organization.
- ❑ Development of evaluation system to assess impact and needed changes of training and development strategies.

Transform the Structures

Structure should now follow form. Global companies need to be both centralized and decentralized; vertical and horizontal barriers must be eliminated; all former functional activities need to be welded into a seamless whole; communication must be quick but complete. Mechanisms that favor or support a single national culture must be dismantled.

Structure casts a powerful directive on an organization's life and people. Structure determines the degree of internal control, the manner in which people work, the locus of power, the lines of communication, the decision-making process, and how knowledge is managed in the organization.

An organization seeking to go global must transform its present international or multinational form and structure into a global one so that there is a global integration of corporate functions. Structures that maximize worldwide operations and functions and enhance global universality while allowing for local diversity should be created. The business dimension of global linking and leveraging must be stronger than geographic or functional dimensions. An integrated global strategy means integration across businesses within each country, as well as integration within each business across countries.

Globalize All Learnings

Continuously learning about and continuously improving globalization activities are the core for continuous improvement and innovation. Learning must be weaved throughout every program and operation of the global organization. Learning should be seen as the critical source for continued global success. The organization should seek to (1) become a global learning organization, (2) globalize the design, delivery, and evaluation of all training programs, and (3) globalize all learning materials.

Create Short-Term Successes Along the Globalization Journey

Because it takes time and much effort to become a global organization, the change effort risks losing momentum if there are no short-term goals to meet and celebrate. Most people won't stay on the long march unless the journey has some short-term successes. Creating short-term wins is different from just hoping for them. The globalization coalition should actively look for ways to obtain, demonstrate, and measure clear success caused by the globalization efforts (for example, increased profits, greater utilization of R&D, greater cultural diversity, new products and/or services, and greater linking and leveraging of resources).

Consolidate Progress Achieved and Push for Continued Movement Toward Global Status

After a few months of hard work, the globalization advocates may be tempted to declare victory when first signs of transformation have occurred. While celebrating a win is fine, "declaring the war won can be catastrophic," declares Kotter. "Until changes sink deeply into a company's culture . . . new (changes) are fragile and subject to regression" [1, p. 66].

Instead of declaring victory, leaders of successful globalization efforts should use the credibility afforded by short-term gains to tackle even bigger problems. They should go after systems and structures that are not consistent with the new vision and have not been confronted before. They should pay greater attention to who is promoted, who is hired, and how people are being developed. They should understand that becoming a global company takes not months but years—and even then is never fully finished.

Anchor Globalization Throughout the Corporation's Culture

In the final analysis, the reality of the global organization sticks when it becomes institutionalized, when it becomes subconscious and automatic. Until the new behaviors are rooted in corporate norms and shared values, the various elements of the globalization process may be subject to retrogression as soon as the pressure for change is removed.

Two factors are particularly important in institutionalizing change in the corporate culture: (a) a conscious attempt to show people how the new approaches, behaviors, and attitudes have helped improve individual and corporate performance and (b) taking sufficient time to make sure the next generation of top-management leaders are committed to and implement the new global way of thinking and operating.

Global Success!

The next century will undoubtedly be even more global than the last few years of this century. Although non-global and global companies exist side by side as we close the twentieth century, in the twenty-first century only companies that have evolved to global status will survive. Non-global companies simply will not be able to compete with the power and competitive advantages of global companies. The choice, therefore, is not whether to globalize but how and how soon. Only a few companies have successfully and totally achieved global status. The challenges are awesome, the difficulties immense, but the opportunities are endless and wonderful. Good luck on your journey to the global twenty-first century!

References

1. Kotter, J. "Leading Change: Why Transformation Efforts Fail." *Harvard Business Review,* Mar.–Apr. 1995, pp. 59–67.
2. Maruca, R. F. "The Right Way to Go Global: An Interview with Whirlpool CEO David Whitwam." *Harvard Business Review,* Vol. 72, No. 2, 1994, pp. 135–145.
3. Rhinesmith, S. "An Agenda for Globalization." *Training & Development,* Vol. 45, No. 2, Feb. 1991, pp. 22–29.
4. Odenwald, S. *Global Training: How to Design Training for a Multinational Corporation.* Homewood, Ill.: Irwin Professional Publishing, 1993.
5. Ohmae, K. *The Borderless World.* New York: Harper, 1990.

APPENDIX

GlobalSuccess *Capability and Readiness Profile*

Overview and Introduction

Six major dimensions of the organization are assessed in the *GlobalSuccess* Capability and Readiness Profile instrument: (1) global corporate culture, (2) global human resources, (3) global strategies, (4) global operations, (5) global structure, and (6) global learning. Completing the profile and reviewing your responses will help you assess the current level of globalization in your organization. The strengths and weaknesses identified through this instrument can serve as a foundation in determining the overall globality of your company, as well as indicate what steps could be taken to improve each of the six global dimensions.

Below is a list of various statements about your organization. Read each statement carefully and decide the extent to which it actually applies to your organization. Use the following scale:

4 = Applies totally (global status)
3 = Applies to a great extent (multinational status)
2 = Applies to a moderate extent (international status)
1 = Applies to little or no extent (domestic status)

I. Global Culture

In this organization . . .

1. ______A global vision is shared by top management and employees.
2. ______There is a global mind-set through which we see the world without boundaries or cultural biases.
3. ______Global ideas of cultural sensitivity, customization, timeliness, and worklife quality are valued.
4. ______We participate regularly in global conferences and read global publications.
5. ______We search worldwide to identify global best practices.
6. ______Policies and procedures enhance global thinking and global action.
7. ______Company heroes and leaders share global experiences and model global behavior.

______**Global Culture Score** (sum of answers to Global Culture questions)

II. Global Human Resources

In this organization . . .

1. ______"Glob-able" competencies have been identified for management and non-management positions.
2. ______We recruit worldwide for the best people.
3. ______Training programs are offered in cross-cultural communication, global issues, and languages.
4. ______The global activities of the company are highlighted in company meetings and publications.
5. ______Overseas experiences are valued and supported by predeparture and repatriation programs.
6. ______Future company leaders receive global assignments as part of the global career path.
7. ______Performance and reward systems are globally standardized and locally tailored.

______**Global Human Resources Score** (sum of answers to Human Resources questions)

III. Global Strategies

In this organization . . .

1. ______There is a clear global mission built on global values and norms.
2. ______We systematically undertake an analysis of global opportunities and threats.
3. ______Specific global goals and performance targets are established.
4. ______We identify global alternatives and make strategic worldwide choices.
5. ______Global plans with possible contingencies and global alliances are regularly developed.
6. ______Implementation of the global strategy is accomplished through alignment and integration of resources and organizational units.
7. ______We continuously evaluate, modify, and reapply our global strategy.

______**Global Strategies Score** (sum of answers to Global Strategies questions)

IV. Global Operations

In this organization . . .

1. ______Research and development is centralized near world-class research sites.
2. ______Flexible-manufacturing systems allow us to integrate global production.
3. ______Product development strategies are made to accommodate for diversity, innovation, scope, and design.
4. ______Service and product quality is benchmarked against global standards.
5. ______Financial planning is built on worldwide access to capital, favorable tax exposure, flexibility, and speed.
6. ______We market and advertise global products and services that are customized to meet the local cultural expectations.
7. ______There is an appropriate mix between global and local distribution systems.

8. ______Global sales include customer education and world-class customer service.
9. ______There is a standardized global communication system for gathering, processing, and distributing information.

______**Global Operations Score** (sum of answers to Global Operations questions)

V. Global Structure

In this organization . . .

1. ______We globally integrate functions and operations on a worldwide basis.
2. ______Many programs are implemented by global project teams.
3. ______Acquiring, storing, and distributing knowledge is globally valued.
4. ______Our structure is boundaryless, streamlined, and seamless.
5. ______The location and layout of facilities recognize the importance of culture, costs, workforce quality, and market.

______**Global Structure Score** (sum of answers to Global Structure questions)

VI. Global Learning

In this organization . . .

1. ______Learning is encouraged and rewarded at the individual and group levels.
2. ______We build learning into all global business goals and operations.
3. ______Technology is utilized to enhance both learning and knowledge management for staff on a worldwide basis.
4. ______We acculturize and globalize the design, delivery, and evaluation of our training programs.
5. ______Learning materials, including videos and software, are developed to be effective in different cultural settings.

______**Global Learning Score** (sum of answers to Global Learning questions)

______**TOTAL SCORE FOR 6 DIMENSIONS OF GLOBALITY**

Profile Results and Interpretation

141–160	=	**Global Status**
101–140	=	**Multinational Status**
61–100	=	**International Status**
Below 61	=	**Domestic Status**

Index

F

G

H

X

Y